2nd Ukrainian Natural Language Processing Workshop (UNLP 2023)

Dubrovnik, Croatia
5 May 2023

ISBN: 978-1-7138-7388-4

Printed from e-media with permission by:

Curran Associates, Inc.
57 Morehouse Lane
Red Hook, NY 12571

Some format issues inherent in the e-media version may also appear in this print version.

Printed with permission by Curran Associates, Inc. (2023)

For permission requests, please contact the Association for Computational Linguistics at the address below.

Association for Computational Linguistics
209 N. Eighth Street
Stroudsburg, Pennsylvania 18360

Phone: 1-570-476-8006
Fax: 1-570-476-0860

acl@aclweb.org

Additional copies of this publication are available from:

Curran Associates, Inc.
57 Morehouse Lane
Red Hook, NY 12571 USA
Phone: 845-758-0400
Fax: 845-758-2633
Email: curran@proceedings.com
Web: www.proceedings.com

EACL 2023

The Second Ukrainian Natural Language Processing Workshop (UNLP 2023)

Proceedings of the Workshop

May 5, 2023

Welcome to UNLP 2023

We warmly welcome you to the Second Ukrainian Natural Language Processing Workshop, held on May 5, 2023, in conjunction with EACL 2023!

The workshop brings together academics, researchers, and practitioners in the fields of natural language processing and computational linguistics who work with the Ukrainian language or do cross-Slavic research that can be applied to the Ukrainian language.

The Ukrainian NLP community has only started forming in recent years, with most of the projects done by isolated groups of researchers. The UNLP workshop provides a platform for discussion and sharing of ideas, encourages collaboration between different research groups, and improves the visibility of the Ukrainian research community.

This year, fifteen papers were accepted to be presented at the workshop. The papers present novel research in the areas of grammatical error correction, large language models, word and text embeddings, coreference resolution, summarization, and news classification. More than half of the papers present new datasets for the Ukrainian language, which is vital for further advances in any low-resource language. We are grateful to the program committee for their careful and thoughtful reviews of the papers submitted this year!

The Second UNLP features the first Shared Task on Grammatical Error Correction for Ukrainian. The shared task had two tracks: GEC-only and GEC+Fluency. The participating systems were expected to make the text grammatical or both grammatical and fluent, depending on the track. It was exciting to watch six teams compete and set the state-of-the-art results for Ukrainian GEC!

We believe that the UNLP 2023 shared task was instrumental in facilitating research on grammatical error correction for the Ukrainian language. All six competing systems were openly published, four teams submitted papers that were accepted to the UNLP workshop, and the CodaLab environment where the shared task was held remains open for further submissions.

UNLP 2023 will host two amazing keynote speeches by Mona Diab and Gulnara Muratova. The speakers will inspire the audience with their work on low-resource and endangered languages.

We are looking forward to the workshop and anticipate lively discussions covering a wide range of topics!

Organizers of UNLP 2023,
Mariana Romanyshyn, Oleksii Ignatenko, Oleksiy Syvokon, Andrii Hlybovets, Oleksii Molchanovskyi

Organizing Committee

Organizing Committee

Mariana Romanyshyn, Grammarly
Oleksii Molchanovskyi, Ukrainian Catholic University
Oleksiy Syvokon, Microsoft
Andrii Hlybovets, National University of Kyiv-Mohyla Academy
Oleksii Ignatenko, Ukrainian Catholic University

Program Committee

Program Committee

Andrii Babii, Kharkiv National University of Radio Electronics
Andrii Liubonko, Grammarly
Anna Rogers, University of Copenhagen
Artem Chernodub, Grammarly
Bogdan Babych, Heidelberg University
Bogdana Oliynyk, National University of Kyiv-Mohyla Academy, Silesian University of Technology
Dmytro Karamshuk, Facebook
Igor Samokhin, Grammarly
Julia Rogushina, Institute of software systems
Kostiantyn Omelianchuk, Grammarly
Maksym Tarnavskyi, Ukrainian Catholic University
Nataliia Cheilytko, Friedrich Schiller University Jena
Natalia Grabar, CNRS STL UMR8163, Université de Lille
Natalia Kotsyba, Insitute of Ukrainian, NGO; Samsung R&D Poland
Oleksandr Marchenko, Taras Shevchenko National University of Kyiv
Oleksandr Skurzhanskyi, Grammarly
Oleksii Turuta, Kharkiv National University of Radio Electronics
Olena Siruk, Bulgarian Academy of Sciences, Institute of Mathematics and Informatics
Olha Kanishcheva, University of Jena
Ruslan Chornei, National University of Kyiv-Mohyla Academy
Serhii Havrylov, University of Edinburgh, Institute for Language, Cognition and Computation
Svitlana Galeshchuk, PSL/Paris Dauphine, West Ukrainian National University, BNP Paribas
Taras Lehinevych, National University of Kyiv-Mohyla Academy
Taras Shevchenko, Giphy
Tatjana Scheffler, Ruhr-Universität Bochum
Thierry Hamon, LISN, Universite Paris-Saclay & Universite Sorbonne Paris Nord
Veronika Solopova, Freie Universität Berlin
Volodymyr Taranukha, Taras Shevchenko National University of Kyiv
Vsevolod Domkin, m8nware
Yevhen Kupriianov, National Technical University Kharkiv Polytechnic Institute"
Yuliia Makohon, Semantrum LLC

Table of Contents

Program

Friday, May 5, 2023

09:00 - 09:10	*Opening Remarks*
09:10 - 09:55	*Keynote Speech: Mona Diab*
09:55 - 10:50	*Morning Session: New Datasets*
	Silver Data for Coreference Resolution in Ukrainian: Translation, Alignment, and Projection Pavlo Kuchmiichuk
	The Parliamentary Code-Switching Corpus: Bilingualism in the Ukrainian Parliament in the 1990s-2020s Olha Kanishcheva, Tetiana Kovalova, Maria Shvedova and Ruprecht von Waldenfels
	Creating a POS Gold Standard Corpus of Modern Ukrainian Vasyl Starko and Andriy Rysin
10:50 - 11:20	*Morning Break*
11:20 - 12:05	*Keynote Speech: Gulnara Muratova*
12:05 - 12:55	*Morning Session: New Directions*
	The Evolution of Pro-Kremlin Propaganda From a Machine Learning and Linguistics Perspective Veronika Solopova, Christoph Benzmüller and Tim Landgraf
	Extension Multi30K: Multimodal Dataset for Integrated Vision and Language Research in Ukrainian Nataliia Saichyshyna, Daniil Maksymenko, Oleksii Turuta, Andriy Yerokhin, Andrii Babii and Olena Turuta
	Exploring Word Sense Distribution in Ukrainian with a Semantic Vector Space Model Nataliia Cheilytko and Ruprecht von Waldenfels
12:55 - 14:25	*Lunch*

Friday, May 5, 2023 (continued)

14:25 - 16:00 *Afternoon Session: Shared Task*

UA-GEC: Grammatical Error Correction and Fluency Corpus for the Ukrainian Language
Oleksiy Syvokon, Olena Nahorna, Pavlo Kuchmiichuk and Nastasiia Osidach

The UNLP 2023 Shared Task on Grammatical Error Correction for Ukrainian
Oleksiy Syvokon and Mariana Romanyshyn

Comparative Study of Models Trained on Synthetic Data for Ukrainian Grammatical Error Correction
Maksym Bondarenko, Artem Yushko, Andrii Shportko and Andrii Fedorych

A Low-Resource Approach to the Grammatical Error Correction of Ukrainian
Frank Palma Gomez, Alla Rozovskaya and Dan Roth

RedPenNet for Grammatical Error Correction: Outputs to Tokens, Attentions to Spans
Bohdan Didenko and Andrii Sameliuk

15:50 - 16:00 *Best Paper and Thank You*

16:00 - 16:30 *Afternoon Break*

16:30 - 18:00 *Afternoon Session: UberText*

Introducing UberText 2.0: A Corpus of Modern Ukrainian at Scale
Dmytro Chaplynskyi

GPT-2 Metadata Pretraining Towards Instruction Finetuning for Ukrainian
Volodymyr Kyrylov and Dmytro Chaplynskyi

Learning Word Embeddings for Ukrainian: A Comparative Study of FastText Hyperparameters
Nataliia Romanyshyn, Dmytro Chaplynskyi and Kyrylo Zakharov

Friday, May 5, 2023 (continued)

	Contextual Embeddings for Ukrainian: A Large Language Model Approach to Word Sense Disambiguation Yurii Laba, Volodymyr Mudryi, Dmytro Chaplynskyi, Mariana Romanyshyn and Oles Dobosevych
	Abstractive Summarization for the Ukrainian Language: Multi-Task Learning with Hromadske.ua News Dataset Svitlana Galeshchuk
18:00 - 18:10	*Closing Words*

Introducing UberText 2.0: A Corpus of Modern Ukrainian at Scale

Dmytro Chaplynskyi
Lang-uk
Kyiv, Ukraine
chaplinsky.dmitry@gmail.com

Abstract

This paper addresses the need for massive corpora for a low-resource language and presents the publicly available UberText 2.0 corpus for the Ukrainian language and discusses the methodology of its construction. While the collection and maintenance of such a corpus is more of a data extraction and data engineering task, the corpus itself provides a solid foundation for natural language processing tasks. It can enable the creation of contemporary language models and word embeddings, resulting in a better performance of numerous downstream tasks for the Ukrainian language. In addition, the paper and software developed can be used as a guidance and model solution for other low-resource languages. The resulting corpus is available for download on the project page. It has 3.274 billion tokens, consists of 8.59 million texts and takes up 32 gigabytes of space.

1 Introduction

In this paper, we introduce UberText 2.0, which is the new and extended version of UberText, a corpus of modern Ukrainian texts designed to meet various NLP needs.

Modern development of word embeddings (Bojanowski et al., 2017), transformers (Devlin et al., 2019), neural machine translators (NLLB Team et al., 2022), speech-to-text models (Radford et al., 2022), and question answering systems (Yang et al., 2019) opens new horizons for natural language processing. Most of the models mentioned above rely heavily on the availability of corpora for a target language. While it is not usually a problem to obtain such a dataset for languages such as English, Chinese or Spanish, for low-resource languages, the absence of publicly available corpora is a severe barrier for researchers.

Different approaches can be used to overcome this problem. Researchers might use multilingual transformers to achieve sub-optimal performance for low-resource languages (Rust et al., 2021). Alternatively, they might rely on the publicly available multilingual corpora, such as Wikipedia (Al-Rfou' et al., 2013), Common Crawl (Grave et al., 2018), or Oscar (Srinath et al., 2021), or collect their own corpus using web crawling technologies. The latter approach requires a lot of data engineering to combat noisy data and extract relevant texts in the target language. While many authors follow this path, it shifts the attention from the target task, requires specific skills, and takes time to collect the data rather than make use of it.

To enable researchers to work on large language models or perform a data mining on texts, we release a high-quality corpus for the Ukrainian language at scale and a model solution that can be applied to other low-resource languages.

The core concept of our corpus is that the same data, once collected and processed, can be later used to produce various deliverables suitable for different computational linguistics tasks. The corpus size, the additional layers (like POS tags and lemmas), and its availability for direct download make it an invaluable dataset. At the same time, the data model behind it and its flexible architecture allows exporting the corpus version pinpointed to a particular task or research need.

The pipeline behind the corpus simplifies data collection, pre- and post-processing, and export of the deliverables, helping set up a regular release cycle so that end users can use the fresh copy of the data or update their models built on the previous versions when needed. Such deliverables can include:

- Raw texts with markup and complete metadata
- Cleansed and filtered texts
- Tokenized version of the corpus (with or without punctuation)
- Lemmatized version of the corpus
- Lemma frequencies, n-grams, and other lists

Proceedings of the Second Ukrainian Natural Language Processing Workshop (UNLP), pages 1–10
May 5, 2023 ©2023 Association for Computational Linguistics

as well as other deliverables or subcorpora, obtained by filtering original texts based on such metadata as date, author, or source.

2 Background

The Ukrainian language is a morphologically rich language of the synthetic type, spoken by more than 40 million people. Historically, it took shape in different centers, which influenced modern Ukrainian as we know it. While it is one of the most widely spoken Slavic languages, it can still be considered a low-resource language and is underrepresented in modern NLP research. The reason is the lack of publicly available corpora tailored to different needs. It can be speculated with a high degree of confidence that similar issues exist in other languages. We want to address this gap for the Ukrainian language and propose a model solution that can be reused for other languages.

Existing corpora are scattered across quite a wide range. On one end, we have relatively small, well-balanced corpora such as Brown (Francis and Kucera, 1979), BRUK (Starko et al., 2016-2023), or any national corpus collected by a dedicated team. On the other end, we have gigantic corpora, such as OSCAR (Abadji et al., 2022) and Common Crawl [1], which have been collected fully automatically. In between these two extremes, there are many corpus projects that may be used either as the main data source or as supplementary material, depending on the task at hand.

In our opinion, each corpus should have a clear contract with the end user that specifies the guarantees and promises it fulfills, the availability of the data, the functionality offered on top of the data (e.g., a corpus manager or extra layers), frequency of updates, and the methodology behind the data collection and processing. This will allow the researcher to pick the right tool for the job and understand the limits of this tool. To meet the requirements of modern computational linguistics, we establish the following contract for the corpus:

- Massive
- Freely available for download under a permissive license
- Built from modern language data and sufficiently representative
- Maintains a decent level of text quality and internal quality control procedures
- Has additional layers, e.g., lemmatization, POS tags, et cetera. This approach allows for various corpus mining tasks, building the lemma frequency dictionaries by POS tags.

3 Related work

Most existing corpora for the Ukrainian language do not meet all the criteria outlined above, particularly when it comes to the scale and availability of the data for direct download.

Corpora unavailable for download:

- Zvidusil created by Kotsyba et al. (2018) corpus contains 2.8 billion tokens collected primarily in an automated fashion. The last update to the corpus was made in 2017.
- General Regionally Annotated Corpus of Ukrainian (GRAC-16) collected by team of Shvedova et al. (2017-2023) has almost 1.9 billion tokens, is updated twice a year, and has extensive meta-information on the texts.
- The Ukrainian Text Corpus (KUM) by Darchuk (2017) contains about 120 million tokens and is only accessible through a limited corpus manager.
- The Ukrainian Web Corpus of Leipzig University [2] only provides samples of up to 1 million words.
- The Corpus of the Chtyvo Library [3] contains 6.6GB of OCRed texts of mediocre quality.
- Araneum Ucrainicum Beta, corpus by Benko (2014) has around 5,249 million of tokens, only available for the registered users through the corpus manager [4]
- ukTenTen: Ukrainian corpus from the Web has about 3,280 million of tokens, available for subscribed users through a corpus manager[5]

Corpora available for download of smaller size:

- Brown-UK by Starko et al. (2016-2023), a well-balanced national high-quality corpus, is available for download, with around one million words.
- UberText 1.0[6], is the previous version of the corpus presented in this paper. It has around 665 million tokens, and consists of shuffled

[1] https://commoncrawl.org

[2] http://corpora.informatik.uni-leipzig.de/

[3] http://korpus.org.ua/

[4] http://aranea.juls.savba.sk/guest/

[5] https://www.sketchengine.eu/uktenten-ukrainian-corpus/

[6] https://lang.org.ua/en/corpora/

sentences. UberText 1.0 wasn't updated since 2016.

4 The Corpus

To address the issues of availability and scale and allow researchers to train large language models for Ukrainian, we release a new version of UberText. The new version shares some sources and texts with UberText 1.0, but all of them were re-crawled and pre-processed.

The total size of the corpus after post-processing and filtering is:

- 8,592,389 texts
- 156,053,481 sentences
- 2,489,454,148 tokens
- 32 gigabytes of text

In addition to releasing texts, we have developed and open-sourced a software solution[7] that helps manage the data sources and update the corpus database, perform quality assurance tasks, calculate statistics, pre- and post-process texts, and export data in various formats.

4.1 Corpus composition

UberText 2.0 has five subcorpora:

- *news* (short news, longer articles, interviews, opinions, and blogs) scraped from 38 central, regional, and industry-specific news websites;
- *fiction* (novels, prose, and some poetry) scraped from two public libraries;
- *social* (264 public telegram channels), acquired from the project TGSearch;
- *wikipedia* — the Ukrainian Wikipedia as of January 2023;
- *court* (decisions of the Supreme Court of Ukraine), received upon request for public information.

Table 1 presents statistical information on the subcorpora.

All the entries of the corpus are stored as separate documents in a document-oriented database and have a title (where possible), the text itself, and meta-information: author, source or publisher, URL of the original article or text, main picture, date of publication, tags or categories of the text, and more. Some subcorpora have additional meta-fields specific to the domain, e.g., court decisions have information on the judge and the geographic region.

[7] https://github.com/lang-uk/lang.org.ua/tree/master/languk/corpus

The original texts' markup (headers of various levels, ordered and unordered lists, emphases, etc) is preserved where possible by converting the HTML of the article to the markdown format using html2text library[8]. Markdown allows keeping some structure of the text (for example, headers and subheaders). Also, it is human-readable and can be easily stripped afterward with the help of Markdown library[9].

4.2 Data collection

UberText 2.0 utilizes the Scrapy framework and ecosystem to crawl texts from the web. A dedicated spider is written for each source to capture only the text of an article and meta-information about it but not the boilerplate of the webpage. Extra effort is made to exclude repetitive elements from the article texts, like "subscribe to our social networks" or "also read" calls to action, during the crawling stage.

Such subcorpora as *court*, *wikipedia*, and *social* are also collected using the Scrapy spiders to keep things consistent and manageable even though their data is obtained or downloaded in machine-readable formats in bulk. A custom fork of a gensim's Wikipedia reader was created[10] for better parsing the Ukrainian Wikipedia dump, primarily to deal with accented characters and to process Wikipedia section names in Ukrainian correctly.

The Wikipedia dump was downloaded from the Wikimedia download page[11]; a dump of public telegram channels was received from the TgSearch[12] project; court decisions were obtained from "Court on the Palm" project[13], in the RTF format with a CSV index. Court decisions were initially published by the State Judicial Administration of Ukraine on the National Open Data Portal[14]. Figure 2 demonstrates the manager of the spiders used in the project.

4.3 Data model

MongoDB[15] was selected to efficiently store the massive number of texts together with numerous

[8] https://github.com/Alir3z4/html2text/

[9] https://python-markdown.github.io

[10] https://gist.github.com/dchaplinsky/f7bf86837837778f75b704ef57e3811c

[11] https://dumps.wikimedia.org/backup-index.html

[12] https://tgsearch.com.ua

[13] https://conp.com.ua

[14] https://data.gov.ua/organization/derzhavna-sudova-administratsiia-ukrayiny

[15] https://www.mongodb.com

Figure 1: Data flow diagram and processing pipeline

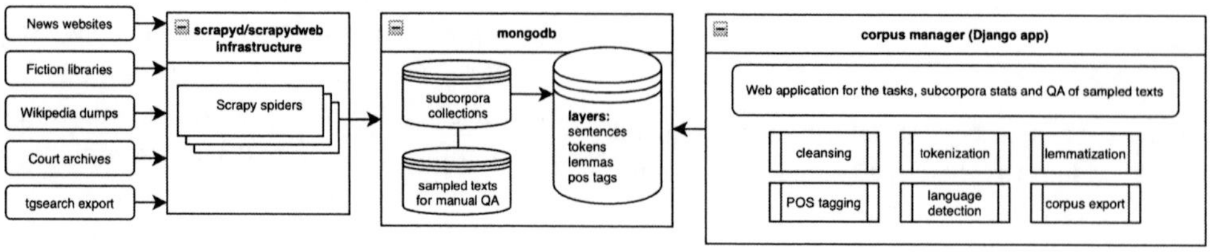

Table 1: Subcorpora of UberText 2.0 with time spans and additional statistics on the number of articles and tokens. The number of texts and tokens are measured before filtering, except when explicitly stated otherwise

Subcorpora	time span	# of sources	# of texts	# of tokens
news	2000-2023	38	7,208,299	2,172,526,177
fiction	n/a	2	23,796	253,321,894
court	2007-2021	1	111,658	285,252,442
wikipedia	2004-2023	1	2,819,395	499,603,082
social	2018-2022	264	885,314	63,472,353
total	-	-	11,048,462	3,274,175,948
total after filtering	-	-	8,592,389	2,489,454,148

meta-fields. Also, MongoDB has native support for efficient data compression algorithms, which helps reduce storage requirements and make the whole system scalable.

Each subcorpus has its collection, and the schemaless nature of MongoDB allows for different sets of meta-fields.

Separate collections are created to store the additional layers (such as the normalized, tokenized, and lemmatized versions of the texts and information on the UD POS tags and features) for each text. Figure 1 demonstrates the general architecture of the system and the data model.

A data model like this enables the "collect and process once/reuse many times" concept. It also makes it possible to release incremental updates to the corpus for which only the newly added texts need to be processed.

4.4 Pre-processing

Once a new batch of texts is collected and added to the corpus database, the corpus editor can launch a set of pre-processing jobs:

- Markdown removal and normalization of the texts (unification of hyphens, apostrophes, and Ukrainian diacritics, fixes for encoding issues and word wraps, etc.)
- Language detection
- Segmentation into sentences
- Tokenization (with preserved punctuation)
- Lemmatization
- POS tagging.

The results of these jobs are saved to the corresponding layers and linked to the original texts. Markdown removal is accomplished with the help of the markdown python library[16]. Normalization, sentence segmentation, tokenization and lemmatization are covered by the nlp-uk-api wrapper[17] over nlp-uk[18] groovy library.

Language detection is performed by CLD3 library[19] to allow filtering out non-Ukrainian texts at later stages.

Finally, POS-tagging is done with a fork of the UDPipe[20] tuned for Ukrainian and the corresponding model[21]. Since the tag and the features for one word of text are much longer than the word itself, the tagging results are converted into a more compact textual format to reduce the storage requirements[22].

[16] https://python-markdown.github.io
[17] https://github.com/arysin/nlp_uk_api
[18] https://github.com/brown-uk/nlp_uk
[19] https://github.com/google/cld3
[20] https://github.com/mova-institute/udpipe
[21] mova.institute analyzer
[22] https://github.com/lang-uk/lang.org.ua/blob/master/languk/corpus/ud_converter.py

4.5 Post-processing and export

Once all texts in the corpus are processed and results are stored in the corresponding layers, the corpus editor can initiate the export of deliverables. The post-processing is being done during the execution of the export job and might include the following:

- Filtering by the subcorpora, individual source of the text, or any other filtering over the meta-information. For example, we might export only the texts published over the last two years.
- Additional filtering by the detected language of the text and/or its length. Some texts (especially from Wikipedia) might be too short or unfinished, and some (especially from news websites) might be in Russian or English. To improve the quality of the exported corpus, we usually filter by the combined text length of the title and text (> 100 characters) and only accept the texts where CLD3 is confident in the language.
- Selection of the layer and transformation to a desired format. Some tasks might require tokenized texts with no markup and no punctuation, split by sentence. Some can benefit from the unaltered texts with the markup. Some require unique sentences only or lemmatized texts.
- Compression of the output stream (bzip2 or lzma2).

Figure 5 reflects the corpus export settings available.

Finally, there is a separate class of export tasks: frequency dictionaries built on n-grams of tokens or lemmas. These require additional calculation during the export and rely on the pre-computed layers. Figure 6 shows the settings available for the frequency dictionary export task.

The existing architecture of the corpus software allows for adding more layers, filters, and output formats without the need to rebuild the whole corpus. That helps deliver massive amounts of data tailored to particular research needs in a very short time. For example, the complete export of all subcorpora currently takes around 24 hours on a very modest hardware.

4.6 Data quality

Maintaining the desired quality of the data in a massive corpus is hard, especially when it is collected from sources the corpus editors do not control. Of course, the amount of data collected can smooth some issues. Still, extra measures can be applied to improve the quality of data. In UberText 2.0, we use the following:

- Texts are collected using custom spiders written for each data source. That allows us to filter out boilerplate texts of webpages or overused fragments like "join us on Patreon." with the help of handcrafted CSS and XPATH selectors. In the case of the *social* subcorpus, we apply additional filtering to exclude Telegram channels that are only posted in Russian or considered to be propaganda by the media-monitoring organizations [23].
- When the text source crawling is complete, the spider automatically samples texts, including the oldest, the shortest, and the longest ones, texts with no title or body, and a random sample. Later volunteers manually review those sampled texts and report the issues found to the GitHub repository. Figures 3 and 4 show the stats of the data sources and available text samples under each source.
- The developer of the spider additionally verifies that the spider works correctly before starting a major update of the corpus. This helps account for design or page structure changes.
- During the post-processing stage, texts that are not in Ukrainian or are too short are dropped.

4.7 Release cycle

When we created UberText 1.0, it took much manual labor to prepare the initial deliverables. The old corpus architecture did not allow for quick updates of the texts from the sources or the export of texts into a different format. Therefore, the work on the new corpus version started with the architecture and pipeline revamp. With these changes, we can update the corpus database and the list of deliverables quickly. We aim for the annual update of the corpus and its deliverables. This way, the end-users might refer to a particular version of the corpus to make their research reproducible. New deliverables may be added between the releases to fulfill particular research needs.

We also plan to add more data sources, for example, websites and social media, to keep up with the quickly changing vocabulary of the Ukrainian

[23] Detector Media

language. This will help to increase the size of the corpus and capture the effect of historical changes on the Ukrainian language.

5 Intended usage and cooperation

We successfully used developers' preview of the corpus in various tasks:

- building the first flair embeddings (Akbik et al., 2018) of the Ukrainian language[24] and training compact downstream models like POS[25] and NER[26] on these embeddings;
- training fastText vectors of a high quality (Romanyshyn et al., 2023);
- training lean language models for a Ukrainian speech-to-text project[27];
- training models for punctuation restoration[28];
- training GPT-2 models of different sizes for the Ukrainian language and fine-tuning for various tasks using instructions (Kyrylov and Chaplynskyi, 2023);
- fine-tuning *paraphrase-multilingual-mpnet-base-v2* sentence transformer on the sentences mined from the corpus to achieve better performance on WSD task (Laba et al., 2023).

We cooperate with teams of researchers to train transformer models like GPT-2 proposed by Radford et al. (2019), BERT by Devlin et al. (2019), RoBERTa by Liu et al. (2019) and ELECTRA by Clark et al. (2020) and are open to further collaborations.

We also share the texts of the corpora with the GRAC project[29] to improve the coverage of this vital corpus and make modern texts accessible to linguists, translators, and students through a user-friendly corpus manager[30].

6 Conclusions and Future Work

To build a massive corpus of high-quality texts for a low-resource language, researchers must have a clear contract of what the corpus guarantees and does not guarantee, a methodology, data sources, and a clear pipeline. Proper pipeline implementation will allow for updating the corpus and its deliverables with minimum manual labor. While implementation of such a pipeline and required infrastructure is more related to data engineering and programming rather than to NLP, the impact on the natural language processing for a target language can be enormous. When collected and made available, a good corpus is a solid foundation for myriads of computational linguistics tasks, multiplying the impact on the industry.

Corpora for low-resource languages can also be included in the datasets used to train multilingual word embedding models, such as XLM-RoBERTa proposed by Conneau et al. (2020).

To continue the effort made for UberText, we are planning to:

- set up a regular annual release cycle for UberText;
- collaborate with more researchers, contributing the corpus for various NLP tasks for the Ukrainian language;
- train and release modern word embeddings and models for downstream tasks.

Limitations

When working on the corpus and the software pipeline, we found some obstacles that might affect the reproducibility of the results for other low-resource languages. While the software created is available for reuse under a permissive license, it relies on other programming components, which might not be available for the target language. For example, text segmentation, tokenization, and lemmatization might be very language-specific. We use the nlp-uk package, which wraps the LanguageTool library[31]. A similar wrapper should be developed or integrated for languages other than Ukrainian. The same applies to the UDPipe library[32] and the model used for automatic POS tagging. Other solutions, like SpaCy[33], can be integrated instead. Also, as mentioned above, creating and maintaining a corpus of such scale requires additional knowledge in data retrieval and data engineering.

Ethics Statement

Our paper aims to bring greater visibility to the Ukrainian research community and foster connections within the ACL community. Furthermore, we

[24] https://huggingface.co/lang-uk/flair-uk-forward

[25] https://huggingface.co/lang-uk/flair-uk-pos

[26] https://huggingface.co/lang-uk/flair-uk-ner

[27] https://huggingface.co/Yehor/kenlm-ukrainian

[28] https://huggingface.co/dchaplinsky/punctuation_uk_bert

[29] http://uacorpus.org/Kyiv/en/

[30] https://parasol.vmguest.uni-jena.de/grac_crystal/#dashboard?corpname=grac16

[31] https://languagetool.org

[32] https://ufal.mff.cuni.cz/udpipe

[33] https://spacy.io

acknowledge the potential broader impact of our research on other low-resource languages and believe that our ideas, methodology, and open-source code are applicable and could be utilized to benefit other languages and communities. We recognize the scarcity of academic papers in the ACL Anthology related to the Ukrainian language or produced by Ukrainian researchers.

We take copyright concerns seriously and have made every effort to ensure that the collection of the texts for our corpus does not violate the law. The texts were collected from various web resources and we have preserved their authorship whenever possible. We believe that our use of these texts falls within the bounds of fair use and Ukrainian copyright law, which specifies that certain objects are not protected by copyright. For example, news or other facts of the nature of ordinary press information, official documents of a political, legislative, administrative, and judicial nature, such as laws, decrees, resolutions, decisions, state standards, drafts, and official translations, are not protected by copyright. Additionally, we are willing to remove any texts from our corpus upon request from the authors or right owners.

Acknowledgments

We want to thank Andriy Rysin for his contribution to the nlp-uk-api project and support of the Ukrainian language in the LanguageTool project, Kyrylo Zakharov for his work on spiders and help with access to the decisions of the Supreme Court of Ukraine and archive of public Telegram channels, Maria Shvedova and Vasyl Starko for their inspirational work on GRAC and BRUK corpora, Mariana Romanyshyn, Volodymyr Kirilov, Nataliia Romanyshyn, Yehor Smoliakov, Yuriy Paniv, and Stefan Schweter for their feedback and ongoing collaborations on developers' preview of the corpus data.

References

Julien Abadji, Pedro Ortiz Suarez, Laurent Romary, and Benoît Sagot. 2022. Towards a cleaner document-oriented multilingual crawled corpus. In *Proceedings of the Thirteenth Language Resources and Evaluation Conference*, pages 4344–4355, Marseille, France. European Language Resources Association.

Alan Akbik, Duncan Blythe, and Roland Vollgraf. 2018. Contextual string embeddings for sequence labeling. In *COLING 2018, 27th International Conference on Computational Linguistics*, pages 1638–1649.

Rami Al-Rfou', Bryan Perozzi, and Steven Skiena. 2013. Polyglot: Distributed word representations for multilingual NLP. In *Proceedings of the Seventeenth Conference on Computational Natural Language Learning*, pages 183–192, Sofia, Bulgaria. Association for Computational Linguistics.

Vladimír Benko. 2014. Aranea: Yet another family of (comparable) web corpora. volume 8655.

Piotr Bojanowski, Edouard Grave, Armand Joulin, and Tomas Mikolov. 2017. Enriching word vectors with subword information. *Transactions of the Association for Computational Linguistics*, 5:135–146.

Kevin Clark, Minh-Thang Luong, Quoc V. Le, and Christopher D. Manning. 2020. ELECTRA: Pre-training text encoders as discriminators rather than generators. In *ICLR*.

Alexis Conneau, Kartikay Khandelwal, Naman Goyal, Vishrav Chaudhary, Guillaume Wenzek, Francisco Guzmán, Edouard Grave, Myle Ott, Luke Zettlemoyer, and Veselin Stoyanov. 2020. Unsupervised cross-lingual representation learning at scale. In *Proceedings of the 58th Annual Meeting of the Association for Computational Linguistics*, pages 8440–8451, Online. Association for Computational Linguistics.

Nataliia Darchuk. 2017. Mozhlyvosti semantychnoyi rozmitky korpusu ukrainskoyi movy (kum). *Naukovyi chasopys Natsionalnoho pedahohichnoho universytetu im. M.P. Drahomanova*, abs/1911.02116:18—28.

Jacob Devlin, Ming-Wei Chang, Kenton Lee, and Kristina Toutanova. 2019. BERT: Pre-training of deep bidirectional transformers for language understanding. In *Proceedings of the 2019 Conference of the North American Chapter of the Association for Computational Linguistics: Human Language Technologies, Volume 1 (Long and Short Papers)*, pages 4171–4186, Minneapolis, Minnesota. Association for Computational Linguistics.

W. N. Francis and H. Kucera. 1979. Brown corpus manual. Technical report, Department of Linguistics, Brown University, Providence, Rhode Island, US.

Edouard Grave, Piotr Bojanowski, Prakhar Gupta, Armand Joulin, and Tomas Mikolov. 2018. Learning word vectors for 157 languages. In *Proceedings of the Eleventh International Conference on Language Resources and Evaluation (LREC 2018)*, Miyazaki, Japan. European Language Resources Association (ELRA).

Natalia Kotsyba, Bohdan Moskalevskyi, and Mykhailo Romanenko et al. 2018. Laboratorija ukrajins'koji.

Volodymyr Kyrylov and Dmytro Chaplynskyi. 2023. GPT-2 metadata pretraining towards instruction finetuning for Ukrainian. In *Proceedings of the Second Ukrainian Natural Language Processing Workshop*, pages 32–40, Dubrovnik, Croatia. Association for Computational Linguistics.

Yurii Laba, Volodymyr Mudryi, Dmytro Chaplynskyi, Mariana Romanyshyn, and Oles Dobosevych. 2023. Contextual embeddings for Ukrainian: A large language model approach to word sense disambiguation. In *Proceedings of the Second Ukrainian Natural Language Processing Workshop*, pages 11–19, Dubrovnik, Croatia. Association for Computational Linguistics.

Yinhan Liu, Myle Ott, Naman Goyal, Jingfei Du, Mandar Joshi, Danqi Chen, Omer Levy, Mike Lewis, Luke Zettlemoyer, and Veselin Stoyanov. 2019. Roberta: A robustly optimized BERT pretraining approach. *CoRR*, abs/1907.11692.

NLLB Team, Marta R. Costa-jussà, James Cross, Onur Çelebi, Maha Elbayad, Kenneth Heafield, Kevin Heffernan, Elahe Kalbassi, Janice Lam, Daniel Licht, Jean Maillard, Anna Sun, Skyler Wang, Guillaume Wenzek, Al Youngblood, Bapi Akula, Loic Barrault, Gabriel Mejia Gonzalez, Prangthip Hansanti, John Hoffman, Semarley Jarrett, Kaushik Ram Sadagopan, Dirk Rowe, Shannon Spruit, Chau Tran, Pierre Andrews, Necip Fazil Ayan, Shruti Bhosale, Sergey Edunov, Angela Fan, Cynthia Gao, Vedanuj Goswami, Francisco Guzmán, Philipp Koehn, Alexandre Mourachko, Christophe Ropers, Safiyyah Saleem, Holger Schwenk, and Jeff Wang. 2022. No language left behind: Scaling human-centered machine translation.

Alec Radford, Jong Wook Kim, Tao Xu, Greg Brockman, Christine McLeavey, and Ilya Sutskever. 2022. Robust speech recognition via large-scale weak supervision.

Alec Radford, Jeff Wu, Rewon Child, David Luan, Dario Amodei, and Ilya Sutskever. 2019. Language models are unsupervised multitask learners.

Nataliia Romanyshyn, Dmytro Chaplynskyi, and Kyrylo Zakharov. 2023. Learning word embeddings for Ukrainian: A comparative study of fastText hyperparameters. In *Proceedings of the Second Ukrainian Natural Language Processing Workshop*, pages 20–31, Dubrovnik, Croatia. Association for Computational Linguistics.

Phillip Rust, Jonas Pfeiffer, Ivan Vulić, Sebastian Ruder, and Iryna Gurevych. 2021. How good is your tokenizer? on the monolingual performance of multilingual language models. In *Proceedings of the 59th Annual Meeting of the Association for Computational Linguistics and the 11th International Joint Conference on Natural Language Processing (Volume 1: Long Papers)*, pages 3118–3135, Online. Association for Computational Linguistics.

Maria Shvedova, Ruprecht von Waldenfels, Sergiy Yarygin, Andriy Rysin, Vasyl Starko, and Tymofij Nikolajenko et al. 2017-2023. GRAC: General regionally annotated corpus of Ukrainian.

Mukund Srinath, Shomir Wilson, and C Lee Giles. 2021. Privacy at scale: Introducing the PrivaSeer corpus of web privacy policies. In *Proceedings of the 59th Annual Meeting of the Association for Computational Linguistics and the 11th International Joint Conference on Natural Language Processing (Volume 1: Long Papers)*, pages 6829–6839, Online. Association for Computational Linguistics.

Vasyl Starko, Andriy Rysin, Olha Havura, and Nataliia Cheilytko et al. 2016-2023. BRUK: Braunskyi korpus ukrainskoi movy.

Wei Yang, Yuqing Xie, Aileen Lin, Xingyu Li, Luchen Tan, Kun Xiong, Ming Li, and Jimmy Lin. 2019. End-to-end open-domain question answering with BERTserini. In *Proceedings of the 2019 Conference of the North American Chapter of the Association for Computational Linguistics (Demonstrations)*, pages 72–77, Minneapolis, Minnesota. Association for Computational Linguistics.

A Screenshots of the system

Figure 2: ScrapydWeb webapp to manage corpus spiders

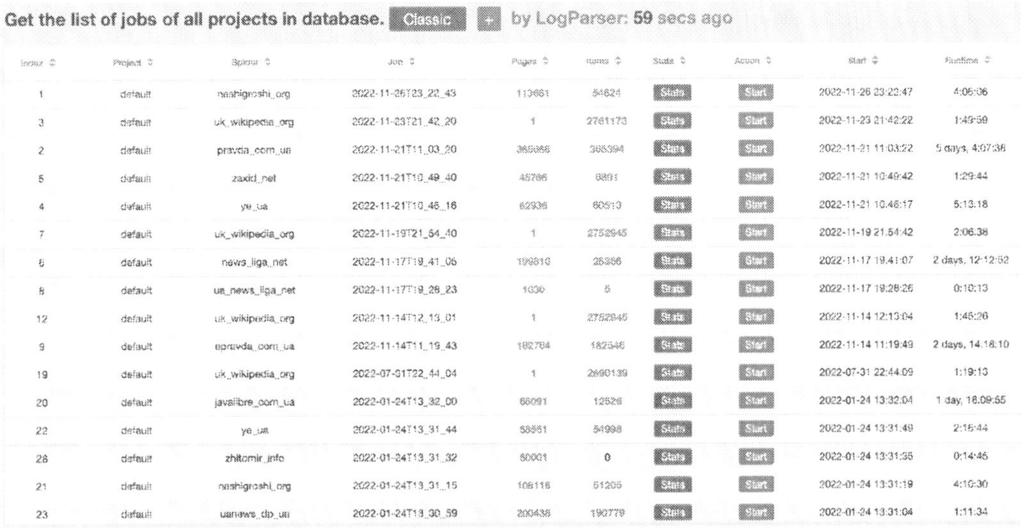

Get the list of jobs of all projects in database. Classic + by LogParser: 59 secs ago

Index	Project	Spider	Job	Pages	Items	Stats	Action	Start	Runtime
1	default	nashigroshi_org	2022-11-26T23_22_43	113661	54624	Stats	Start	2022-11-26 23:22:47	4:05:06
3	default	uk_wikipedia_org	2022-11-23T21_42_20	1	2761173	Stats	Start	2022-11-23 21:42:22	1:49:59
2	default	pravda_com_ua	2022-11-21T11_03_20	365068	365394	Stats	Start	2022-11-21 11:03:22	5 days, 4:07:38
5	default	zaxid_net	2022-11-21T10_49_40	45786	6891	Stats	Start	2022-11-21 10:49:42	1:29:44
4	default	ye_ua	2022-11-21T10_46_16	62936	60613	Stats	Start	2022-11-21 10:46:17	5:13:18
7	default	uk_wikipedia_org	2022-11-19T21_54_40	1	2752945	Stats	Start	2022-11-19 21:54:42	2:06:38
6	default	news_liga_net	2022-11-17T19_41_05	199810	26366	Stats	Start	2022-11-17 19:41:07	2 days, 12:12:52
8	default	ua_news_liga_net	2022-11-17T19_28_23	1030	5	Stats	Start	2022-11-17 19:28:26	0:10:13
12	default	uk_wikipedia_org	2022-11-14T12_13_01	1	2752945	Stats	Start	2022-11-14 12:13:04	1:45:26
9	default	epravda_com_ua	2022-11-14T11_19_43	182764	182546	Stats	Start	2022-11-14 11:19:48	2 days, 14:18:10
19	default	uk_wikipedia_org	2022-07-31T22_44_04	1	2690139	Stats	Start	2022-07-31 22:44:09	1:19:13
20	default	javalibre_com_ua	2022-01-24T13_32_00	66091	12526	Stats	Start	2022-01-24 13:32:04	1 day, 18:09:55
22	default	ye_ua	2022-01-24T13_31_44	53861	54998	Stats	Start	2022-01-24 13:31:49	2:15:44
26	default	zhitomir_info	2022-01-24T13_31_32	60001	0	Stats	Start	2022-01-24 13:31:35	0:14:46
21	default	nashigroshi_org	2022-01-24T13_31_15	106116	51205	Stats	Start	2022-01-24 13:31:19	4:10:30
23	default	uanews_dp_ua	2022-01-24T13_30_59	200438	190779	Stats	Start	2022-01-24 13:31:04	1:11:34

Figure 3: Internal corpus manager and QA tool

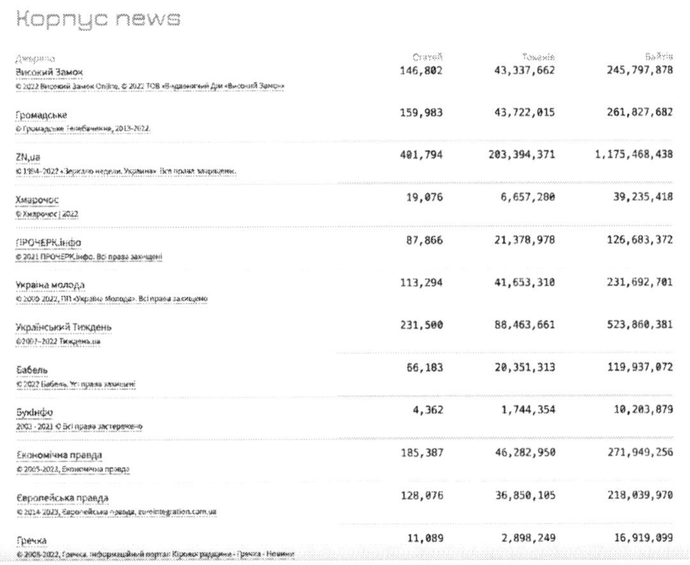

Корпус news

Джерело	Статей	Токенів	Байтів
Високий Замок	146,802	43,337,662	245,797,878
Громадське	159,983	43,722,015	261,827,682
ZN,ua	401,794	203,394,371	1,175,468,438
Хмарочос © Хмарочос | 2022	19,076	6,657,280	39,235,418
ПРОЧЕРК.інфо	87,866	21,378,978	126,683,372
Україна молода	113,294	41,653,310	231,692,701
Український Тиждень	231,500	88,463,661	523,860,381
Бабель	66,183	20,351,313	119,937,072
Букінфо	4,362	1,744,354	10,203,879
Економічна правда	185,387	46,282,950	271,949,256
Європейська правда	128,076	36,850,105	218,039,970
Гречка	11,089	2,898,249	16,919,099

Figure 4: Details about corpus source and text samples

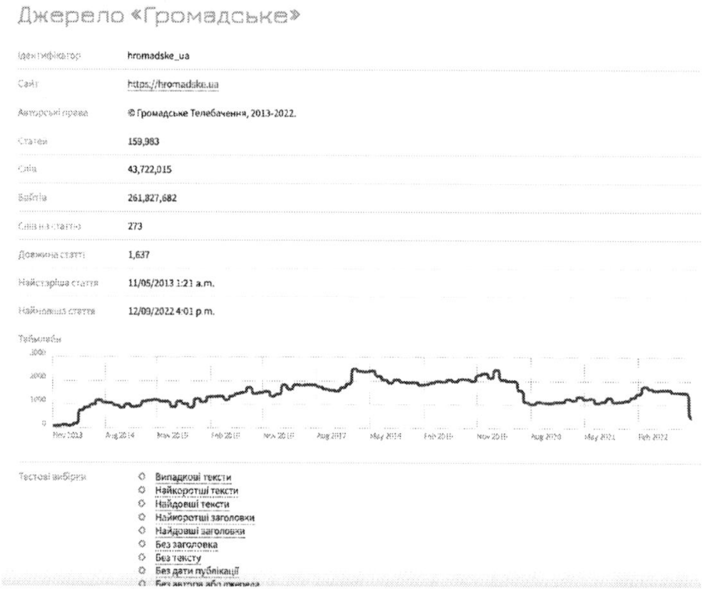

Figure 5: Corpus export task options

Figure 6: Lemma frequency export options

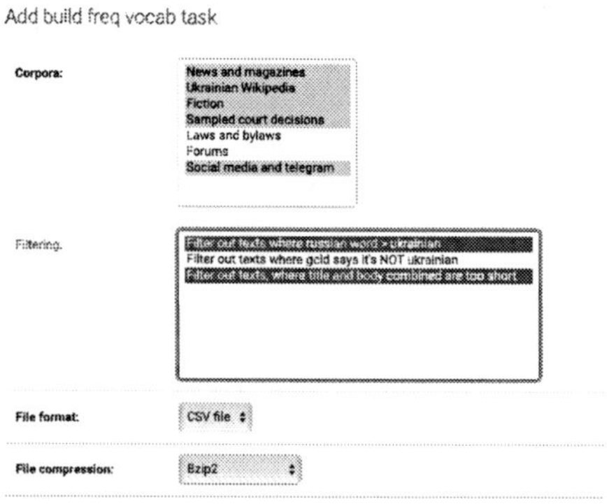

Contextual Embeddings for Ukrainian: A Large Language Model Approach to Word Sense Disambiguation

Yurii Laba
The Machine Learning Lab at
Ukrainian Catholic University,
Lviv, Ukraine
laba@ucu.edu.ua

Volodymyr Mudryi
Independent Researcher,
Lviv, Ukraine
vova.mudruy@gmail.com

Dmytro Chaplynskyi
Lang-uk
Kyiv, Ukraine
chaplinsky.dmitry@gmail.com

Mariana Romanyshyn
Grammarly
Kyiv, Ukraine
mariana.scorp@gmail.com

Oles Dobosevych
The Machine Learning Lab at
Ukrainian Catholic University,
Lviv, Ukraine
dobosevych@ucu.edu.ua

Abstract

This research proposes a novel approach to the Word Sense Disambiguation (WSD) task in the Ukrainian language based on supervised fine-tuning of a pre-trained Large Language Model (LLM) on the dataset generated in an unsupervised way to obtain better contextual embeddings for words with multiple senses. The paper presents a method for generating a new dataset for WSD evaluation in the Ukrainian language based on the SUM dictionary. We developed a comprehensive framework that facilitates the generation of WSD evaluation datasets, enables the use of different prediction strategies, LLMs, and pooling strategies, and generates multiple performance reports. Our approach shows 77,9% accuracy for lexical meaning prediction for homonyms.

1 Introduction

Word Sense Disambiguation (WSD) task involves identifying a polysemic word's correct meaning in a given context. A task of WSD is applicable in various NLP fields Sharma and Niranjan (2015), such as information retrieval, machine translation Neale et al. (2016), and question answering. For well-resourced languages, this problem has many different approaches for solving that demonstrate competitive results Navigli (2009).

However, this task has received relatively little attention in the Ukrainian language due to the absence of sense-annotated datasets. To address this issue, we propose a novel approach to the WSD task based on fine-tuning a pre-trained Large Language Model (LLM) to obtain better contextual embeddings for words with multiple senses.

In this research, we present a method for generating a new dataset for WSD evaluation in the Ukrainian language, which includes lemmas, example sentences, and lexical meanings based on the SUM dictionary, of NAS of Ukraine (ULIF-NASU). This dataset is used to evaluate the effectiveness of our proposed method. For supervised LLM fine-tuning, we generate the dataset in an unsupervised way based on UberText Chaplynskyi (2023).

Additionally, we have developed a comprehensive framework [1] that facilitates the generation of WSD evaluation datasets, enables the use of different prediction strategies, LLMs, or pooling strategies, and generates multiple performance reports.

2 Related works

Early approaches in WSD utilized the concept of word embeddings, which were generated using pre-trained algorithms such as Word2Vec Mikolov et al. (2013) or Glove Pennington et al. (2014). However, these static word embeddings have a notable problem that all senses of a homonym word must share a single vector. To address this issue, several researchers have proposed techniques for capturing polysemy and generating more informative embeddings Faruqui et al. (2014) or Speer et al. (2017). Recently, there has been a trend toward utilizing contextual embeddings generated by LLMs instead of pre-trained word embeddings. These contextual embeddings provide a more nuanced representation of words, capturing context-specific information. As a result, a simple approach such as kNN can be used in combination with these embeddings to predict word senses in Word Sense Disambiguation tasks accurately Wiedemann et al. (2019).

WSD can be approached as a binary classifica-

[1] More details in Appendix A

Proceedings of the Second Ukrainian Natural Language Processing Workshop (UNLP), pages 11–19

tion problem. One such approach was proposed by Huang et al. (2019), which involved adding a classification head to the BERT model Devlin et al. (2018). The model takes a pair of sentences as input, with one sentence containing the target word and the other providing one of the possible definitions of the target word. The model then predicts whether the target word in the sentence has the same meaning as the definition.

Another noteworthy approach to Word Sense Disambiguation is the one presented by Barba et al. (2021), where the model not only takes into account the contextual information of the target word, but also the explicit senses assigned to neighboring words.

Despite the high performance of the previously mentioned supervised approaches for Word Sense Disambiguation, their reliance on a large amount of annotated sense data can pose a challenge for their application to under-resourced languages. In contrast, unsupervised methods can also be applied to WSD tasks. One of the earliest and most well-known solutions is using sense definitions and semantic relations from lexical graph databases such as Babelfy Moro et al. (2014). However, recent works such as Huang et al. (2019) have shown that LLM-based solutions outperform those methods.

Given the limitations of prior research, particularly the shortage of annotated corpora in the Ukrainian language, we present our proposed solution of supervised fine-tuning of an LLM on a dataset generated in an unsupervised way. Additionally, we have prepared a validation dataset for the Ukrainian WSD task, derived from the SUM (Dictionary of Ukrainian Language) dictionary of NAS of Ukraine (ULIF-NASU).

Our approach will enhance the model's understanding of semantic word meaning and improve the performance of the Word Sense Disambiguation task in the Ukrainian language.

3 Evaluation Dataset

To assess the efficacy of our methodology for addressing the Ukrainian WSD task, we have established a validation dataset based on the SUM dictionary. The SUM dictionary is an appropriate resource as it employs componential analysis, a linguistic methodology used to differentiate common language phenomena such as polysemy and homonymy, by evaluating the presence or absence of shared semantic features among compared units. Therefore, the dataset derived from the SUM dictionary is well-suited for evaluating the performance of our approach. According to Ukrainian Lingua-Information Fund (2022), the examples in the SUM dictionary were taken from a broad selection of resources, including fiction (from the end of the 18th century to the present day), Ukrainian translations of the Bible, folklore, publicistic, scientific, and popular scientific works, the language of the mass media, the language of the Internet, etc. Unfortunately, at the moment of publication, there is only part of the dictionary available (until word ПІДКУРЮВАЧ (en: lighter, translit: pidkuryuvach)).

The dataset was constructed by extracting each lemma, its lexical meaning, and examples of usage related to that meaning. While building the evaluation dataset, the lemmas with single possible lexical senses were filtered out, and the resulting dataset consisted of 78,000 samples. Further data cleaning was performed to remove lemmas with a length of fewer than three characters, lemmas with missing senses or examples, lemmas that belong to functional parts of speech, and lemmas which lexical meaning reference for another lemma. After cleaning, the dataset consisted of 42,000 samples, with each sample consisting of a lemma, one of the possible lexical meanings of the lemma, and examples of this meaning. Assembling the dataset involved part-of-speech (POS) detection for each lemma using the Stanza library Qi et al. (2020), and this information was utilized in the subsequent evaluation table.

During our experiments, we observed that many lemmas in the Ukrainian language have multiple similar lexical meanings, which significantly complicates the task, the examples presented in Table 1. To address this issue, we built a dataset focusing on homonymy rather than polysemy.

Homonyms are unrelated words with the same written and spelling form but different lexical meanings. To construct a dataset of homonyms, we first filtered out lemmas with fewer than two entries in the SUM dictionary. Then, for each remaining lemma, we concatenated all the lexical meanings and examples of usage of each separate homonym. The resulting dataset consisted of 2,882 homonym samples, each sample including the lemma, its possible meanings, and examples for each meaning (see Table 2). We used this dataset for further model evaluation.

Lemma	Meaning	Example
КОСА (en: braid, transl: kosa)	Заплетене волосся (en: Braided hair)	Очі в неї були великі, дві чорні коси, перекинуті наперед, обрамляли лице. (en: Her eyes were large, two black braids, thrown forward, framed her face.)
КОСА (en: braid, transl: kosa)	Довге волосся (en: Long hair)	Густі, золото-жовті коси буйними хвилями спадали на її груди і плечі. (en: Thick, golden-yellow braids fell in wild waves on her chest and shoulders.)

Table 1: Examples from polysemy dataset (similar lexical meanings)

4 Approach

4.1 Task Definition

In our approach to Word Sense Disambiguation, for each homonym l (target word), we have identified a set of possible lexical meaning groups, denoted as

$$G_l = \{g_{l_1}, ..., g_{l_n}\}$$

Each lexical meaning group g_{l_i}, comprises all the possible lexical meanings of a particular lemma corresponding to the homonym. Our objective is to predict the correct lexical meaning group g_{l_i}, from all the possible lexical meaning groups of the lemma G_l, based on a list of examples of the lemma's usage.

To accomplish this, we first calculate embeddings for the sentence example and obtain the target word embedding from it using various pooling strategies, which will be described later. Subsequently, we measure the cosine similarity between the obtained embedding of the target word and the embeddings of each lexical meaning group. The lexical meaning group with the highest cosine similarity is considered to be the predicted context. Figure 1 demonstrates an example of the single lemma prediction process utilizing our approach.

4.2 Evaluation

In order to evaluate the performance of our WSD approach, we have chosen to utilize the accuracy metric. Specifically, for each sample in the dataset, we compare the predicted context of the lemma (see Figure 1) with the ground truth context derived from the corresponding example. Any instances where the predicted context matches the ground truth context are considered correct predictions, and the overall accuracy is calculated based on the total number of correct predictions.

4.3 Embedding calculation

In the context of natural language processing (NLP), word embeddings have emerged as a powerful technique to represent words in a numerical form, which can then be leveraged to perform various NLP tasks, including Word Sense Disambiguation. Each word is mapped to a high-dimensional vector of real numbers in word embeddings, which encodes its semantic and syntactic information based on its context in a given corpus. By capturing words' intrinsic meaning and contextual usage, word embeddings have demonstrated their effectiveness in various NLP applications, including WSD Huang et al. (2019).

In NLP, one of the most effective approaches for generating high-quality contextualized word embeddings is leveraging pre-trained LLMs such as RoBERTa Liu et al. (2019) or GPT-2 Radford et al. (2019). LLMs allow the calculation of word embeddings for individual words or entire sentences. For instance, the BERT (Bidirectional Encoder Representations from Transformers) base model Devlin et al. (2018) employs 12 layers of transformer encoders, which utilize a multi-head attention mechanism to learn context-dependent representations of input tokens. The resultant output vector of each token from each layer of the BERT model can be used as a word embedding.

Various pooling strategies can be applied to generate embeddings for individual words or entire sentences, but determining the most effective strategy for a particular task requires experimental investigation. In this study, we conducted experiments to compare the performance of different pooling methods, including:

1. Mean pooling - computes the average of the embeddings for each token from the last hidden state of the model. The last hidden state

Lemma	Meaning	Example
КОСА (en: braid, transl: kosa)	[Заплетене волосся (en: Braided hair), Довге волосся (en: Long hair)]	[Очі в неї були великі, дві чорні коси, перекинуті наперед, обрамляли лице. (en: Her eyes were large, two black braids, thrown forward, framed her face.); Густі, золото-жовті коси буйними хвилями спадали на її груди і плечі. (en: Thick, golden-yellow braids fell in wild waves on her chest and shoulders.)]
КОСА (en: scythe, transl: kosa)	[Сільськогосподарське знаряддя для косіння трави, збіжжя тощо, що має вигляд вузького зігнутого леза, прикріпленого до держака. (en: An agricultural tool for mowing grass, grain, etc., having the form of a narrow bent blade attached to a handle.)]	[Внук косу несе в росу. (en: A grandson carries a scythe into the dew.)]

Table 2: Examples from the homonym dataset

corresponds to the sequence of hidden states at the output of the model's final layer.

2. Max pooling - extracts the maximum value of the embeddings for each token from the last hidden state of the model.

3. Mean Max pooling - calculates the average and maximum values of the embeddings for each token from the last hidden state of the model and concatenates the resulting vector.

4. Concatenate pooling - concatenates the embeddings from the last four hidden states.

5. Last four or two pooling - sums the embeddings from the last four or two hidden states.

Based on our experiments, we concluded that the mean pooling shows the best results in the WSD task for the Ukrainian language (see Table 3).

Our research aimed to determine the most effective LLM for generating contextual embeddings. To achieve this, we conducted experiments using a range of multilingual LLMs and evaluated their performance without fine-tuning. Our results in Table 3 demonstrates that one of the SBERT models Reimers and Gurevych (2019), namely paraphrase-multilingual-mpnet-base-v2 (PMMBv2), produced the highest quality contextual embeddings for our WSD task on a homonym dataset. Interestingly, our findings suggest that the SBERT model, initially designed to improve the semantic representation of entire sentences, can also significantly enhance the semantic representation of individual words.

5 Embeddings improvement

5.1 Dataset for fine-tuning

In order to enhance the quality of embeddings and to achieve superior performance on words with multiple lexical senses, we opted to fine-tune our best model, PMMBv2, as a means to improve its efficiency. Typically, researchers rely on supervised datasets such as Semcor Miller et al. (1993) or SemEval-2007 Pradhan et al. (2007) to enhance WSD task performance, consisting of pairs of sentences and a sense for a particular lemma, along with binary labels indicating the usage of a lemma in that particular context. Unfortunately, no such dataset is available for the Ukrainian language, leading us to pursue fine-tuning our model using a dataset generated using our proposed unsupervised method.

Our dataset samples consist of an anchor, a positive, and a negative example. To define positive and

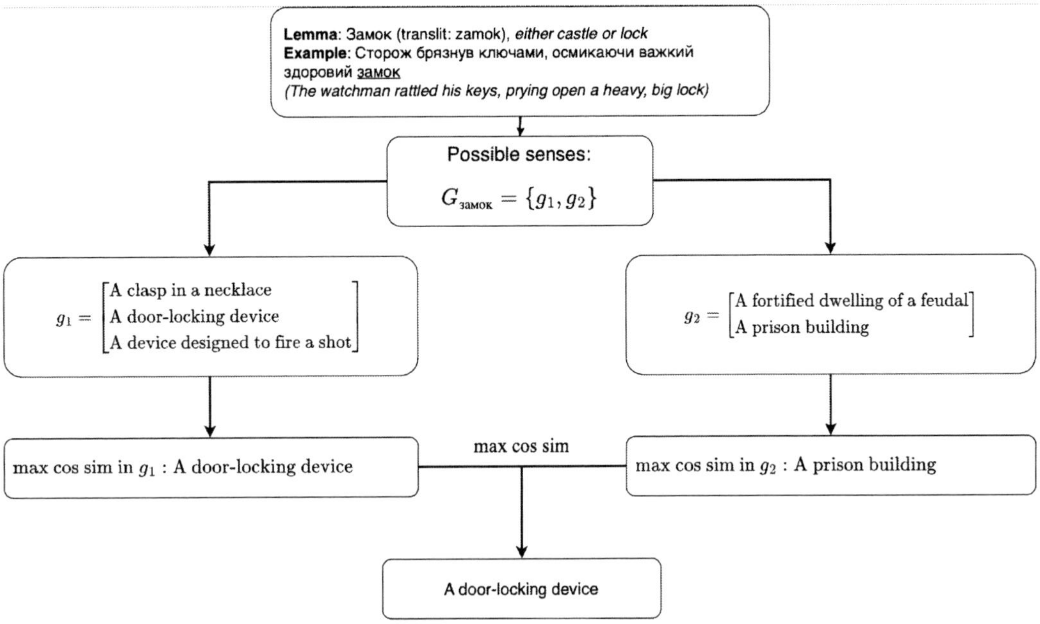

Figure 1: Prediction Logic for Lemma "Замок" (translit: zamok). In Ukrainian, the lemma "zamok" has two possible meanings. The first one means a castle, and the second is a lock. In this figure, we depicted prediction logic given an example, lemma of interest, and possible senses.

negative examples relative to the anchor sentence for the WSD task, we determined that the positive sample should be a sentence with a lemma used in the same context as in the anchor sentence. In contrast, the negative sample should be a lemma used in a different context.

In order to acquire a suitable dataset, an entirely unsupervised methodology was employed. The Developers' preview of UberText 2.0 Chaplynskyi (2023), which comprises of texts from Ukrainian periodicals, was utilized to gather a vast number of Ukrainian language sentences. Subsequently, we filtered out sentences that did not contain any lemmas from our homonym evaluation dataset (Evaluation Dataset). We removed outliers based on criteria such as length and the presence of punctuation symbols or digits. We also employed langdetect Shuyo (2010) to remove non-Ukrainian language samples.

Each dataset sample was then represented as an embedding using ukr-roberta Radchenko (2020). We calculated the cosine distance between the anchor embedding and all other sentences in the dataset containing the required lemma. We then assumed that the sample with the highest cosine similarity would be the positive sample - containing a lemma used in the same context as in the anchor sentence and that the sample with the lowest cosine similarity would be the negative sample, containing a lemma used in a different context.

This dataset is available in two sizes, consisting of ~190,000 and ~1,200,000 triplet pairs obtained from UberText 2.0.

We assessed the suitability of our dataset for fine-tuning by selecting a subset of examples to determine if target lemmas in positive and negative instances have distinct lexical meanings. After sampling approximately 100 examples, we found that 13.1% of the samples constituted relevant triplets. In the Conclusion section of this paper, we will provide future works for enhancing the dataset's quality.

5.2 Loss

Given that we had access to a suitable dataset, we opted to employ the TripletMarginLoss Balntas et al. (2016) for fine-tuning our neural network.

The Triplet Margin Loss function is used to optimize a neural network by minimizing the distance between the embedding of an anchor sentence and that of a positive example while maximizing the distance between the anchor and a negative example. The loss function is defined as follows:

$$max(||a - p|| - ||a - n|| + M, 0)$$

Model	Mean	Max	Mean Max	Concatenat	Last four	Last two
bert-base-multilingual-cased	0.602	0.601	0.622	0.576	0.579	0.590
xlm-roberta-base	0.529	0.492	0.501	0.534	0.531	0.533
xlm-roberta-large	0.547	0.495	0.502	0.576	0.581	0.576
xlm-roberta-base-uk	0.528	0.491	0.501	0.535	0.533	0.535
ukr-roberta	0.580	0.559	0.570	0.572	0.570	0.582
paraphrase-multilingual-mpnet-base-v2	**0.735**	0.718	0.716	0.644	0.636	0.656

Table 3: Word Sense Disambiguation (WSD) Accuracy for Ukrainian language with Different Pooling Strategies and Pretrained Models without fine-tuning.

where a, p, and n are the embeddings of the anchor, positive, and negative sentences, respectively, and M is a margin hyperparameter that ensures that the positive example is at least closer to the anchor than the negative example. We used Euclidean distance as the distance metric in our experiments and set $M = 1$.

5.3 Training process

During the model's training, we monitored the performance of Word Sense Disambiguation accuracy on 20% of the SUM evaluation dataset to assess if it was being improved with the training process. We used 1% of a fine-tuning dataset to calculate training metrics and the rest 99% for training. We employed an early stopping mechanism based on the WSD accuracy on SUM based evaluation dataset. A batch size of 32 and the Adam optimizer with a learning rate of 2e-6 were used for the model optimization. Furthermore, we applied linear learning rate warm-up over the first 10% of the training data.

6 Results

The Table 4 presents the performance evaluation of our proposed method on the SUM evaluation dataset for homonyms.

We started with the Babelfy as a baseline, which was manually validated on 10% of the randomly sampled portion from the WSD evaluation dataset. Next, we tested a vanilla PMMBv2 model without fine-tuning, followed by a fine-tuned version of the PMMBv2 model using the proposed approach. The models fine-tuned by our approach outperform both Babelfy and vanilla PMMBv2 models. We observed that a larger dataset for fine-tuning led to better accuracy.

We assume that a model trained on a larger dataset, which also has a larger average distance between positive and negative examples, generates better homonym-specific embeddings. We also observed that the model PMMBv2 tuned on 1,2M triplets with filtering out pairs with a small difference (less than 0.3) between the cosine similarity of the anchor and positive examples and that of the anchor and negative examples, resulting in the best accuracy.

As the dataset used for training our model was constructed in an unsupervised manner, there existed a possibility of the model being biased towards the most frequently occurring senses of a given lemma. To assess this, we evaluated the model's accuracy based on the frequency of sense usage referring to the SUM dictionary (see Table 5). Our findings showed that the PMMBv2 model tuned on $\sim$1,2M triplets with filtering performed better for the less commonly occurring senses. Therefore, we can infer that the fine-tuned model not only considers the context but also makes predictions that are not solely based on the popularity of a sense.

We have evaluated our approach on the polysemy dataset to investigate the correlation between the performance of the model on homonyms and polysemous lemmas. The Table 6 shows the accuracy of the model on the polysemy dataset, where we have examined the model's ability to predict the first 2/3/all lexical meanings of each lemma. How-

Model	Overall acc.	Noun acc.	Verb acc.	Adj. acc.	Adv. acc.
Babelfy baseline	0.526	-	-	-	-
PMMBv2	0.735	0.767	0.668	0.752	0.593
PMMBv2 tuned on $\sim$190K triplets	0.77	0.819	0.685	0.743	0.562
PMMBv2 tuned on $\sim$1,2M triplets	0.778	**0.825**	**0.698**	**0.761**	0.531
PMMBv2 tuned on $\sim$1,2M triplets with filtering	**0.779**	0.824	0.693	0.759	**0.607**

Table 4: Accuracy on the WSD homonym evaluation dataset for Ukrainian Language using Babelfy, PMMBv2, and models fine-tuned by the proposed approach.

Frequency of sense usage	PMMBv2	PMMBv2 tuned on $\sim$1,2M triplets with filtering
1	0.76	0.799
2	0.703	0.754
3	0.666	0.773

Table 5: Accuracy on the WSD evaluation dataset for the Ukrainian Language based on the frequency of sense usage for the PMMBv2 baseline and fine-tuned version.

ever, we have observed a decrease in performance when evaluating the polysemy dataset, despite using better homonym-specific embeddings achieved through fine-tuning. We hypothesize that this may be due to the challenge of distinguishing between similar meanings for polysemous words (see Table 1). Furthermore, our observations indicate that the model PMMBv2, fine-tuned on 1,2M triplets with filtering out pairs, exhibits an even greater decrease in performance when applied to the polysemy dataset compared to PMMBv2 fine-tuned on 1,2M triplets without filtering.

7 Conclusion

Our research proposes a novel approach for solving the WSD task in under-resourced languages such as Ukrainian. We used a supervised approach to fine-tune LLMs on the unsupervised dataset generated by our method.

Furthermore, we built an evaluation dataset based on the SUM dictionary, which other researchers can use for evaluating the WSD task in the Ukrainian language.

We implemented the U-WSD framework during the research, which preprocess and generate evaluation and fine-tuning datasets, perform inference, and measure performance.

Our approach achieved 77.9% accuracy on the homonym dataset, surpassing graph-based methods such as Babelfy.

Future work aims to enhance the quality of the fine-tuning dataset by employing several measures. These measures include the removal of nearly identical anchor and positive examples, the exclusion of named entities detected as the target lemma, and the sampling of a more uniformly representative subset of examples for each lemma. We also want to improve the target lemma detection algorithm. Additionally, we plan to explore more advanced embedding comparison mechanisms beyond cosine similarity.

Limitations

The proposed approach has several limitations. Firstly, the approach is evaluated on a relatively small dataset of homonyms, which contains example from fiction, folklore, etc. Our dataset might not represent the entire Ukrainian language. Additionally, we focus only on homonymy, which may limit the approach's applicability to real-world scenarios where both homonymy and polysemy are present.

During our research on WSD, we discovered a lack of bias control in the SUM and UberText datasets. This deficiency presents a potential issue of such as gender, race, or socioeconomic status biases in our model.

Recreating the fine-tuning process requires a GPU with sufficient memory, such as the NVIDIA T4 GPU with 16 GB of memory on the AWS in-

Model	First 2 senses	First 3 senses	All senses
PMMBv2	0.682	0.637	0.608
PMMBv2 tuned on ∼190K triplets	**0.702**	**0.66**	**0.632**
PMMBv2 tuned on ∼1,2M triplets	0.7	0.656	0.629
PMMBv2 tuned on ∼1,2M triplets with filtering	0.689	0.646	0.618

Table 6: Accuracy on the WSD polysemy evaluation dataset for Ukrainian Language using, PMMBv2, and models fine-tuned by the proposed approach.

stance g4dn.xlarge.

To use the proposed approach for languages other than Ukrainian, a dictionary with lemmas and their lexical meanings, mechanisms to classify parts of speech, and a large dataset with sentences from various areas to cover lemmas with different meanings are needed.

Ethics Statement

Our objective is to increase the accessibility of NLP research by prioritizing under-resourced languages, with a particular focus on Ukrainian language research. Through the development of generalizable approaches, we hope to create solutions that can be applied to a variety of languages beyond Ukrainian. We are also mindful of the potential real-world impact of our research, and we strive to ensure that our work contributes to the advancement of society. Finally, we believe in the importance of engaging with the broader NLP community, particularly the global ACL community, to promote collaboration and knowledge-sharing.

References

Vassileios Balntas, Edgar Riba, Daniel Ponsa, and Krystian Mikolajczyk. 2016. Learning local feature descriptors with triplets and shallow convolutional neural networks. In *Bmvc*, volume 1, page 3.

Edoardo Barba, Luigi Procopio, and Roberto Navigli. 2021. Consec: Word sense disambiguation as continuous sense comprehension. In *Proceedings of the 2021 Conference on Empirical Methods in Natural Language Processing*, pages 1492–1503.

Dmytro Chaplynskyi. 2023. Introducing UberText 2.0: a corpus of modern Ukrainian at scale. In *Proceedings of the Second Ukrainian Natural Language Processing Workshop*, pages 1–10, Dubrovnik, Croatia. Association for Computational Linguistics.

Jacob Devlin, Ming-Wei Chang, Kenton Lee, and Kristina Toutanova. 2018. Bert: Pre-training of deep bidirectional transformers for language understanding. *arXiv preprint arXiv:1810.04805*.

Manaal Faruqui, Jesse Dodge, Sujay K Jauhar, Chris Dyer, Eduard Hovy, and Noah A Smith. 2014. Retrofitting word vectors to semantic lexicons. *arXiv preprint arXiv:1411.4166*.

Luyao Huang, Chi Sun, Xipeng Qiu, and Xuanjing Huang. 2019. Glossbert: Bert for word sense disambiguation with gloss knowledge. *arXiv preprint arXiv:1908.07245*.

Yinhan Liu, Myle Ott, Naman Goyal, Jingfei Du, Mandar Joshi, Danqi Chen, Omer Levy, Mike Lewis, Luke Zettlemoyer, and Veselin Stoyanov. 2019. Roberta: A robustly optimized bert pretraining approach. *arXiv preprint arXiv:1907.11692*.

Tomas Mikolov, Kai Chen, Greg Corrado, and Jeffrey Dean. 2013. Efficient estimation of word representations in vector space. *arXiv preprint arXiv:1301.3781*.

George A Miller, Claudia Leacock, Randee Tengi, and Ross T Bunker. 1993. A semantic concordance. In *Human Language Technology: Proceedings of a Workshop Held at Plainsboro, New Jersey, March 21-24, 1993*.

Andrea Moro, Alessandro Raganato, and Roberto Navigli. 2014. Entity linking meets word sense disambiguation: a unified approach. *Transactions of the Association for Computational Linguistics*, 2:231–244.

Roberto Navigli. 2009. Word sense disambiguation: A survey. *ACM computing surveys (CSUR)*, 41(2):1–69.

Steven Neale, Luís Gomes, Eneko Agirre, Oier Lopez de Lacalle, and António Branco. 2016. Word sense-aware machine translation: Including senses as contextual features for improved translation models. In *Proceedings of the Tenth International Conference on Language Resources and Evaluation (LREC'16)*, pages 2777–2783.

Ukrainian Lingua-Information Fund of NAS of Ukraine (ULIF-NASU). 2010. Словник української мови [Dictionary of the Ukrainian language], volume 20 of Словники України [Dictionaries of Ukraine]. Наук. думка [Nauk. dumka], Kyiv.

Jeffrey Pennington, Richard Socher, and Christopher D Manning. 2014. Glove: Global vectors for word representation. In Proceedings of the 2014 conference on empirical methods in natural language processing (EMNLP), pages 1532–1543.

Sameer Pradhan, Edward Loper, Dmitriy Dligach, and Martha Palmer. 2007. Semeval-2007 task-17: English lexical sample, srl and all words. In Proceedings of the fourth international workshop on semantic evaluations (SemEval-2007), pages 87–92.

Peng Qi, Yuhao Zhang, Yuhui Zhang, Jason Bolton, and Christopher D Manning. 2020. Stanza: A python natural language processing toolkit for many human languages. arXiv preprint arXiv:2003.07082.

Vitalii Radchenko. 2020. Youscan. https://youscan.io/blog/ukrainian-language-model/.

Alec Radford, Jeffrey Wu, Rewon Child, David Luan, Dario Amodei, Ilya Sutskever, et al. 2019. Language models are unsupervised multitask learners. OpenAI blog, 1(8):9.

Nils Reimers and Iryna Gurevych. 2019. Sentence-bert: Sentence embeddings using siamese bert-networks. arXiv preprint arXiv:1908.10084.

Neetu Sharma and Prof. S. Niranjan. 2015. Applications of word sense disambiguation: A historical perspective. INTERNATIONAL JOURNAL OF ENGINEERING RESEARCH TECHNOLOGY (IJERT) NCETEMS-2015 (Volume 3-Issue 10).

Nakatani Shuyo. 2010. Language detection library for java. http://code.google.com/p/language-detection/.

Robyn Speer, Joshua Chin, and Catherine Havasi. 2017. Conceptnet 5.5: An open multilingual graph of general knowledge. In Proceedings of the AAAI conference on artificial intelligence, volume 31.

NAS of Ukraine Ukrainian Lingua-Information Fund. 2022. Ulif. https://en.ulif.org.ua/.

Gregor Wiedemann, Steffen Remus, Avi Chawla, and Chris Biemann. 2019. Does bert make any sense? interpretable word sense disambiguation with contextualized embeddings. arXiv preprint arXiv:1909.10430.

A U-WSD framework

During our research, we implemented the framework to aid in working with models and evaluating their performance in the WSD task for the Ukrainian language, which is available at `https://github.com/YuriiLaba/U-WSD`. This framework consists of three main parts: (1) cleaning and generation of the SUM dataset, (2) embedding calculation and prediction running, and (3) performance metric evaluation.

The first part includes various dataset-cleaning techniques, such as filtering by the length of the lemma, selecting the first n senses or examples for each lemma, and more. Additionally, this part allows the generation of a dataset with lexical meanings for each lemma separately or grouping meanings at the homonym level.

The second part enables the selection of different models and pooling strategies for calculating embeddings for lexical meanings and examples. Finally, the third part generates a performance report based on the part of speech, lemma frequency which is obtained from the Ubertext dataset Chaplynskyi (2023), and different numbers of top n lexical senses of a lemma.

Learning Word Embeddings for Ukrainian: A Comparative Study of FastText Hyperparameters

Nataliia Romanyshyn*
Ukrainian Catholic University
Lviv, Ukraine
romanyshyn.n@ucu.edu.ua

Dmytro Chaplynskyi*
Lang-uk
Kyiv, Ukraine
chaplinsky.dmitry@gmail.com

Kyrylo Zakharov
Court on the Palm
Kyiv, Ukraine
kirillzakharov13@gmail.com

Abstract

This study addresses the challenges of learning unsupervised word representations for the morphologically rich and low-resource Ukrainian language. Traditional models that perform decently on English do not generalize well for such languages due to a lack of sufficient data and the complexity of their grammatical structures. To overcome these challenges, we utilized a high-quality, large dataset of different genres for learning Ukrainian word vector representations. We found the best hyperparameters to train fastText language models on this dataset and performed intrinsic and extrinsic evaluations of the generated word embeddings using the established methods and metrics. The results of this study indicate that the trained vectors exhibit superior performance on intrinsic tests in comparison to existing embeddings for Ukrainian. Our best model gives 62% Accuracy on the word analogy task. Extrinsic evaluations were performed on two sequence labeling tasks: NER and POS tagging (83% spaCy NER F-score, 83% spaCy POS Accuracy, 92% Flair POS Accuracy).

1 Introduction

Word embeddings (Almeida and Xexéo, 2019) are fixed-length vector representations of words that have a variety of applications in natural language processing (NLP) tasks, including semantic text similarity (Nguyen et al., 2019), word sense disambiguation (Ruas et al., 2019), text classification (Mandelbaum and Shalev, 2016), question answering (Shen et al., 2017). Word embedding techniques rely on the distributional hypothesis – the assumption that the meaning of a word is captured by the contexts in which it appears (Harris, 1954).

Even though unsupervised word embeddings can be learned directly from raw texts, gathering a significant amount of data for their training remains an immense challenge for low-resource languages such as Ukrainian. Moreover, Ukrainian is a morphologically rich language; its nouns decline for 7 cases, three genders, and two numbers. Adjectives agree with nouns in case, gender, and number. Verbs conjugate for four tenses, two voices, and two numbers. Ukrainian verbs come in aspect pairs: perfective and imperfective. Not surprisingly, traditional models that give excellent results for English may not be able to generalize well for highly inflected languages, such as Ukrainian, without special tuning.

To address these challenges, we worked with a high-quality, large dataset of different genres for learning vector representations of words in the Ukrainian language. We identified the best hyperparameters to train fastText language models on this dataset and performed the intrinsic and extrinsic evaluations of the generated word embeddings using firmly established methods and metrics. Furthermore, the obtained vectors were compared with the ones previously published by the Facebook team[1] (Grave et al., 2018) and those trained using the default hyperparameters. Our optimized models outperformed the baseline models by **7.1%** in Accuracy on the word analogy task, and showed a **6.4%** improvement compared to the Ukrainian word embeddings published by Grave et al. (2018).

The novel contributions of this work are:

- Conducted the first study of effects of various hyperparameters for fastText word embeddings in the Ukrainian language.
- Created and made publicly available the largest collection of pre-trained Ukrainian word embeddings. The best models are available on the Hugging Face platform[2], and others upon request.
- Presented a new word analogy dataset for

*These authors contributed equally to this work.

[1] https://fasttext.cc/docs/en/crawl-vectors.html

[2] https://huggingface.co/dchaplinsky/fasttext_uk

Proceedings of the Second Ukrainian Natural Language Processing Workshop (UNLP), pages 20–31
May 5, 2023 ©2023 Association for Computational Linguistics

Ukrainian[3].

- Provided the first formal analysis of Ukrainian word vectors utilizing intrinsic and extrinsic approaches.

The obtained results allow NLP practitioners to reduce the computational resources and time required to develop algorithms for solving applied NLP tasks.

The rest of the paper is organized as follows. Section 2 contains an overview of related work. Section 3 presents the data collection and preprocessing techniques. We describe the methodology for learning word vectors and conducted experiments in Section 4. Section 5 describes the evaluation methods and obtained results. We conclude and present future work in Section 6.

2 Related work

A standard approach (Miaschi and Dell'Orletta, 2020) for learning non-contextual word representations is to train a log-bilinear model based on the continuous bag-of-words (cbow) or the skip-gram architectures. An example of such a language model is word2vec, described by Mikolov et al. (2013a). It learns continuous representations of words using a shallow neural net. Mikolov et al. (2013b) showed that these representations capture syntactic and semantic regularities in language decently, and presented a novel method — word analogies — for evaluating word embeddings based on vector arithmetic.

Word2vec's main drawback is that it ignores the word's internal structure that contains rich information. This knowledge could be beneficial in computing representations of uncommon or misspelled words and for morphologically rich languages like Ukrainian. To address this issue, the fastText method (Bojanowski et al., 2017) proposed to take word morphology into account by representing each word as a bag of character n-grams. They evaluated the fastText model on nine languages exhibiting different morphologies, but Ukrainian was omitted.

Grave et al. (2018) developed and released fastText language models for 157 languages, including Ukrainian, but they did not provide any evaluation of the embeddings for this language. They used Wikipedia, which is of limited diversity, and quite noisy data from the Common Crawl (CC) project[4] for learning their word vectors. Another shortcoming is that they did not optimize subword size and employed character n-grams of size 5–5 for all languages. Also, the authors concluded that the quality of the obtained vectors for low-resource languages is significantly worse than for high-resource ones.

Novotný et al. (2021) discovered that subword sizes have a significant impact on the Accuracy of fastText language models, and their optimization enhanced the Accuracy on word analogy tasks by up to 14%. The authors proposed a simple n-gram coverage model and discovered the optimal subword sizes on the English, German, Czech, Italian, Spanish, French, Hindi, Turkish, and Russian word analogy tasks. We utilized their findings for Czech and Russian as they also belong to the Slavic language group.

In the current study, we evaluate how the corpus size, specific models, and set of hyperparameters affect the quality of Ukrainian word embeddings for different NLP tasks. Also, we conduct a proper evaluation of the proposed by Grave et al. (2018) word embeddings for Ukrainian and compare them with our results.

3 Training Dataset

This section presents our datasets and preprocessing techniques.

3.1 Corpus Selection

Currently available corpora for the Ukrainian language include:

- Zvidusil[5] corpus, which contains 2,8 billion tokens. Around ten text sources of Zvidusil are collected by the specialized parsers. The rest is retrieved automatically using SpiderLing[6];
- General Regionally Annotated Corpus of Ukrainian (GRAC)[7], collected by Shvedova et al. (2017-2022). It consists of approximately 890 million tokens and has various genre coverage, good general quality, and unique texts;
- other corpora[8] of a smaller size.

[3]https://github.com/lang-uk/vecs/blob/master/test/test_vocabulary.txt

[4]https://commoncrawl.org

[5]https://mova.institute/

[6]http://corpus.tools/wiki/SpiderLing

[7]http://uacorpus.org/

[8]http://uacorpus.org/Kyiv/ua/other-ukrainian-corpora

General corpora statistics are summarized in Table 1.

Table 1: Statistical information on Zvidusil and GRAC corpora.

Corpus	Zvidusil	GRAC
# of tokens	2,848,203,658	889,097,859
# of sentences	155,821,729	55,324,205
# of documents	6,936,227	113,569

Unfortunately, neither Zvidusil nor GRAC datasets are open-source and available for direct download.

Therefore, we decided to use other corpora — UberText 1.0[9] and the developer preview of UberText 2.0[10]. We summarize these datasets in Table 2.

UberText 1.0 is the smaller one and includes 11 news websites spanning 2006-2016, Ukrainian Wikipedia as of 2016, and fiction. UberText 2.0 — the bigger one, at the moment of the experiment, consisted of 30 news websites spanning 2000-2021, Ukrainian Wikipedia as of 2021, and a bigger subcorpus of fiction. The final version of the UberText 2.0 corpus is a subject of a separate paper (Chaplynskyi, 2023); here, we only cover the essential aspects of its composition and preprocessing.

Table 2: Training datasets description. The **# of words** indicates the vocabulary size of the models trained on this dataset and equals to the number of unique tokens.

Corpus	UberText 1.0	UberText 2.0
# of tokens	665,322,645	1,589,010,407
# of words	1,758,917	2,665,029
# of sentences	48,522,905	126,696,187
Size	8.4 GB	20.1 GB

Both datasets were collected using custom-written spiders for the Scrapy[11] framework to parse publicly available sources of Ukrainian texts.

The selection of sources covers modern vocabulary of the Ukrainian language and, therefore, is helpful for the downstream tasks. All the texts were converted from the HTML markup to Markdown standard using html2text[12] to maintain the basic structure of headers and sub-headers.

In comparison to UberText 1.0, the second version provides the following improvements:

- more sources of texts;
- texts that were added to the existing sources since 2016;
- better internal structure and meta information on texts (authorship, tags, images).

It was a deliberate decision not to include Common Crawl or Oscar[13] corpora data into UberText because of their aggregated nature and instead focus on individual sources of texts rather than deal with noisy input.

3.2 UberText Preprocessing

All the texts were preprocessed using the nlp-uk[14] library, a wrapper for the LanguageTool[15]; the following techniques were applied:

1. cleansing — removal of Markdown tags, fix for broken encodings, normalization of the hyphens, apostrophes, fixes for mixed Latin/Cyrillic texts, fixes for simple word wraps;
2. rating for the number of used Ukrainian and Russian dictionary words and characters specific to Ukrainian and Russian alphabets;
3. tokenization into paragraphs, sentences, and words using the LanguageTool tokenizer for the Ukrainian language;
4. removal of punctuation marks.

No changes were made to the word capitalization in texts.

During the export of the texts, the following filters were applied:

- Texts with a substantial amount of Russian words (over 25%) were removed to exclude articles wholly or partially written in Russian.
- Articles shorter than 100 characters were also removed.

[9] https://lang.org.ua/static/downloads/corpora/ubercorpus.txt.tokenized.noemptylines.no_markdown.txt.bz2

[10] https://lang.org.ua/static/downloads/corpora/ubertext.fiction_news_wikipedia.filter_rus+short.tokens.txt.bz2

[11] https://scrapy.org

[12] https://pypi.org/project/html2text/

[13] https://oscar-corpus.com

[14] https://github.com/brown-uk/nlp_uk

[15] https://github.com/languagetool-org/languagetool

4 Embedding methods

While recent advances in NLP have been dominated by transformer-based language models, there is still a place for simpler models like continuous bag-of-words (cbow) and skipgram (Mikolov et al., 2013a) in certain scenarios. These models offer several advantages over more complex ones, particularly in low-resource settings. For one, they are computationally efficient and can be trained on smaller datasets. Additionally, they offer greater interpretability and transparency, making it easier to understand how the model makes its predictions.

Given these advantages, we choose to use cbow and skipgram methods for obtaining context-independent word embeddings for our study.

Cbow model learns to predict a target word based on its context, using the sum of the background vectors. A predefined window size surrounding the target word represents the neighboring terms taken into account.

Skipgram is another architecture for creating word embeddings. The model uses a target word for predicting the context by summing the log probabilities of the surrounding words to the left and right of the target word.

For the study, we have chosen the fastText[16] implementation of these models, where morphology is taken into account. Each word is represented as a bag of character n-grams (i.e., subwords), and the word vector is obtained by taking the sum of the vectors of the character n-grams appearing in that particular word (Bojanowski et al., 2017). While being the golden implementation, it has two shortcomings that weren't described in the project documentation:

- has a hyperparameter wordNgram that does not impact the training;
- it lacks the implementation of the cbow algorithm with positional weights, called cbow weighted in what follows. Such an algorithm was first described in the work of Grave et al. (2018) and used to train reference word vectors, available for 157 languages. To overcome this issue, we have switched to an alternative implementation described in the paragraph below.

Cbow with positional weights is a variation of the cbow model that modifies the input vectors of context words to better depict the relationship between the target and context words based on their relative positions (Novotný et al., 2022). The authors noted that the positional model more than doubles the training time since, for each gradient update of an input vector, we also need to update the weights of a positional vector. We utilized the implementation of the positional weighted model presented in the paper mentioned above.

4.1 Baseline

In order to compare learned embeddings, we trained the fastText model on our dataset UberText 2.0 (20.1 GB) with default parameters, but the vector dimension was fixed to 300 instead of 100. We introduce this model as a "Baseline".

4.2 Hyperparameter tuning

We decided to add the following modifications to the Baseline model for obtaining high-quality word vectors:

1. more epochs for training; by default, the fastText library trains for five epochs;
2. more negative samples; by default, it samples five negative examples;
3. use different character n-grams size instead of the default range of 3–6;
4. also utilize the cbow model for learning word vectors; the default is the skipgram variant.

The increment in the number of the training epochs and negative samples refers to the results of Grave et al. (2018) experiments, which show that although such adjustments increase training time, they result in a significant increase in Accuracy. Subword ranges were chosen based on Novotný et al. (2021) reported accuracies on word analogies for Czech and Russian, which are the most related to Ukrainian among the studied languages.

In Table 3, we have collected all selected options for training fastText vectors for the current study. To find the best setting, we explored 32 combinations of parameters for learning word representations.

Since the cbow weighted model requires much time to learn, we did not train it on all combinations of parameters but used the best one according to our previous evaluation on other models and their performance on the word analogies. Therefore, subword range 2-5 and 15 negative samples were

[16] https://fasttext.cc/

Table 3: Selected parameters to study their impact on Ukrainian vectors' quality. Subword refers to the min and max character n-gram.

Model	Epochs	Subword	Negative Sampling
cbow	10	2-5	10
skipgram	15	2-6	15
		4-6	
		5-6	

used. Also, following the Grave et al. (2018) experiment setup, we trained word vectors with character n-grams of length five only and ten negative samples. As mentioned in Novotný et al. (2022), the positional model can benefit from a larger context window. Therefore, we set it to 15, as the optimal context window size defined by the authors.

To run the training on all the combinations of hyperparameters, we wrote the software[17] that can be quickly deployed on any server with enough RAM, effectively turning that server into a computational node that picks the next available task from the pool. That allowed us to quickly deploy it to the farm of seven servers and parallelize the grid search.

4.3 The impact of training data size

Another experiment was conducted to investigate the result stated by Bojanowski et al. (2017) regarding the impact of training data size on the quality of produced vectors. They argued that high-performing word embeddings can be constructed on a corpus of a restricted size while still performing well on previously unseen data. For the purpose of investigating this claim, we utilized the smaller corpus UberText 1.0 (8.4 GB) and trained with optimized parameters and hyperparameters on intrinsic and extrinsic tasks. See more details in Sections 5.1.2 and 5.2.3.

4.4 Estimating the hyperparameter significance

The quality of calculated word vectors was measured with the Accuracy and F1 score. Both metrics are continuous variables expressed in a range from 0 to 1. Therefore we used a Beta regression to regress the hyperparameters. It is assumed that the model's dependent variable is beta-distributed and that its value is related to a set of independent variables through a linear predictor with unknown coefficients and a link function (logit in our case). Calculations were made with betareg package (Zeileis et al., 2016) in the R environment for statistical computing (R Core Team, 2013).

5 Evaluation

In this section, we describe various evaluation metrics on trained word vectors. Prior work on evaluation of the embeddings can be divided into intrinsic and extrinsic evaluation methods (Torregrossa et al., 2021). We start with the intrinsic evaluation on the word analogy task, then continue with named entity recognition (NER) and part-of-speech (POS) tagging for extrinsic estimation.

5.1 Intrinsic Evaluation

Intrinsic evaluators directly measure the syntactic and semantic relationship between word vectors. For this study, we intrinsically evaluated our models on the word analogy task, also known as analogical reasoning, introduced by Mikolov et al. (2013b). In the test set, a triplet of words `A`, `B`, `C` is given, and the goal is to find the fourth word `D`, where `A` is to `B` as `C` to `D`. An example of such an analogy question is Kyiv relates to Ukraine as Madrid to `prediction`, where the correct answer is Spain.

5.1.1 Word Analogy Dataset

We developed the word analogy dataset for Ukrainian[18], which includes 23,970 questions on 12 topics. More precisely, analogy questions are represented by the relations shown in Table 4. To create a dataset, the following methods were used:

- GraphQL requests to WikiData[19] to obtain information about countries, capitals, nationalities, regions, currencies, and relations between them;
- PyMorphy2[20] library with Ukrainian dictionaries[21] installed to generate singular-plural, opposite, comparative, adjective-adverb, superlative, past tense-present, and verb-noun pairs, inflecting the manually crafted list of popular lemmas to generate a unique pair;

[17] https://github.com/lang-uk/fasttext-vectors-uk

[18] https://github.com/lang-uk/vecs/blob/master/test/test_vocabulary.txt

[19] https://www.wikidata.org/wiki/Wikidata:Main_Page

[20] https://github.com/kmike/pymorphy2

[21] https://pypi.org/project/pymorphy2-dicts-uk/

- the family relations were created manually.

Table 4: Word analogy dataset. Questions denote the number of word pairs to compare, and unique pairs denote the number of unique word pairs.

Relations	# of questions	# of unique pairs
country : capital	4,271	137
country : region	2,038	117
country : nationality	10,359	2,732
country : currency	729	28
family relations	400	21
singular : plural	1,225	36
adjective : adverb	961	32
opposite	625	26
comparative	400	21
superlative	1,089	33
past tense : present	1,089	33
verb : noun	784	29

To evaluate the vector model, a separate library was written[22] to read the dataset, load vectors, and run the intrinsic tests using gensim utilities [23]. Additional logic was added to the evaluation script to make it case-insensitive. The word vector model is tested on each topic separately and on all questions to get the total analogy score. The answer is considered correct if it occurs in the first n predictions (in our case, n = 4).

5.1.2 Results for Intrinsic Evaluation

Table 5 compares the Accuracy scores for the baseline models with default hyperparameters and the optimized models for different train datasets and algorithms.

Overall, it can be seen that the optimized skipgram model increases Accuracy by **7.1%** compared to the baseline model and by **6.4%** compared to the Grave et al. (2018) Ukrainian word embeddings. Models with larger training data (UberText 2.0) generally outperform models built with UberText 1.0. In terms of architecture selection, the skipgram model shows better results than the cbow one for the word analogy task. The same is supported by the regression analysis. Table 8 (Appendix A) provides estimated coefficients and their significance.

The Accuracy significantly depends on the selected model (skipgram is better) and the corpus size. Also, results can be improved by increasing the number of training epochs. The pseudo R-squared for the regression model is 0.957.

5.2 Extrinsic Evaluation

Extrinsic evaluation measures the contribution of the word vectors to a specific downstream task. The comparison result depends on the nature of these tasks and cannot be used as a metric for the quality of embeddings. Nevertheless, comparing performance across tasks may provide insight into the information encoded by embeddings (Schnabel et al., 2015).

We performed experiments on two sequence labeling models: NER and POS tagging. Named entity recognition is a standard NLP task that can identify entities discussed in a text document. Part-of-speech tagging is the process of labeling a word in the text with a particular part of speech based on both its context and definition.

5.2.1 Data

The datasets for extrinsic evaluation were derived from publicly available GitHub repositories:

NER. Ukrainian corpus for named entities recognition[24] comprises 238,927 tokens from 264 text samples. The primary source of the data is the open Brown Corpus of Ukrainian[25], including texts of different genres. The 6,751 entities are annotated by four classes for recognizing locations (LOC) — 4,390 entities, persons (PERS) — 1,616, organizations (ORG) — 780, and miscellaneous (MISC) — 660. We exploit the standard division into dev/test sets at 70%/30% for the training and validation of our models.

POS tagging. Ukrainian Universal Dependencies (UD) corpus[26] was developed by a non-profit organization Institute for Ukrainian[27]. The data follows the CoNLL-U format (Buchholz and Marsi, 2006). UD Ukrainian consists of 122K tokens in 7,000 sentences of different genres — fiction, news, opinion articles, Wikipedia, legal documents, letters, posts, and comments spanning the previous 15 years and the early twentieth century. The current study utilized the proposed data split between

[22] `https://github.com/lang-uk/vecs`

[23] `https://radimrehurek.com/gensim/models/keyedvectors.html#gensim.models.keyedvectors.KeyedVectors.most_similar`

[24] `https://github.com/lang-uk/ner-uk`

[25] `https://github.com/brown-uk/corpus`

[26] `https://github.com/UniversalDependencies/UD_Ukrainian-IU`

[27] `https://mova.institute/`

Table 5: Evaluated the Accuracy of word embeddings trained with default and optimized hyperparameters. Top Accuracy is marked in bold.

	Training Dataset	Model	Subword	Negative Sampling	Epochs	Intrinsic Accuracy
Grave et al. (2018)	Wikipedia+CC	cbow weighted	5-5	10	10	0.579
Our baselines	UberText 2.0	skipgram	3-6	5	5	0.575
	UberText 2.0	cbow	3-6	5	5	0.449
Our optimized	UberText 2.0	skipgram	2-5	15	15	**0.616**
	UberText 1.0	skipgram	2-5	15	10	0.573
	UberText 2.0	cbow	4-6	15	15	0.492
	UberText 1.0	cbow	5-6	15	15	0.473

Table 6: F1 scores for NER task for word embeddings trained with default and optimized hyperparameters. The top F1 score is marked in bold.

	Training Dataset	Model	Subword	Negative Sampling	Epochs	NER SpaCy F1
Grave et al. (2018)	Wikipedia+CC	cbow weighted	5-5	10	10	0.792
Our baselines	UberText 2.0	cbow	3-6	5	5	0.824
	UberText 2.0	skipgram	3-6	5	5	0.816
Our optimized	UberText 1.0	cbow	5-6	15	15	**0.827**
	UberText 2.0	cbow	2-6	10	10	0.826
	UberText 1.0	skipgram	2-5	15	15	0.824
	UberText 2.0	skipgram	2-5	15	15	0.818

train/dev/test at 75%/10%/15% balanced in genre and complexity.

5.2.2 Models

In order to conduct an extrinsic evaluation, we need to load our learned word vectors as input features into a blank model. In the current study, we exploit spaCy[28] and flair[29] (Akbik et al., 2019) libraries as they both support Ukrainian language and usage of custom word embeddings.

spaCy is a free and open-source software library that provides various practical tools for text processing. We used it for training both NER and POS tagging models. In spaCy, it is implemented by the `ner` and `morphologizer pipeline` components. The `morphologizer` aims to predict morphological features and coarse-grained POS tags following the Universal Dependencies grammar; we used only part-of-speech predictions for our evaluation.

flair is a simple framework for state-of-the-art NLP built directly on PyTorch. We trained a BiLSTM-CRF sequence tagger using the flair for the POS task. In contrast to spaCy, in flair, we can use the ability of custom fastText embeddings to get the representations for out-of-vocabulary (OOV) words, loading word vectors in the `.bin` file that contains the model parameters along with the vectors for all n-grams.

All models were trained with the default hyperparameters using early stopping callback and evaluated on the test set. Metrics were F1 for the NER model and the Accuracy for the POS taggers.

5.2.3 Results for Extrinsic Evaluation

We observed minor improvements in the quality of the word embeddings for the NER task. Table 6 shows no significant advances, and the F1 scores for different models are roughly the same.

This is confirmed by the regression analysis. The estimated coefficients do not significantly differ from zero (see Table 9, Appendix A).

Improvements in optimized models for POS tagging tasks also can be considered modest. SpaCy POS accuracy showed almost no increase with model optimization, and the accuracy of flair POS increased by only **2.8%** compared to the cbow base-

[28]`https://spacy.io/`

[29]`https://github.com/flairNLP/flair`

Table 7: Accuracy scores for POS tagging tasks performed with spaCy and flair. Top Accuracy is marked in bold.

	Training Dataset	**Model**	**Subword**	**Negative Sampling**	**Epochs**	**POS SpaCy Accuracy**
Grave et al. (2018)	Wikipedia+CC	cbow weighted	5-5	10	10	0.824
Our baselines	UberText 2.0	cbow	3-6	5	5	0.825
	UberText 2.0	skipgram	3-6	5	5	0.822
Our optimized	UberText 2.0	cbow	2-6	10	10	**0.827**
	UberText 2.0	skipgram	2-5	15	10	0.826
	UberText 1.0	skipgram	2-5	15	10	0.823
	UberText 1.0	cbow	2-6	10	10	0.823
	Training Dataset	**Model**	**Subword**	**Negative Sampling**	**Epochs**	**POS Flair Accuracy**
Grave et al. (2018)	Wikipedia+CC	cbow weighted	5-5	10	10	**0.94**
Our baselines	UberText 2.0	cbow	3-6	5	5	0.893
	UberText 2.0	skipgram	3-6	5	5	0.881
Our optimized	UberText 2.0	cbow	2-6	15	15	0.918
	UberText 2.0	skipgram	2-6	10	15	0.912
	UberText 1.0	cbow	2-6	10	15	0.911
	UberText 1.0	skipgram	2-5	10	15	0.899

line. Accuracy scores are presented in Table 7. Pseudo R-squared is 0.110.

Nevertheless, regression models for the grid of hyperparameters show that the flair POS model Accuracy is better using cbow and cut down choosing a high minimum subword number and the low subword range (Table 10, Appendix A), and the spaCy POS model can be improved by enlarging the training dataset and shows the same tendency for subwords like flair POS does (Table 11, Appendix A). The pseudo R-squared for both models is 0.304 and 0.918, respectively.

We examined that the performance on downstream models is inconsistent across tasks and with intrinsic evaluations, as was previously discovered by Schnabel et al. (2015).

6 Conclusions and Future work

In this paper, we reviewed various aspects of learning word embeddings, including the quality and the quantity of the corpus texts, the choice of the word embeddings algorithm, and its hyperparameters. Those variations were tested on real-world texts and NLP tasks, and the performance of the resulting word embeddings was carefully measured. During the research, more than forty variants of word vectors were trained and evaluated using the clean framework, which consists of one intrinsic and three extrinsic tests.

The evaluation of the resulting word embeddings has indicated that:

- The best hyperparameters based on intrinsic evaluation are:
  - 2-5 subword size, 15 negative samples and epochs for the skipgram model[30];
  - 4-6 subword size, 15 negative samples and epochs for the cbow model[31].
- While the trained vectors have shown visibly better performance on the intrinsic tests, this performance does not correlate much with the extrinsic evaluation results.
- The correlation between the hyperparameters and the results of the extrinsic tests exists but has no significant impact on the corresponding metrics.

Additionally, we found that the reference implementation of the fastText algorithm misses a vital part: the cbow weighted version, which makes it

[30] https://huggingface.co/dchaplinsky/fasttext_uk

[31] https://huggingface.co/dchaplinsky/fasttext_uk_cbow

hard to reproduce the Grave et al. (2018) results on our corpus.

In the paper, we suggest a methodology to build and test word embeddings for low-resource languages, provide the code for training and evaluation, and describe the required data. Such an approach allows conducting similar experiments for other languages and sets a good performance baseline for Ukrainian, allowing us to revisit the results on an even bigger corpus.

Similar methods can be used to train other word vectors, such as classical word2vec (Mikolov et al., 2013a), GloVe (Pennington et al., 2014), or more recent alternatives like LexVec[32] or Floret[33].

Limitations

During the research, we met some of the limitations which might affect the reproducibility of the paper results:

1. The need for a significantly large corpus of good quality may affect reproducibility for other low-resource languages. Researchers might use one of the existing noisy corpora (such as OSCAR[34]) and apply extensive filtering, use Wikipedia, or collect their corpus using web scraping.
2. As fastText word vectors can be trained only on the CPU and require a lot of RAM, access to the modern server time is needed. For this paper, the farm of 7 servers was utilized for training word vectors and running the evaluation.
3. The implementation of the cbow with positional weights had an issue with the memory allocation for the random weights initialization, so we patched the implementation to make it work on a server with 128GB of RAM.
4. The resulting embeddings for the Ukrainian language require about 8 GB of disk storage; therefore, training and evaluation of tens of thousands of them imposes a visible requirement for data storage.

Ethics Statement

We acknowledge that there is a lack of papers in the ACL Anthology that mention the Ukrainian language or are authored by researchers affiliated with Ukrainian universities.

We believe our paper will increase the visibility of the Ukrainian research community and will help build connections with the ACL community.

Furthermore, we acknowledge the potential broader impact of our research on other low-resource, morphologically rich languages. We believe that our methods and findings are generalizable and can be applied to benefit other languages and communities.

[32]https://github.com/alexandres/lexvec

[33]https://github.com/explosion/floret

[34]https://oscar-project.org/

References

Alan Akbik, Tanja Bergmann, Duncan Blythe, Kashif Rasul, Stefan Schweter, and Roland Vollgraf. 2019. FLAIR: An easy-to-use framework for state-of-the-art NLP. In *Proceedings of the 2019 Conference of the North American Chapter of the Association for Computational Linguistics (Demonstrations)*, pages 54–59, Minneapolis, Minnesota. Association for Computational Linguistics.

Felipe Almeida and Geraldo Xexéo. 2019. Word embeddings: A survey. *CoRR*, abs/1901.09069.

Piotr Bojanowski, Edouard Grave, Armand Joulin, and Tomas Mikolov. 2017. Enriching word vectors with subword information. *Transactions of the Association for Computational Linguistics*, 5:135–146.

Sabine Buchholz and Erwin Marsi. 2006. CoNLL-X shared task on multilingual dependency parsing. In *Proceedings of the Tenth Conference on Computational Natural Language Learning (CoNLL-X)*, pages 149–164, New York City. Association for Computational Linguistics.

Dmytro Chaplynskyi. 2023. Introducing UberText 2.0: a corpus of modern Ukrainian at scale. In *Proceedings of the Second Ukrainian Natural Language Processing Workshop*, pages 1–10, Dubrovnik, Croatia. Association for Computational Linguistics.

Edouard Grave, Piotr Bojanowski, Prakhar Gupta, Armand Joulin, and Tomas Mikolov. 2018. Learning word vectors for 157 languages. In *Proceedings of the Eleventh International Conference on Language Resources and Evaluation (LREC 2018)*, Miyazaki, Japan. European Language Resources Association (ELRA).

Zellig Harris. 1954. Distributional structure. *Word*, 10(2-3):146–162.

Amit Mandelbaum and Adi Shalev. 2016. Word embeddings and their use in sentence classification tasks. *CoRR*, abs/1610.08229.

Alessio Miaschi and Felice Dell'Orletta. 2020. Contextual and non-contextual word embeddings: an in-depth linguistic investigation. In *Proceedings of the*

5th Workshop on Representation Learning for NLP, pages 110–119, Online. Association for Computational Linguistics.

Tomas Mikolov, Kai Chen, Greg S. Corrado, and Jeffrey Dean. 2013a. Efficient estimation of word representations in vector space.

Tomas Mikolov, Wen-tau Yih, and Geoffrey Zweig. 2013b. Linguistic regularities in continuous space word representations. In *Proceedings of the 2013 Conference of the North American Chapter of the Association for Computational Linguistics: Human Language Technologies*, pages 746–751, Atlanta, Georgia. Association for Computational Linguistics.

Hien T. Nguyen, Phuc H. Duong, and Erik Cambria. 2019. Learning short-text semantic similarity with word embeddings and external knowledge sources. *Knowledge-Based Systems*, 182:104842.

Vít Novotný, Eniafe Festus Ayetiran, Dalibor Bačovský, Dávid Lupták, Michal Štefánik, and Petr Sojka. 2021. One size does not fit all: Finding the optimal subword sizes for FastText models across languages. In *Proceedings of the International Conference on Recent Advances in Natural Language Processing (RANLP 2021)*, pages 1068–1074, Held Online. INCOMA Ltd.

Vít Novotný, Michal Štefánik, Eniafe Festus Ayetiran, Petr Sojka, and Radim Řehůřek. 2022. When fasttext pays attention: Efficient estimation of word representations using constrained positional weighting. *JUCS - Journal of Universal Computer Science*, 28(2):181–201.

Jeffrey Pennington, Richard Socher, and Christopher Manning. 2014. GloVe: Global vectors for word representation. In *Proceedings of the 2014 Conference on Empirical Methods in Natural Language Processing (EMNLP)*, pages 1532–1543, Doha, Qatar. Association for Computational Linguistics.

R Core Team. 2013. R: A language and environment for statistical computing.

Terry Ruas, William Grosky, and Akiko Aizawa. 2019. Multi-sense embeddings through a word sense disambiguation process. *Expert Systems with Applications*, 136:288–303.

Tobias Schnabel, Igor Labutov, David Mimno, and Thorsten Joachims. 2015. Evaluation methods for unsupervised word embeddings. In *Proceedings of the 2015 Conference on Empirical Methods in Natural Language Processing*, pages 298–307, Lisbon, Portugal. Association for Computational Linguistics.

Yikang Shen, Wenge Rong, Nan Jiang, Baolin Peng, Jie Tang, and Zhang Xiong. 2017. Word embedding based correlation model for question/answer matching. In *Proceedings of the Thirty-First AAAI Conference on Artificial Intelligence*, AAAI'17, page 3511–3517. AAAI Press.

Maria Shvedova, Ruprecht von Waldenfels, Sergiy Yarygin, Andriy Rysin, Vasyl Starko, and Tymofij Nikolajenko et al. 2017-2022. GRAC: General regionally annotated corpus of Ukrainian.

François Torregrossa, Robin Allesiardo, Vincent Claveau, Nihel Kooli, and Guillaume Gravier. 2021. A survey on training and evaluation of word embeddings. *International Journal of Data Science and Analytics*, 11(2):85–103.

Achim Zeileis, Francisco Cribari-Neto, Bettina Gruen, Ioannis Kosmidis, Alexandre B Simas, Andrea V Rocha, and Maintainer Achim Zeileis. 2016. Package 'betareg'. *R package*, 3(2).

A Regression Analysis

Table 8: Beta regression coefficients for the model predicting the mean Accuracy for word analogy task.

component	term	estimate	std.error	statistic	p.value
mean	**(Intercept)**	**-0.2554787**	**0.0558844**	**-4.5715534**	**0.0000048**
mean	Cbow weighted	-0.0217421	0.0333612	-0.6517183	0.5145829
mean	**Skipgram**	**0.4838693**	**0.0164096**	**29.4869395**	**0.0000000**
mean	**Epochs**	**0.0053332**	**0.0023039**	**2.3148724**	**0.0206199**
mean	Subword 2-6	-0.0081295	0.0230823	-0.3521978	0.7246899
mean	Subword 3-6	-0.0398978	0.0507995	-0.7853973	0.4322207
mean	Subword 4-6	0.0035476	0.0237927	0.1491042	0.8814714
mean	Subword 5-5	-0.0106454	0.0398361	-0.2672294	0.7892926
mean	Subword 5-6	-0.0294700	0.0229863	-1.2820653	0.1998197
mean	**UberText 2.0**	**0.0640098**	**0.0207206**	**3.0891944**	**0.0020070**
mean	Negative sampling	0.0022902	0.0033095	0.6919969	0.4889393
precision	**(phi)**	**1528.2850428**	**305.5581464**	**5.0016177**	**0.0000006**

Table 9: Beta regression coefficients for the model predicting the mean F1 score for NER task.

component	term	estimate	std.error	statistic	p.value
mean	**(Intercept)**	**1.6216440**	**0.0666023**	**24.3481651**	**0.0000000**
mean	Cbow weighted	-0.0075895	0.0397626	-0.1908713	0.8486264
mean	Skipgram	-0.0178466	0.0195245	-0.9140592	0.3606857
mean	Epochs	0.0029815	0.0027425	1.0871598	0.2769662
mean	Subword 2-6	0.0371129	0.0275649	1.3463850	0.1781784
mean	Subword 3-6	-0.0361289	0.0602330	-0.5998193	0.5486267
mean	Subword 4-6	0.0002828	0.0282246	0.0100184	0.9920066
mean	Subword 5-5	-0.0324346	0.0474000	-0.6842734	0.4938025
mean	Subword 5-6	0.0102150	0.0273104	0.3740327	0.7083800
mean	UberText 2.0	0.0108599	0.0246912	0.4398274	0.6600621
mean	Negative sampling	-0.0049084	0.0039411	-1.2454404	0.2129699
precision	(phi)	1902.8778974	380.5287293	5.0006156	0.0000006

Table 10: Beta regression coefficients for the model predicting the mean Accuracy score for SpaCy POS tagging.

component	term	estimate	std.error	statistic	p.value
mean	**(Intercept)**	**1.5293970**	**0.0138662**	**110.2966659**	**0.0000000**
mean	Cbow weighted	-0.0051336	0.0083367	-0.6157876	0.5380347
mean	Skipgram	-0.0049324	0.0040683	-1.2123932	0.2253619
mean	Epochs	0.0003477	0.0005735	0.6062589	0.5443429
mean	**Subword 2-6**	**-0.0118624**	**0.0057226**	**-2.0729047**	**0.0381811**
mean	Subword 3-6	-0.0080235	0.0126195	-0.6357997	0.5249070
mean	Subword 4-6	-0.0099378	0.0058999	-1.6843804	0.0921082
mean	Subword 5-5	-0.0066263	0.0099457	-0.6662503	0.5052511
mean	Subword 5-6	-0.0081829	0.0057037	-1.4346837	0.1513773
mean	**UberText 2.0**	**0.0209113**	**0.0051287**	**4.0773230**	**0.0000456**
mean	Negative sampling	-0.0002691	0.0008203	-0.3280957	0.7428393
precision	**(phi)**	**41970.9373563**	**8394.1353521**	**5.0000310**	**0.0000006**

Table 11: Beta regression coefficients for the model predicting the mean Accuracy score for Flair POS tagging.

component	term	estimate	std.error	statistic	p.value
mean	**(Intercept)**	**2.3223858**	**0.0854556**	**27.1765257**	**0.0000000**
mean	**Cbow weighted**	**-0.2127466**	**0.0544897**	**-3.9043446**	**0.0000945**
mean	**Skipgram**	**-0.2372245**	**0.0246544**	**-9.6219977**	**0.0000000**
mean	Epochs	0.0001504	0.0035905	0.0418964	0.9665813
mean	Subword 2-6	0.0017537	0.0383267	0.0457572	0.9635038
mean	**Subword 3-6**	**-0.1959644**	**0.0775663**	**-2.5264110**	**0.0115235**
mean	**Subword 4-6**	**-0.5094930**	**0.0359537**	**-14.1708221**	**0.0000000**
mean	Subword 5-5	0.0316722	0.0640241	0.4946926	0.6208171
mean	**Subword 5-6**	**-0.5957699**	**0.0344968**	**-17.2702724**	**0.0000000**
mean	UberText 2.0	0.0246145	0.0320123	0.7689059	0.4419491
mean	Negative sampling	0.0063355	0.0049368	1.2833240	0.1993786
precision	**(phi)**	**1631.2103337**	**326.2489973**	**4.9998938**	**0.0000006**

GPT-2 Metadata Pretraining Towards Instruction Finetuning for Ukrainian

Volodymyr Kyrylov
Università della Svizzera italiana
vol@wilab.org.ua

Dmytro Chaplynskyi
lang-uk
chaplinsky.dmitry@gmail.com

Abstract

We explore pretraining unidirectional language models on 4B tokens from the largest curated corpus of Ukrainian, UberText 2.0. We enrich document text by surrounding it with weakly structured metadata, such as title, tags, and publication year, enabling metadata-conditioned text generation and text-conditioned metadata prediction at the same time. We pretrain GPT-2 Small, Medium, and Large models on a single GPU, reporting training times, BPC on BrUK, BERTScore, and BLEURT on titles for 1000 News from the Future. Next, we venture to formatting POS and NER datasets as instructions, and train low-rank attention adapters, performing these tasks as constrained text generation. We release our models for the community at https://github.com/proger/uk4b.

1 Introduction

Large language models provide a text-based user interface to perform multiple language processing tasks. The release of UberText 2.0 (Chaplynskyi, 2023) is a milestone that unlocks pretraining experiments of language models on curated Ukrainian texts. Coupled with recent improvements to hardware and software, we can train larger models on a single consumer GPU from scratch.

Our contributions are:

- techniques to train language models on UberText 2.0 under 1B parameters on consumer hardware setting a baseline of 0.69 BPC on a subset of BrUK;
- a method to add new tasks from document metadata in pretraining compared to finetuning larger models for sequence generation explicitly;
- exploration of tagging tasks formatted as instructions using low-rank adapters compared to traditional sequence tagging methods.

2 Related Work

Radford and Narasimhan (2018) show that a single pretrained causal Transformer (Vaswani et al., 2017) decoder-only model on as much as 5 GB of books with 124M parameters can be finetuned for many downstream tasks. Devlin et al. (2019) show that using an bidirectional encoder-only model improves performance for tasks where bidirectional context is important, like question answering. Radford et al. (2019) discover that models pretrained on 40 GB of curated internet text and scaled up to over 1B parameters are able to perform multiple tasks in zero shot scenario. 100x larger models trained on larger dataset exhibit few shot learning abilities of new tasks at the cost of impressive engineering efforts (Brown et al., 2020; Chowdhery et al., 2022). These ideas guide us towards seeking large text corpora and training Transformers on them.

Kaplan et al. (2020) and Hoffmann et al. (2022) observe that bigger models converge to the same validation loss much faster in the same wall clock time. They fit a power law curve between a power of the model size, dataset size, or compute time and performance ($l = ax^{b<1} + c$) into runtime metrics collected from running a large number of experiments. The power laws suggest that the returns from increasing model, data, or compute diminish after a certain point. Caballero et al. (2022) present a smoothly broken neural scaling law equation, suggesting a scaling speedup laying further ahead past the currently accepted inflection region. Sorscher et al. (2022) suggest a way to beat scaling laws by using careful data selection methods on vision tasks. These ideas give us the insight that we should use the biggest models possible for our compute budget.

It's not only compute that's important. While the work of Radford et al. (2019) discovered prompts that drove the model to perform tasks like sum-

Proceedings of the Second Ukrainian Natural Language Processing Workshop (UNLP), pages 32–39
May 5, 2023 ©2023 Association for Computational Linguistics

marization, Schick and Schütze (2021) introduce pattern-exploiting training that reformulates sentences into cloze tasks on purpose. It is beneficial to curate examples of natural language instructions to save compute.

Instruction finetuning datasets, such as The Flan Collection, released by Longpre et al. (2023), curate massive amounts of task-specific datasets and provide a pipeline to reformulate tasks into natural language using seqio introduced in Roberts et al. (2022). Flan T5 demonstrates that you can achieve higher performance on multiple NLP tasks at once with smaller models in 1.5B–11B range using such data curation methods. These ideas inspire us to leverage metadata and attempt to formulate NLP tasks using natural language.

Techniques like sequence length warmup (Li et al., 2022), gradient clipping (Graves, 2013) enable training stability. Dettmers et al. (2022) enable memory savings by quantizing gradient statistics. Katharopoulos et al. (2020) explore a recurrent formulation of attention with lower computational complexity, and Schlag et al. (2021) view it as fast weight programmers improving capacity of attention in the recurrent setting. Tillet et al. (2019) provide a programming language to implement high performing kernels quickly. Dao et al. (2022) demonstrate how to significantly speed up computation of self-attention and allow much larger context sizes than 1024 or 2048 tokens. Finally, Geiping and Goldstein (2022) demonstrate achieving competitive pretraining speed and performance on a single GPU in 24 hours with a BERT-like model. Notably, these two advancements, the release of PyTorch 2.0 and Andrej Karpathy's nanoGPT tweets, encouraged us to try pretraining from scratch.

Low-rank adaptation methods presented in Hu et al. (2022) and extended in Valipour et al. (2022) enable finetuning of large pretrained models on consumer hardware by updating only a small fraction of extra parameters, suggesting we can efficiently maintain adapters for many tasks in memory at once and achieve better finetuning performance.

Shen et al. (2022) observe that smaller models optimize faster in the beginning of training and propose grafting parameters of a smaller network onto a larger one to continue training after some time. We keep this idea in mind for the future.

3 Pretraining

3.1 Dataset Preparation

We produce a tokenizer from the Wikipedia subset of the corpus using SentencePiece (Kudo and Richardson, 2018) on the document level, including whitespace symbols like newlines and byte-level fallback, totaling 50257 tokens[1]. We include additional special tokens, like <|transcribe|>, reserved for future use. Every document is Unicode-normalized using ftfy[2]. We tokenize the News, Fiction and Wikipedia subsets of UberText 2.0 in parallel using Datasets (Lhoest et al., 2021).

When tokenizing each document we prepend `title`, year part of `date_of_publish` and `tags` document metadata fields prefixed by тема: ("topic: "), рік: ("year: ") and мітки: ("tags: ") strings in randomized order, separated by newlines from each other, and by double newlines from the body. The metadata is repeated at the end of the document as well after a double newline. After the metadata suffix we append one <|endoftext|> token. Following Geiping and Goldstein (2022) we remove all documents that have a ratio of characters to tokens higher than 0.4.

The resulting dataset has 4,299,910,622 training tokens. 4,194,956 tokens are set aside for validation. All document tokens are concatenated together into a single binary file with 2 bytes per token. We name this dataset `uk4b` in our experiments.

3.2 Model

We choose a Transformer decoder based on GPT-2 (Radford et al., 2019). The decoder contains two embedding tables, one for each of 50257 tokens and one for each of 1024 possible token positions. At input, every token in a sequence is represented using a sum of the token embedding and its corresponding position embedding. Input goes through N blocks, consisting of a residually connected multi head self-attention layer, followed by layer normalization and a residually connected linear layer, followed by another layer normalization. Latent representation is projected back to token ids using a linear layer with weights tied to the token embedding table.

Attention heads are constrained to use only tokens earlier in a sequence. This enables us to use an

[1] Original GPT-2 uses 50000 BPE tokens + 256 for each byte + 1 for <|endoftext|>

[2] `https://ftfy.readthedocs.io`

Model	Size	BrUK$_{29k}$ bpc↓	uk4b validation loss↓	uk4b training tokens (compute optimal)	ETA 3090-hours
LSTM	5.7M	0.82	-	-	-
GPT-2 Small$_+$	123M	0.72	2.38	6.87B (2.29B)	35
GPT-2 Medium$_+$	355M	0.70	2.10	6.29B (6.85B)	89
GPT-2 Large$_l$	774M	**0.69**	1.82	21.4B (15.4B)	492$_\dagger$

Table 1: Intrinsic evaluation of trained models. $_+$ means the model uses an output projection layer with a dimension rounded up to the next multiple of 8 to enable tiling optimizations, and biases from all attention, linear and layer normalization layers have been removed. $\cdot_l$ means the model uses layer normalization of token and position embeddings. $\cdot_\dagger$ denotes that the time estimate for Large is computed for a 772M $_+$-type model with 2048 tokens per forward pass. LSTM is trained on a different train/validation split of UberText 2.0 than uk4b and is available at `https://huggingface.co/lang-uk/flair-uk-forward`.

autoregressive text completion objective computed in *parallel for all tokens* in a batch.

Our implementation is based on nanoGPT.[3] We rely on PyTorch (Paszke et al., 2019) 2.0 compiler and FlashAttention (Dao et al., 2022).

We pretrain three model variants: Small, Medium and Large.

Small has 12 layers, 12 attention heads and 768 embedding dimension totaling 124M parameters. We do not use the bias in attention, linear layer and layer normalization for speed. We use AdamW $\beta_1 = 0.9, \beta_2 = 0.95$, weight decay of 1e-2. Learning rate is linearly warmed up for 1000 steps from 6e-5 to 6e-4 and then back for 13000 more steps. We clip gradients at 2-norm of 1.

We use a batch size of 512 with sequence length 1024.

Medium has 24 layers, 16 attention heads and 1024 embedding dimension totaling 354M parameters, without bias. According to Chinchilla Approach 2 (Hoffmann et al., 2022)[4] compute optimal estimate we need to train on 6.85B tokens, requiring 13066 gradient updates. We round it up to 13100 updates. We train Medium and Small for the same amount of time to compare wall clock time on RTX 3090. Small and Medium vocabulary size is expanded to 50304 to enable tiling optimizations[5]

Large has 774M parameters: 36 layers, 20 attention heads and 1280 embedding dimension. We used bias in all layers in this model. We train Large for 10M forward passes on a single A100. Compute optimal estimate for Large is 15.4B tokens, requiring roughly 29.5K gradient updates. At 2048 tokens per iteration this requires 7.5M forward passes. The training was started with 8-bit AdamW (Dettmers et al., 2022) and continued with 32-bit AdamW following divergence. We used a maximum learning rate of 2.5e-4. As an artifact, this model additionally includes layer normalization in Embedding layers.

Large model uses standard PyTorch initialization for all layers, Small and Medium use GPT-2 initialization. We use bfloat16 adaptive mixed precision in all runs. Loss curves are available on Figure 1. Sequences of tokens are randomly sampled from the dataset during training.

One epoch of uk4b requires 8202 gradient updates. Compute optimal training tokens estimate assumes tokens are not repeated, which is not the case for our experiment.

3.3 Evaluation

To perform instrinsic evaluation, we use a subset of BrUK corpus of contemporary Ukrainian by Starko et al. (2016-2023). To avoid overlap with training data, we choose sentences split using a toolkit by Rysin (2022) that do not appear in UberText 2.0, ending up with 28643 test sentences. We call this dataset BrUK$_{29k}$. As a baseline, we include a character-level 1-layer LSTM (Hochreiter and Schmidhuber, 1997) with hidden size 1024 trained for 20 epochs (364B characters) on another variant of UberText 2.0 using an implementation provided by Akbik et al. (2018). We report bits per character and training statistics in Table 1 (Mielke, 2019).

3.4 Metadata Prediction

To evaluate metadata prediction, we sample 1000 News Articles from the Future using an in-domain news source.

We perform decoding of the Large model

[3] `https://github.com/karpathy/nanoGPT`

[4] Estimated using code from `https://github.com/karpathy/nanoGPT/blob/master/scaling_laws.ipynb`

[5] Once again thanks to @karpathy: `https://twitter.com/karpathy/status/1621578354024677377`

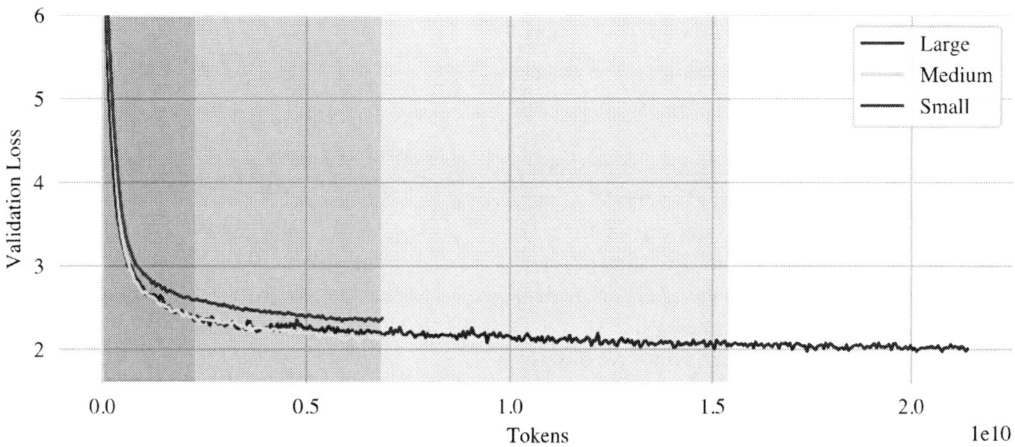

Figure 1: Validation loss curves against training tokens seen by models. Shaded regions denote compute optimal training times for Small, Medium and Large estimated using Chinchilla (Hoffmann et al., 2022).

prompted by article content followed by two newlines and prompt tokens тема: ("topic: ") or мітки: ("tags: ").

We report BERTScore using xlm-roberta-large (Zhang* et al., 2020) and BLEURT using BLEURT-20 model (Sellam et al., 2020; Pu et al., 2021) for title prediction task in Table 2. To compare, we take mBART-50 (Tang et al., 2021), which is an encoder-decoder model pretrained on multiple languages and finetune it on news articles from UberText 2.0. We remove all text from mBART output after the first sentence.

For tag prediction, we measure and report intersection over union and accuracy between sets of reference and hypothesis tags constructed by splitting the tag string by commas and downcasing.

Table 2: Metadata Prediction results on 1000 News Articles from the Future, Greedy Decoding. mBART is finetuned on 1000 news articles from UberText 2.0.

Titles	BERTScore F1	BLEURT mean
GPT-2 Small 123M	0.90	0.54
GPT-2 Medium 355M	0.91	0.57
GPT-2 Large 774M	0.91	0.59
mBART 610M	**0.94**	**0.74**
Tags	IOU	Accuracy
GPT-2 Small 123M	0.47	0.64
GPT-2 Medium 355M	0.54	0.71
GPT-2 Large 774M	0.56	0.71

4 Finetuning

4.1 Low-Rank Adaptation

When finetuning for a new task, we add low-rank decomposed clones of query W_q and key W_k input projection weights for each attention head, summing their activations with original queries and keys, as suggested by Hu et al. (2022) using their provided code. This method is based on an observation that overparametrized models reside in a low intrinsic dimension by Li et al. (2018). Practically, this allows us to finetune large models on consumer GPUs by updating only a small amount of parameters. The pretrained model remains frozen, allowing operation of multiple adaptation modules on a single GPU at once.

4.2 Instruction Datasets

Wei et al. (2021) has shown that finetuning large models on instruction datasets improves their zero-shot performance. In aspiration to this work, we prepare POS (Kotsyba et al., 2018) and lang-uk[6] NER datasets in instruction format to evaluate our model on these tasks in a finetuned setting.

For each example, we prefix the input sentence by a prompt token речення: ("sentence: "), provide the input sentence and put a task prompt проаналізуй: ("analyze: ") on a new line followed by a response. We format ground truth responses to contain observed words interspersed with hidden labels: part-of-speech tags in case of POS and named entity labels in case of NER. Word

[6] https://lang.org.ua

tokenization depends on the task, making the task harder than pointwise token projection as the model needs to learn arbitrary tokenization. We ensure hidden labels use exactly one token. We prompt the hidden label prompt by a / token. This encoding reminds us of a text representation of observed-hidden sequences in hidden Markov models.

We intercalate all examples with an <|endoftext|> training and continue training using the same objective using the same data loading process as during pretraining.

During our preliminary experiments, we observe that the model struggles to correctly reproduce the sentence after the prompt in about 1/3rd of the cases, making evaluation impossible without constrained decoding.

To complete POS measurements we provide the model with a oracle-tokenized observed response with hidden labels replaced by a token previously unseen during training[7]. We evaluate by forwarding this string through the model and replacing blanks with highest probability tokens. We effectively use an autoregressive model in a parallel fashion. We do not constrain the set of tokens to choose from after the forward pass. The results in the evaluation are available in Table 3.

Table 3: POS Performance

Model	Accuracy
Flair LSTM Forward/Backward	**0.979**
UDPipe	0.975
GPT-2 Medium Instr. Parallel **(ours)**	0.964
FastText CBOW (flair)	0.940
FastText CBOW (spacy)	0.825

To complete NER evaluations, we provide the model with oracle tokenization, performing constrained greedy decoding. Results of this evaluation are show in Table 4. ELECTRA models are provided by updated work of Schweter (2020).

5 Discussion

We are excited to release a new decoder-only monolingual model trained on curated Ukrainian data to the community.

It took us over a month to pretrain the first Large model successfully and in the process we became aware of possible improvements to the model, such as removing biases. These improvements resulted in a narrow visual gap between Medium and Large,

[7]we choose _ at random

Table 4: NER Performance

Model	F1	Prec	Recall
xlm-roberta-large	**0.92**	**0.92**	**0.91**
xlm-roberta-base	0.89	0.89	0.88
dbmdz/electra-base-ukrainian-cased-discriminator	0.89	0.89	0.89
lang-uk/electra-base-ukrainian-cased-discriminator	0.87	0.87	0.87
youscan/ukr-roberta-base	0.87	0.87	0.86
bert-base-multilingual-cased	0.87	0.88	0.87
Flair LSTM Forward and Backward	0.86	0.86	0.86
GPT-2 Large Instruction Data, Constrained Decoding **(ours)**	0.85	0.86	0.84
FastText CBOW	0.83	0.86	0.80
FastText skipgram	0.82	0.83	0.81

as seen on Figure 1. We were able to report a much lower validation loss on Large due to a spike towards the end of training. Loss curves in Figure 1, bpc values in Table 1 and results on metadata prediction show in Table 2 suggest it might be beneficial to train Medium for longer. We see that using a task specific encoder-decoder model is performing better, possibly leveraging context in both directions when predicting metadata given the document.

While aiming towards a general purpose language agent trained on a single GPU, we are lured by simplicity of formatting tasks as instructions. During our experiments, we observed the model drifting away from the NER task into text generation on long inputs, requiring us to use constrained decoding to "remind" it what the model is supposed to be doing. We achieve a competitive result this way, however would still choose a more traditional approach to solve NER, as confirmed by our measurements in Table 4.

It is suprising to find that POS could be solved by "filling in blanks" by picking maximum probability tokens in parallel. We used that result in Table 3.

There is room for more data to faithfully leverage the prediction of the number of tokens we need to train for to optimally utilize compute. There is more available data in Conneau et al. (2020), Wenzek et al. (2020) and Raffel et al. (2020). We leave filtering this data to future work.

Limitations

We choose to keep bias of UberText 2.0 in the models as is. We observe a gap in performance between our models and task-specific large encoder or encoder-decoder models. While we evaluate document-conditional metadata generation, we do not evaluate metadata-conditioned document generation ability present in our model. Constrained decoding necessary for NER evaluation is a major limitation of our instruction finetuning attempts, suggesting we need to make further improvements to the design of our pretraining corpus for performing multiple tasks with one model. We do not test our model on traditional sequence tagging formulations of POS and NER. Causal language models are useful for tasks like speech recognition and we leave effectiveness of these models on such tasks to future work.

Ethics Statement

We seek to accelerate adoption of larger language models at scale enabling new capabilities for Ukrainian, improving lives of millions of language users. We recognize that our work can be misused to produce fake information and deceptive content and we do not condone such use of our models.

Acknowledgements

Volodymyr would like to thank Kazuki Irie for encouragement to train larger language models sooner and feedback on the early versions of the paper. Róbert Csordás and Aditya Ramesh for discussions about Transformers.

References

Alan Akbik, Duncan Blythe, and Roland Vollgraf. 2018. Contextual string embeddings for sequence labeling. In *COLING 2018, 27th International Conference on Computational Linguistics*, pages 1638–1649.

Tom Brown, Benjamin Mann, Nick Ryder, Melanie Subbiah, Jared D Kaplan, Prafulla Dhariwal, Arvind Neelakantan, Pranav Shyam, Girish Sastry, Amanda Askell, Sandhini Agarwal, Ariel Herbert-Voss, Gretchen Krueger, Tom Henighan, Rewon Child, Aditya Ramesh, Daniel Ziegler, Jeffrey Wu, Clemens Winter, Chris Hesse, Mark Chen, Eric Sigler, Mateusz Litwin, Scott Gray, Benjamin Chess, Jack Clark, Christopher Berner, Sam McCandlish, Alec Radford, Ilya Sutskever, and Dario Amodei. 2020. Language models are few-shot learners. In *Advances in Neural Information Processing Systems*, volume 33, pages 1877–1901. Curran Associates, Inc.

Ethan Caballero, Kshitij Gupta, Irina Rish, and David Krueger. 2022. Broken Neural Scaling Laws. In *NeurIPS ML Safety Workshop*.

Dmytro Chaplynskyi. 2023. Introducing UberText 2.0: a corpus of modern Ukrainian at scale. In *Proceedings of the Second Ukrainian Natural Language Processing Workshop*, pages 1–10, Dubrovnik, Croatia. Association for Computational Linguistics.

Aakanksha Chowdhery, Sharan Narang, Jacob Devlin, Maarten Bosma, Gaurav Mishra, Adam Roberts, Paul Barham, Hyung Won Chung, Charles Sutton, Sebastian Gehrmann, Parker Schuh, Kensen Shi, Sasha Tsvyashchenko, Joshua Maynez, Abhishek Rao, Parker Barnes, Yi Tay, Noam Shazeer, Vinodkumar Prabhakaran, Emily Reif, Nan Du, Ben Hutchinson, Reiner Pope, James Bradbury, Jacob Austin, Michael Isard, Guy Gur-Ari, Pengcheng Yin, Toju Duke, Anselm Levskaya, Sanjay Ghemawat, Sunipa Dev, Henryk Michalewski, Xavier Garcia, Vedant Misra, Kevin Robinson, Liam Fedus, Denny Zhou, Daphne Ippolito, David Luan, Hyeontaek Lim, Barret Zoph, Alexander Spiridonov, Ryan Sepassi, David Dohan, Shivani Agrawal, Mark Omernick, Andrew M. Dai, Thanumalayan Sankaranarayana Pillai, Marie Pellat, Aitor Lewkowycz, Erica Moreira, Rewon Child, Oleksandr Polozov, Katherine Lee, Zongwei Zhou, Xuezhi Wang, Brennan Saeta, Mark Diaz, Orhan Firat, Michele Catasta, Jason Wei, Kathy Meier-Hellstern, Douglas Eck, Jeff Dean, Slav Petrov, and Noah Fiedel. 2022. PaLM: Scaling language modeling with pathways.

Alexis Conneau, Kartikay Khandelwal, Naman Goyal, Vishrav Chaudhary, Guillaume Wenzek, Francisco Guzmán, Edouard Grave, Myle Ott, Luke Zettlemoyer, and Veselin Stoyanov. 2020. Unsupervised cross-lingual representation learning at scale. In *Proceedings of the 58th Annual Meeting of the Association for Computational Linguistics*, pages 8440–8451, Online. Association for Computational Linguistics.

Tri Dao, Daniel Y Fu, Stefano Ermon, Atri Rudra, and Christopher Re. 2022. FlashAttention: Fast and memory-efficient exact attention with IO-awareness. In *Advances in Neural Information Processing Systems*.

Tim Dettmers, Mike Lewis, Sam Shleifer, and Luke Zettlemoyer. 2022. 8-bit optimizers via block-wise quantization. In *International Conference on Learning Representations*.

Jacob Devlin, Ming-Wei Chang, Kenton Lee, and Kristina Toutanova. 2019. BERT: Pre-training of deep bidirectional transformers for language understanding. In *Proceedings of the 2019 Conference of the North American Chapter of the Association for Computational Linguistics: Human Language Technologies, Volume 1 (Long and Short Papers)*, pages 4171–4186, Minneapolis, Minnesota. Association for Computational Linguistics.

Jonas Geiping and Tom Goldstein. 2022. Cramming: Training a language model on a single gpu in one day. *ArXiv*, abs/2212.14034.

Alex Graves. 2013. Generating sequences with recurrent neural networks. *ArXiv*, abs/1308.0850.

Sepp Hochreiter and Jürgen Schmidhuber. 1997. Long short-term memory. *Neural computation*, 9(8):1735–1780.

Jordan Hoffmann, Sebastian Borgeaud, Arthur Mensch, Elena Buchatskaya, Trevor Cai, Eliza Rutherford, Diego de las Casas, Lisa Anne Hendricks, Johannes Welbl, Aidan Clark, Tom Hennigan, Eric Noland, Katherine Millican, George van den Driessche, Bogdan Damoc, Aurelia Guy, Simon Osindero, Karen Simonyan, Erich Elsen, Oriol Vinyals, Jack William Rae, and Laurent Sifre. 2022. An empirical analysis of compute-optimal large language model training. In *Advances in Neural Information Processing Systems*.

Edward J Hu, yelong shen, Phillip Wallis, Zeyuan Allen-Zhu, Yuanzhi Li, Shean Wang, Lu Wang, and Weizhu Chen. 2022. LoRA: Low-rank adaptation of large language models. In *International Conference on Learning Representations*.

Jared Kaplan, Sam McCandlish, T. J. Henighan, Tom B. Brown, Benjamin Chess, Rewon Child, Scott Gray, Alec Radford, Jeff Wu, and Dario Amodei. 2020. Scaling laws for neural language models. *ArXiv*, abs/2001.08361.

Angelos Katharopoulos, Apoorv Vyas, Nikolaos Pappas, and François Fleuret. 2020. Transformers are RNNs: Fast autoregressive transformers with linear attention. In *Proceedings of the 37th International Conference on Machine Learning*, volume 119 of *Proceedings of Machine Learning Research*, pages 5156–5165. PMLR.

Natalia Kotsyba, Bohdan Moskalevskyi, and Mykhailo Romanenko et al. 2018. Laboratorija ukrajins'koji.

Taku Kudo and John Richardson. 2018. SentencePiece: A simple and language independent subword tokenizer and detokenizer for neural text processing. In *Proceedings of the 2018 Conference on Empirical Methods in Natural Language Processing: System Demonstrations*, pages 66–71, Brussels, Belgium. Association for Computational Linguistics.

Quentin Lhoest, Albert Villanova del Moral, Yacine Jernite, Abhishek Thakur, Patrick von Platen, Suraj Patil, Julien Chaumond, Mariama Drame, Julien Plu, Lewis Tunstall, Joe Davison, Mario Šaško, Gunjan Chhablani, Bhavitvya Malik, Simon Brandeis, Teven Le Scao, Victor Sanh, Canwen Xu, Nicolas Patry, Angelina McMillan-Major, Philipp Schmid, Sylvain Gugger, Clément Delangue, Théo Matussière, Lysandre Debut, Stas Bekman, Pierric Cistac, Thibault Goehringer, Victor Mustar, François Lagunas, Alexander Rush, and Thomas Wolf. 2021. Datasets: A community library for natural language processing. In *Proceedings of the 2021 Conference on Empirical Methods in Natural Language Processing: System Demonstrations*, pages 175–184, Online and Punta Cana, Dominican Republic. Association for Computational Linguistics.

Chunyuan Li, Heerad Farkhoor, Rosanne Liu, and Jason Yosinski. 2018. Measuring the intrinsic dimension of objective landscapes. In *International Conference on Learning Representations*.

Conglong Li, Minjia Zhang, and Yuxiong He. 2022. The stability-efficiency dilemma: Investigating sequence length warmup for training GPT models. In *Advances in Neural Information Processing Systems*.

S. Longpre, Le Hou, Tu Vu, Albert Webson, Hyung Won Chung, Yi Tay, Denny Zhou, Quoc V. Le, Barret Zoph, Jason Wei, and Adam Roberts. 2023. The Flan Collection: Designing data and methods for effective instruction tuning. *ArXiv*, abs/2301.13688.

Sabrina J. Mielke. 2019. Can you compare perplexity across different segmentations?

Adam Paszke, Sam Gross, Francisco Massa, Adam Lerer, James Bradbury, Gregory Chanan, Trevor Killeen, Zeming Lin, Natalia Gimelshein, Luca Antiga, Alban Desmaison, Andreas Kopf, Edward Yang, Zachary DeVito, Martin Raison, Alykhan Tejani, Sasank Chilamkurthy, Benoit Steiner, Lu Fang, Junjie Bai, and Soumith Chintala. 2019. PyTorch: An imperative style, high-performance deep learning library. In *Advances in Neural Information Processing Systems*, volume 32. Curran Associates, Inc.

Amy Pu, Hyung Won Chung, Ankur Parikh, Sebastian Gehrmann, and Thibault Sellam. 2021. Learning compact metrics for MT. In *Proceedings of the 2021 Conference on Empirical Methods in Natural Language Processing*, pages 751–762, Online and Punta Cana, Dominican Republic. Association for Computational Linguistics.

Alec Radford and Karthik Narasimhan. 2018. Improving language understanding by generative pretraining.

Alec Radford, Jeff Wu, Rewon Child, David Luan, Dario Amodei, and Ilya Sutskever. 2019. Language models are unsupervised multitask learners.

Colin Raffel, Noam Shazeer, Adam Roberts, Katherine Lee, Sharan Narang, Michael Matena, Yanqi Zhou, Wei Li, and Peter J. Liu. 2020. Exploring the limits of transfer learning with a unified text-to-text transformer. *Journal of Machine Learning Research*, 21(140):1–67.

Adam Roberts, Hyung Won Chung, Anselm Levskaya, Gaurav Mishra, James Bradbury, Daniel Andor, Sharan Narang, Brian Lester, Colin Gaffney, Afroz Mohiuddin, Curtis Hawthorne, Aitor Lewkowycz, Alex Salcianu, Marc van Zee, Jacob Austin, Sebastian Goodman, Livio Baldini Soares, Haitang Hu, Sasha Tsvyashchenko, Aakanksha Chowdhery, Jasmijn Bastings, Jannis Bulian, Xavier Garcia, Jianmo Ni, Andrew Chen, Kathleen Kenealy, Jonathan H. Clark, Stephan Lee, Dan Garrette, James Lee-Thorp,

Colin Raffel, Noam Shazeer, Marvin Ritter, Maarten Bosma, Alexandre Passos, Jeremy Maitin-Shepard, Noah Fiedel, Mark Omernick, Brennan Saeta, Ryan Sepassi, Alexander Spiridonov, Joshua Newlan, and Andrea Gesmundo. 2022. Scaling up models and data with t5x and seqio. *CoRR*, abs/2203.17189.

Andrij Rysin. 2022. nlp_uk: A collection of NLP tools and resources for Ukrainian language processing. `https://github.com/brown-uk/nlp_uk`. Accessed: February 18, 2023.

Timo Schick and Hinrich Schütze. 2021. It's not just size that matters: Small language models are also few-shot learners. In *Proceedings of the 2021 Conference of the North American Chapter of the Association for Computational Linguistics: Human Language Technologies*, pages 2339–2352, Online. Association for Computational Linguistics.

Imanol Schlag, Kazuki Irie, and Jürgen Schmidhuber. 2021. Linear transformers are secretly fast weight programmers. In *International Conference on Machine Learning*.

Stefan Schweter. 2020. Ukrainian ELECTRA model.

Thibault Sellam, Dipanjan Das, and Ankur Parikh. 2020. BLEURT: Learning robust metrics for text generation. In *Proceedings of the 58th Annual Meeting of the Association for Computational Linguistics*, pages 7881–7892, Online. Association for Computational Linguistics.

Sheng Shen, Pete Walsh, Kurt Keutzer, Jesse Dodge, Matthew Peters, and Iz Beltagy. 2022. Staged training for transformer language models. In *Proceedings of the 39th International Conference on Machine Learning*, volume 162 of *Proceedings of Machine Learning Research*, pages 19893–19908. PMLR.

Ben Sorscher, Robert Geirhos, Shashank Shekhar, Surya Ganguli, and Ari S. Morcos. 2022. Beyond neural scaling laws: beating power law scaling via data pruning. In *Advances in Neural Information Processing Systems*.

Vasyl Starko, Andriy Rysin, Olha Havura, and Nataliia Cheilytko et al. 2016-2023. BRUK: Braunskyi korpus ukrainskoi movy.

Yuqing Tang, Chau Tran, Xian Li, Peng-Jen Chen, Naman Goyal, Vishrav Chaudhary, Jiatao Gu, and Angela Fan. 2021. Multilingual translation from denoising pre-training. In *Findings of the Association for Computational Linguistics: ACL-IJCNLP 2021*, pages 3450–3466, Online. Association for Computational Linguistics.

Philippe Tillet, H. T. Kung, and David D. Cox. 2019. Triton: an intermediate language and compiler for tiled neural network computations. *Proceedings of the 3rd ACM SIGPLAN International Workshop on Machine Learning and Programming Languages*.

Mojtaba Valipour, Mehdi Rezagholizadeh, Ivan Kobyzev, and Ali Ghodsi. 2022. DyLoRA: Parameter efficient tuning of pre-trained models using dynamic search-free low-rank adaptation. *ArXiv*, abs/2210.07558.

Ashish Vaswani, Noam Shazeer, Niki Parmar, Jakob Uszkoreit, Llion Jones, Aidan N Gomez, Ł ukasz Kaiser, and Illia Polosukhin. 2017. Attention is all you need. In *Advances in Neural Information Processing Systems*, volume 30. Curran Associates, Inc.

Thomas Wang, Adam Roberts, Daniel Hesslow, Teven Le Scao, Hyung Won Chung, Iz Beltagy, Julien Launay, and Colin Raffel. 2022. What language model architecture and pretraining objective work best for zero-shot generalization? In *International Conference on Machine Learning*.

Jason Wei, Maarten Bosma, Vincent Zhao, Kelvin Guu, Adams Wei Yu, Brian Lester, Nan Du, Andrew M. Dai, and Quoc V. Le. 2021. Finetuned language models are zero-shot learners. *ArXiv*, abs/2109.01652.

Guillaume Wenzek, Marie-Anne Lachaux, Alexis Conneau, Vishrav Chaudhary, Francisco Guzmán, Armand Joulin, and Edouard Grave. 2020. CCNet: Extracting high quality monolingual datasets from web crawl data. In *Proceedings of the 12th Language Resources and Evaluation Conference*, pages 4003–4012, Marseille, France. European Language Resources Association.

Tianyi Zhang*, Varsha Kishore*, Felix Wu*, Kilian Q. Weinberger, and Yoav Artzi. 2020. BERTScore: Evaluating text generation with BERT. In *International Conference on Learning Representations*.

A Bidirectional Finetuning

Wang et al. (2022) presents experiments suggesting it's possible to perform MLM adaptation of causal models with only 1.3x of compute. We attempt to turn our Medium left-to-right model into a bidirectional one by relaxing the causal attention and continuing training the whole model using a masked language modeling objective for 4100 gradient updates. We observe a very sharp drop in the loss, converging to a degenerate solution: the model latches onto reproducing a single word instead of a blank token. We leave comprehensive evaluation of bidirectional adaptation of smaller models to future work.

The Evolution of Pro-Kremlin Propaganda From a Machine Learning and Linguistics Perspective

Veronika Solopova
Freie Universität Berlin, Germany
veronika.solopova@fu-berlin.de

Christoph Benzmüller
Universität Bamberg, Germany
Freie Universität Berlin, Germany
christoph.benzmueller@uni-bamberg.de

Tim Landgraf
Freie Universität Berlin, Germany
tim.landgraf@fu-berlin.de

Abstract

In the Russo-Ukrainian war, propaganda is produced by Russian state-run news outlets for both international and domestic audiences. Its content and form evolve and change with time as the war continues. This constitutes a challenge to content moderation tools based on machine learning when the data used for training and the current news start to differ significantly. In this follow-up study, we evaluate our previous BERT and SVM models that classify Pro-Kremlin propaganda from a Pro-Western stance, trained on the data from news articles and telegram posts at the start of 2022, on the new 2023 subset. We examine both classifiers' errors and perform a comparative analysis of these subsets to investigate which changes in narratives provoke drops in performance.

1 Introduction and Related Work

Fake news has been shown to evolve over time (Adriani, 2019). A piece of news is often modified as it spreads online by malicious users who twist the original information (Guo et al., 2021), while an imperfect replication process by other users leads to further distortion (Zellers et al., 2019). Guo et al. (2021) showed that the disinformation techniques, parts of speech, and keywords stayed consistent during the evolution process, while the text similarity and sentiment changed. Moreover, according to their scoring, the distance between the fake and evolved fake news was more prominent than between the truth and the initial fake news. The evolved ones sound more objective and cheerful and are more difficult to detect. Jang et al., 2018 also observed significant differences between real and fake news regarding evolution patterns. They found that fake news tweets underwent a more significant number of modifications over the spreading process.

Inn case of fake news and disinformation originating in state-run outlets, we talk about propaganda. In this and previous studies, we focus on Russian propaganda. (Kendall, 2014; Chee, 2017; Parlapiano and Lee, 2018). It has been shown that the Russian Presidential Administration exercises coordinated control over media advertising budgets and editorial content whilst maintaining an illusion of media freedom by letting a small number of minor independent media outlets operate (Lange-Ionatamišvili, 2015). Hence, the adaptations to Kremlin's political agenda are an additional factor that contributes to how Russian fake news evolves. Modern Kremlin propaganda fundamentally appeals to former greatness, glorification of the Russian Empire, the victory in World War II, the Soviet Union's past and the narrative of 'Facing the West' (Khrebtan-Hörhager and Pyatovskaya, 2022). Looking at the key narratives between the beginning of 2022, and the start of 2023, after a year of unsuccessful assault we observe several shifts in the narrative. At the beginning of the war, the official goals and objectives were identified by obscure terms such as "denazification" and "demilitarization" of Ukraine. At the same time, a fight against the Neo-Nazis has become an established rhetoric of the highest officials. "American biolabs in Ukraine", "8 years of genocide in Donbas" and the claim that the Ukrainian government is responsible for shelling its own cities (Korenyuk and Goodman, 2022; Opora, 2022) became the most frequent topics.

After almost one year, Russian officials now openly recognize shelling of civilian electric infrastructure (Kraemer, 2022; Luke Harding and Koshiw, 2022; Grynszpan, 2022; Ebel, 2022), while propaganda directed to the external audience becomes majorly blackmail threatening Western countries to prevent them from supplying Ukraine (Faulconbridge, 2022a). As for the internal audience, the main objective is to support mobilisation efforts in Russia (Romanenko, 2022).

In our initial study (Solopova et al., 2023), we proposed two multilingual automated pro-Kremlin

Proceedings of the Second Ukrainian Natural Language Processing Workshop (UNLP), pages 40–48
May 5, 2023 ©2023 Association for Computational Linguistics

propaganda identification methods, based on the multilingual BERT model (Devlin et al., 2018) and Support Vector Machine trained with linguistic features and manipulative terms glossary. Considering the aforementioned transformations, we hypothesised that our models' performance should drop on the 2023 data. In this follow-up study, we measured how the models trained a year ago perform on current news from the same sources. We also analysed how their language changed according to our linguistic feature set.

In Section 2, describe the experimental setup and the new data set. We present our results in comparison to those from 2022 in Section 3. In Section 4 we carried out an error analysis of the SVM and BERT models. For the SVM we contrasted the linguistic feature distributions in the groups of errors. For the BERT model, we applied a simplified word importance approach to gain insight into vocabulary and morpho-syntactical categories. In Section 5, we compare the 2022 and the 2023 data sets to see how propaganda evolved overall in our given context. Finally, we discuss our key findings and draw a conclusion in Section 6.

2 Methods

2.1 Models

In our initial study, we implemented a binary classification using the Support Vector Machine model for input vectors consisting of 41 handcrafted linguistic features and 116 keywords (normalized by the length of the text in tokens). For comparison with learned features, we extracted embeddings using a multilingual BERT model (Devlin et al., 2018) and trained a linear model using these embeddings. In this study, we apply the models to the new data from the same sources to see how resistant such systems are to changes in the data provoked by the changing events of war and adaptations from the Kremlin's propaganda campaign. We evaluate the performance of our models using Cohen's κ (Cohen, 1960), F-measure (Powers, 2008), false positive and false negative rate.

2.2 Data

We automatically scraped articles from online news outlets in Russian, Ukrainian, Romanian, French and English language, attributing each source to either Pro-Kremlin or Pro-Western class. We assigned ground-truth labels without manual labelling, based on journalistic investigations, or, in the case of Romanian data, using proxy websites, which categorize outlets as those containing fake news. We filtered out the news on neutral topics.

For Russian and Ukrainian we also collected posts from Telegram news channels which are the most popular alternative to traditional media. For pro-Western channels, we used those recommended by Ukrainian Center for Strategic Communications[1], while for the Pro-Kremlin stance, we identified one of the biggest Russian channels with a pro-war narrative.

We had 8 data collections from the 23rd of February until the fourth of April, 2022. In 2023, we collected on the 9th of January. Although this particular day can be considered relatively peaceful in terms of war events, this collection contained news about the preceding incidents and overall political analysis.

We made sure to collect from the same sources as the last year. However, French RT was banned from broadcast in Europe. Instead, we scraped a francophone version of the Turkish Anadolu Agency, which evokes Russian versions of the events in its reports. We also completed RainTV with Meduza news in the Russian liberal subset, since at the moment Meduza is a source with the least dubious reputation, widely read by the liberal Russian community. In 2022, we trained the model with 18,229 out of 85k texts to balance out different languages and sources. In 2023, we collected 1400 texts overall. You can find the data and our code in our Github repository[2].

3 Results

The full test in 2022 corresponds to the performance on 8700 samples of the original test set, while the small is a random sampling of the original 2022 test set to correspond to the size of the 2023 set and makes them comparable. Although we also took an average of 5 seeds, the perfect comparison is complicated since we cannot ensure a balanced representation of the test samples from 2022 and 2023 in their complexity. As shown in Table 1, both models stayed accurate on the task. The SVM model on the 2023 data slightly outperforms its small test results from 2022 and even the full test as per κ. It seems quite stable in its false positive rate across the experiments but has a higher false negative rate, especially seen in the 2022 small test

[1] https://spravdi.gov.ua

[2] https://github.com/anonrep/pro-kremlin_propaganda

Model	F1	Cohen's κ	FP%	FN%
SVM 2022 full test	0.88	0.66	8%	3%
SVM 2022 small	0.74	0.5	9.5%	16%
SVM 2023	0.85	0.71	9.5%	4%
BERT 2022 full test	0.92	0.81	2%	2%
BERT 2022 small	0.87	0.74	11%	1.4%
BERT 2023	0.93	0.87	5%	0.8%

Table 1: The Table shows the models' performance on 2022 and 2023 subsets.

results.
The BERT on the 2023 data outperformed both full and small 2022 tests in f1 and κ. On the 2023 data, there are considerably fewer false negatives, while it shows a slight tendency towards false positives. 12 out of 12 news from liberal Russian outlets were labelled as propaganda by both SVM and the BERT. The SVM had difficulty with the Ukrainian Telegram, labelling 50% as propaganda. In terms of the Ukrainian outlets which in 2022 we considered as Pro-Kremlin propaganda, in 'Newsua' both BERT and SVM found no propaganda, while in 'Strana.ua', almost 100% was found to be propaganda by both models.

4 Error analysis

SVM. Regarding the SVM model, some patterns can be observed by looking into the distributions between the true positives, true negatives, false positives, and false negatives. Thus, the number of reports mentioned, positive sentiment, stative verbs and subordinate clauses used all indicate strong similarities in distribution between true positives and false positives. In the case of relative clauses, clauses of condition and time, there is a correlation between both true positives-false positives and also true negatives-false negative pairs. False negatives also have the highest average sentence length. Finally, we observe the highest number of abstract nouns and adjectives in true negatives and false positives, which means it can be a very confusing category in 2023 data. Out of the keywords, the most confusing are 'Europe', 'Kremlin', 'invasion' and to a lesser degree 'Belarus'. For more information see Appendix A.1

BERT. We were inspired by the attribution method (Sundararajan et al., 2017). It is based on integrated gradients and requires retraining of the initial model. This approach is also computationally expensive because it uses back-propagation to calculate word importance. We segmented texts, so that the first segment is the first token of the text, while every next segment will have another next word unmasked until the last segment becomes a full text again. We classify each of them.

$$text = w_0, w_0 + w_1, w_0 + w_1 + w_2... + w_n$$

If the new next word changed the prediction value and its probability, it was recovered into either the list of words inducing pro-Kremlin or Pro-Western prediction, separately for 2022 and 2023. We analysed extracted lists with linguistic features extraction script to see if there are some similarities in how experts and BERT choose propaganda features.
Thus, the first finding is that BERT identifies the names of the sources appearing in the text and connects them to the prediction classes. For instance, 'ziua', the name of a Romanian tabloid is one of the most frequent words we extracted for Romanian words, which changes prediction into 'propaganda'. In contrast 'activenews', a neutral Romanian news outlet always changed prediction value into 'pro-Western stance'. Even more, in 2022 french data a link to Russian 'Ria' news also was accurately determinant for propaganda class. In 2023, the main word indicating propaganda in Russian news was 'main/head', for the French 'authority' and for the Romanian 'treaty'. In contrast, the main words for pro-Western prediction for the Russian were 'announce' and 'sovereign default'. In 2023, the main words indicating propaganda for Romanian were 'sanctions', 'tribunal' and 'war'. In 2022, the word 'war' was actually a determinant for propaganda, while words describing punishment were not typical topics for Romanian media, they were, however, already present in Ukrainian one. It is possible that keywords BERT learnt in one language are projected to others in the multilingual model. In 2023 Pro-Kremlin propaganda in Ukrainian news would focus on the word 'Putin' while predicting for Pro-Western news are

words ‘Ukraine’ and ‘Ukrainians’. In Ukrainian Pro-Western news, words connected to national institutions such as ‘government’, ‘minister’, and ‘state’ are significant.

In the Russian language, a keyword most reliable for prediction of the liberal side is ‘orcs’, the way how Ukrainians call Russian soldiers (while Russia is called ‘Mordor’ by the analogy of Tolkien’s Lord of the Rings).

By classifying the resulting words according to categories of linguistic features, we can see that many categories are matched. The most popular parts of speech are adjectives, abstract and proper nouns, and high-modality words. Many of them express either strongly negative or positive connotations. Similar to our initial study results, reporting words are highly predictive of the Pro-Kremlin stance in the Russian language in 2022.

Syntactical features such as different types of clauses are present to a lesser degree. Hence, morphological information may be used more than syntactical one for predictions.

Some glossary keywords were also used by BERT’s model, e.g., ‘war’, ‘special operation’, ‘DNR’, ‘LNR’, ‘negotiations’, and ‘Kremlin’.

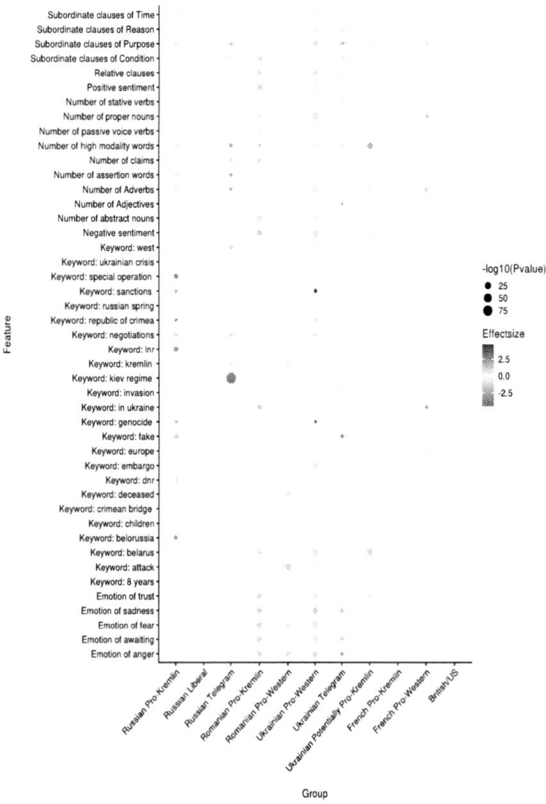

Figure 1: The dot plot shows the comparison between 2022 and 2023 subsets according to linguistic features. The dot size shows P-values while the colour shows the effect size. It represents the difference between the 2023 and 2022 averages, with red indicating growth in usage and blue meaning the drop.

5 Comparative Analyses

We decided to look into the evolution of propaganda, by comparing the averages for each feature between 2022 and 2023 for each subset. We used z-score normalized averages. We could not use medians, which are a better choice, because the data is sparse, most of the medians equal 0, which complicates normalization and significance testing. We chose the Mann-Whitney U-test, as the events are not paired and are not normally distributed. See the comparison in Figure 1. The most substantial difference is seen for the keyword "Kiev Regime", which became a lot more frequent in the Russian Telegram, where users also started discussing more negotiations and ‘the west’, making more claims, and using more assertive words, adverbs and other high-modality words. Russian state-run outlets on the other hand started using considerably less ‘Special military operation’ wording but also dropped the rhetoric of ‘the Republic of Crimea’, ‘LNR’ and ‘DNR’, which the Russian Federation annexed and considers its own regions, rather than independent republics. It also speaks less of negotiations, sanctions, genocide, fake news and Belorussia.

Russian Liberal news did not change its style and narrative, nor did English-speaking, French Pro-Western and French Pro-Kremlin news. Romanian Pro-Kremlin data became less emotional. We can observe a drop in most negative and positive emotions, especially in ‘trust’. There can be seen more abstract nouns and conditional clauses, which are more typical for the Pro-Western narrative but also relative clauses and claims, which can usually be seen more in Pro-Kremlin news. On the other hand, Pro-Western Romanian media has much more negative sentiment than at the beginning of 2022, there is more anger and fear. They talk more about the deceased and the attacks, calling out Kremlin more directly.

Ukrainian Pro-Western news became more neutral, as negative and positive emotions calmed down, particularly trust. There is less mention of genocide, embargo, negotiations and sanctions, which were more important topics for 2022. A rise in the clause of time, adverbs and especially proper nouns is significant, reflecting mostly the discussion around armament supplies.

In Ukrainian Telegram, on the contrary, there is more anger, awaiting, and sadness. The high effect size for the keyword 'fake' reflects Ukrainian efforts to debunk Kremlin propaganda. Stylistically, the language possesses more adjectives, and subordinate clauses of reason, purpose and condition. The potentially Pro-Kremlin news in Ukrainian, which seems to have partly changed their allegiance, shows more emotion of trust and fear, it is in general more expressive, with a higher number of adverbs. It uses the Russian manipulative 'Belorussia' term and 'Belarus' but leans more towards the latter. For comparing the languages see Appendix A.1.

6 Discussion and Conclusion

We applied an SVM with linguistic features and BERT multilingual model trained on the data from the beginning of 2022 to the new data from 2023. Since it is complicated to balance the complexity of the test sets, the true accuracy of the model lies anywhere between the full and the small 2022 test results, depending on how explicit the propaganda is. However, it is still possible to claim that both models successfully accurately identify a pro-Western stance.

Both classifiers are more prone to false positives. As we showcased in the SVM model's error analysis, some distributions of significantly important features from our previous study, like abstract nouns and adjectives, are now similarly distributed between false positives and true positives.

At the same time, the BERT model is prone to attributing the class according to the news source name mentioned, which can lead to the model predicting everything describing or even debunking these outlets as propaganda. Overall, we observed that morphological information may be used more than syntactical one for predictions in BERT, while according to our initial study, a tendency towards some subordinate types distinguishes well the two stances. At the same time, the rise in temporal clauses in pro-Western stance, which in 2022 was highly significant for pro-Kremlin news may explain the higher miss-classification rate of the SVM.

The word 'war' appeared highly predictive for both SVM and BERT. Indeed, at the beginning of the war, this term was avoided by Kremlin officials and even made illegal in Russia (Troianovski and Safronova, 2022; Faulconbridge, 2022b). Hence, it would usually not appear in Pro-Kremlin news that used euphemisms instead.

In the Romanian language, we can see how in 2022, in contrast to other languages, it was a determinant for propaganda, and now it is a determinant for pro-Western news. Consequently, some mistakes may be coming from such terms.

All liberal Russian 2023 news was identified as Pro-Kremlin propaganda by both classifiers. However, they did not change their style since 2022, even though we added Meduza.

Meanwhile, Romanian Pro-Kremlin sources in 2023 became more neutral. Similarly, in Ukrainian 'Newsua' which according to journalistic investigations was flagged as Pro-Kremlin, in 2023 100% of articles were classified as Pro-Western, by both models.

The evolution of war news gives us an insight into deeper-rooted differences between the sides of the conflict. The fact that in the Ukrainian language in 2023, in contrast to 2022, Pro-Kremlin propaganda focuses on what Putin says, while real Ukrainian news almost does not mention him, but instead focuses on the Ukrainian government and Ukrainians themselves reflects how wartime societies evolve.

Overall, both models managed to draw good results on 2023 data, even considering how much topics and linguistic characteristics changed after one year of the war.

Limitations

The classical attribution method may be a more reliable explainability approach for BERT-like models than the one presented. We cannot be sure that these exact words and not them being present in combination with others, or even the length of the text is what changes prediction. In our future work, we want to expand on the explainability and transparency of our algorithms, add more languages and provide a web application interface. The comparability of the performance of the models on the 2022 and 2023 sets still leaves much to be desired. No cleaning nor filtring was performed over the scraped text which can contain irregular symbols left from the website meta-data. At the same time, collaboration with a fact-checking agency would also increase labelling quality.

Ethics Statement

It should be disclosed that the corresponding author is of Ukrainian nationality, although the study is not funded nor in any way affiliated with any governmental or private Ukrainian agency. Our work seeks to contribute to the automated content moderation efforts to protect human moderators from the constant psychological trauma they have to undergo reading toxic and manipulative posts and news. However, an imperfect automated tool may flag neutral content and should not be used to demonetize or ban internet users on social media. Unfortunately, such technology can be used to reinforce eco-chambers if users choose to filter out everything that is, e.g. not Pro-Kremlin propaganda. It can also help create tools which would be able to produce propaganda which will avoid these specific phenomena we describe, and thus make it more difficult to detect.
We also hope to support the general efforts to strengthen European security in the face of the Russian international propaganda campaign, by scaling defensive capacities and increasing citizens' awareness.

Acknowledgements

The author VS would like to express gratitude to fellow researcher Lev Petrov, who actively helped us with the visual component of this paper.

References

Roberto Adriani. 2019. The evolution of fake news and the abuse of emerging technologies. *European Journal of Social Sciences*, 2:32–38.

Foo Yun Chee. 2017. Nato says it sees sharp rise in russian disinformation since crimea seizure. *Reuters*.

Jacob Cohen. 1960. A coefficient of agreement for nominal scales. *Educational and Psychological Measurement*, pages 37–46.

Jacob Devlin, Ming-Wei Chang, Kenton Lee, and Kristina Toutanova. 2018. BERT: pre-training of deep bidirectional transformers for language understanding. *CoRR*, abs/1810.04805.

Francesca Ebel. 2022. Putin admits attacks on civilian infrastructure, asking: 'who started it?'. *The Washington Post*.

Guy Faulconbridge. 2022a. Putin escalates ukraine war, issues nuclear threat to west. *Reuters*.

Guy Faulconbridge. 2022b. Russia fights back in information war with jail warning. *Reuters*.

Emmanuel Grynszpan. 2022. Russian missiles target ukraine civilians and infrastructure. *Le Monde*.

Mingfei Guo, Xiuying Chen, Juntao Li, Dongyan Zhao, and Rui Yan. 2021. How does truth evolve into fake news? an empirical study of fake news evolution. *arXiv*.

S. Mo Jang, Tieming Geng, Jo-Yun Queenie Li, Ruofan Xia, Chin-Tser Huang, Hwalbin Kim, and Jijun Tang. 2018. A computational approach for examining the roots and spreading patterns of fake news: Evolution tree analysis. *Computers in Human Behavior*, 84:103–113.

Bridget Kendall. 2014. Russian propaganda machine 'worse than soviet union. *BBC*.

Julia Khrebtan-Hörhager and Evgeniya Pyatovskaya. 2022. Putin's propaganda is rooted in russian history – and that's why it works. *The Conversation*.

Maria Korenyuk and Jack Goodman. 2022. Ukraine war: 'my city's being shelled, but mum won't believe me'. *BBC*.

Christian Kraemer. 2022. Russian bombings of civilian infrastructure raise cost of ukraine's recovery: Imf. *Reuters*.

Elina Lange-Ionatamišvili. 2015. Analysis of russia's information campaign against ukraine: Examining non-military aspects of the crisis in ukraine from a strategic communications perspectives. *NATO Strategic Communications Centre of Excellence*.

Dan Sabbagh Luke Harding and Isobel Koshiw. 2022. Russia targets ukraine energy and water infrastructure in missile attacks. *The Guardian*.

Civil Network Opora. 2022. War speeches. 190 days of propaganda, or "evolution" of statements by russian politicians. *Ukrainska Pravda*.

Alicia Parlapiano and Jasmine C. Lee. 2018. The propaganda tools used by russians to influence the 2016 election. *The New York Times*.

David Powers. 2008. Evaluation: From precision, recall and f-factor to roc, informedness, markedness & correlation. *Mach. Learn. Technol.*, 2.

Valentyna Romanenko. 2022. Russia issues new guidelines on how to support mobilisation campaign. *Ukrainska Pravda*.

Veronika Solopova, Oana-Iuliana Popescu, Christoph Benzmüller, and Tim Landgraf. 2023. Automated multilingual detection of pro-kremlin propaganda in newspapers and telegram posts. *Datenbank Spektrum*.

Mukund Sundararajan, Ankur Taly, and Qiqi Yan. 2017. Axiomatic attribution for deep networks.

Anton Troianovski and Valeriya Safronova. 2022. Russia takes censorship to new extremes, stifling war coverage. *The New York Times*.

Rowan Zellers, Ari Holtzman, Hannah Rashkin, Yonatan Bisk, Ali Farhadi, Franziska Roesner, and Yejin Choi. 2019. Defending against neural fake news.

A Appendix

A.1 Appendix

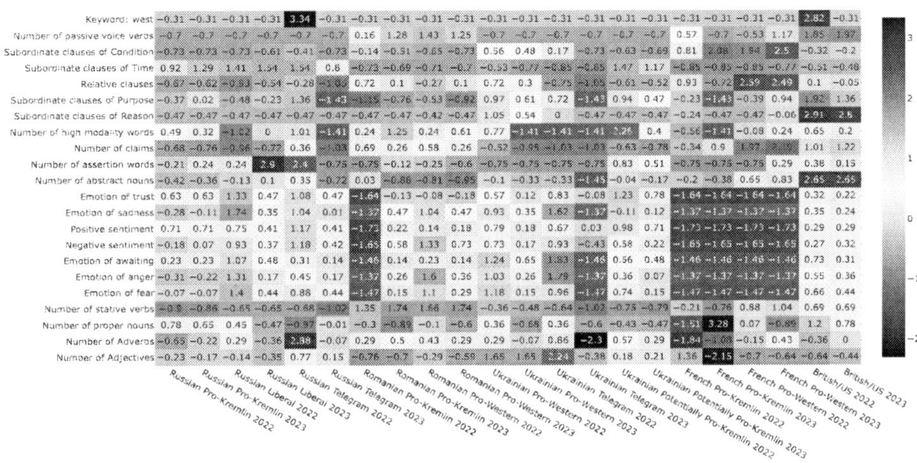

Figure 2: Normalized averages from the Comparative analysis. Linguistic features.

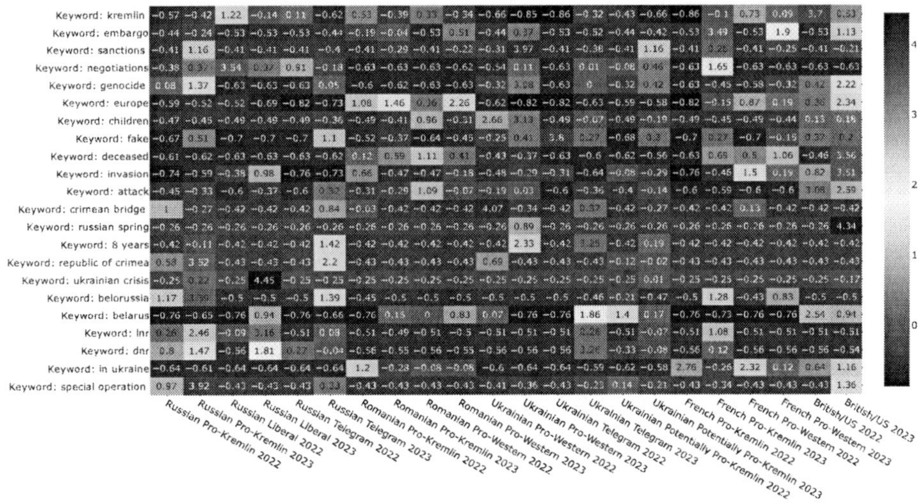

Figure 3: Normalized averages from the Comparative analysis. Keywords.

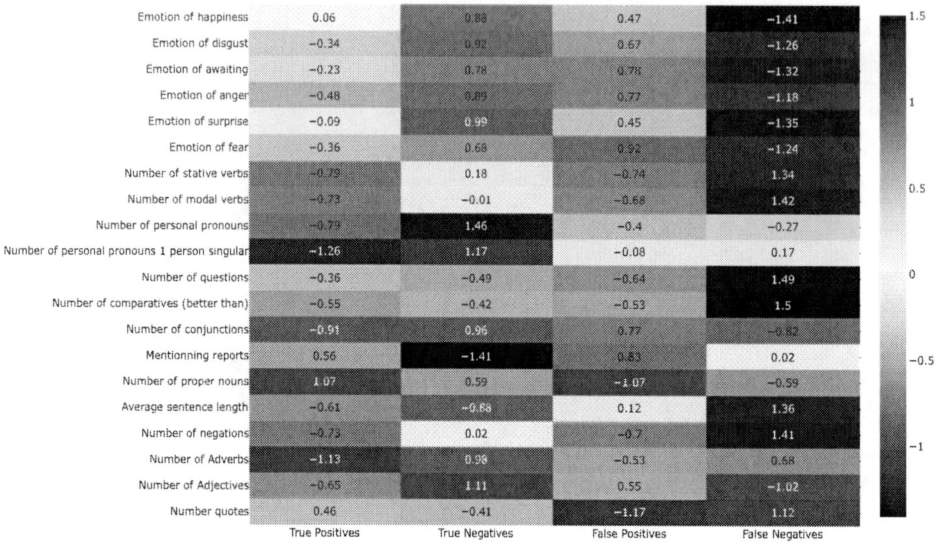

Figure 4: Error analysis. Normalized averages of linguistic features for the groups of errors.

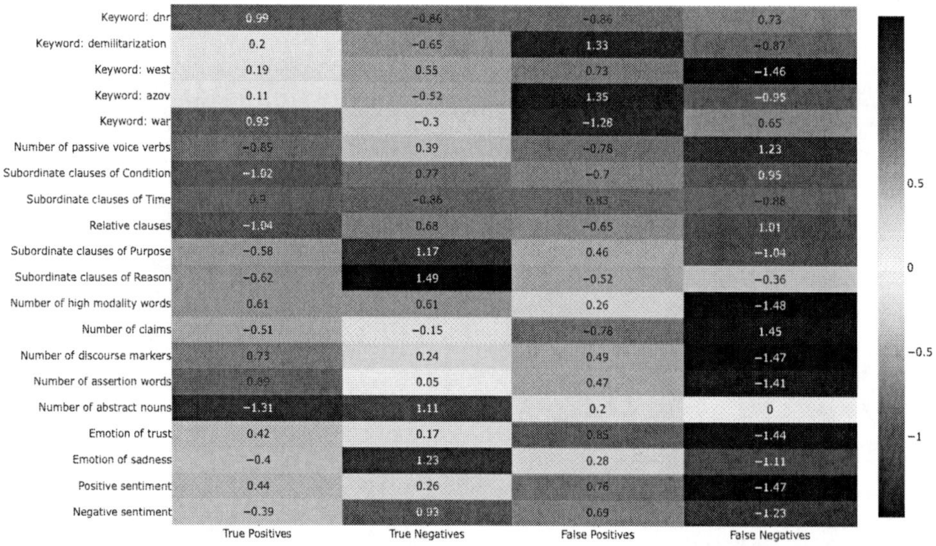

Figure 5: Error analysis. Normalized averages of keyword occurrences for the groups of errors.

Abstractive Summarization for the Ukrainian Language: Multi-Task Learning with Hromadske.ua News Dataset

Svitlana Galeshchuk
Arval BNP Paribas / Rueil-Malmaison, France
West Ukrainian National University / Ternopil, Ukraine
svitlana.galeshchuk@gmail.com

Abstract

Despite recent NLP developments, abstractive summarization remains a challenging task, especially in the case of low-resource languages like Ukrainian. The paper aims at improving the quality of summaries produced by mT5 for news in Ukrainian by fine-tuning the model with a mixture of summarization and text similarity tasks using summary-article and title-article training pairs, respectively. The proposed training set-up with small, base, and large mT5 models produce higher quality résumé. Besides, we present a new Ukrainian dataset for the abstractive summarization task that consists of circa 36.5K articles collected from Hromadske.ua until June 2021.

1 Introduction

Reading a large number of documents is a time-consuming and frequently tedious process that requires a substantial investment of human resources. That is why creating pithy abstracts for financial articles, social media news, or even bug reports originated many real-life use cases for automatic summarization.

In the meantime, the rapid development of AI methodology and the latest NLP progress with large Transformer language models pushed the boundaries of text generation. Producing a résumé for a document constitutes one of the applications for text generation that keeps attracting more attention of the academic community (see Section 2.1) and practitioners.

Abstractive summarization is a generative task that foresees automatic creation of document summary by synthesizing an input while preserving its gist. Observed limitations of language models (see Section 2.1) frequently challenge this definition. Recent papers discuss the problem of information distortion when it comes to solutions for the English language; however, for low-resource languages like Ukrainian the differences between real and expected results might be even more significant. This paper tries to improve the ability of language models to capture a gist of text in order to generate summaries of better quality for news articles in Ukrainian by finetuning the multilingual T5 Transformer on the corpora that exploits training data for both summarization and text similarity tasks simultaneously and thus guiding the model to the essence of each article. The second objective is to construct and introduce the dataset of Ukrainian news that can be further exploited for abstractive summarization.

The next section presents problems of abstractive summarization and discusses mT5 architecture and training. Section 3 focuses on training data, methodology and evaluation strategy. Section 4 concludes with results and discussion.

2 Overview of automatic summarization

2.1 Challenges of Abstractive Summarization

The recent growth of transfer learning solutions with Transformer-like decoder architectures contributed to development of fine-tuned models apt for abstractive summarization (such as BART, T5, GPT). However, current research identifies significant issues which make automatic summarization a challenging task (see the papers that conduct in-depth research on the topic: Erdem et al., 2022; Ji et al., 2023). We highlight the following problems:

• How to evaluate a summary? We address the issues of summary evaluation in Section 3.3.

• Summaries suffer from hallucinations, i.e., information leaked to the output from the outside of source text. However, Cao et al., 2022 find that much hallucinated content is mainly consistent with world knowledge.

• Summaries do not convey a gist of text, which is especially noticeable in multi-document summarization. Our study concentrates on "helping" the mT5 model to pay attention to an essential message

Proceedings of the Second Ukrainian Natural Language Processing Workshop (UNLP), pages 49–53
May 5, 2023 ©2023 Association for Computational Linguistics

expressed in the article.

We can find a plethora of models pre-trained and fine-tuned on English corpora. However, language resources for Ukrainian are still limited, which penalizes models' performance and limits the number of available monolingual solutions. Among language models suitable for summarization BART, PEGASUS, T5 and GPT/GPT-2/GPT-3 are the most well regarded pre-trained solutions as they include a decoder part in their architecture. We use the multilingual T5 model in our experimentation (see Section 2.3).

2.2 Related Works

Training resources for summarization in Ukrainian are limited. XL-SUM (Hasan et al., 2021) multilingual dataset stands for a silver standard as it comprises more than 58K of BBC news articles in Ukrainian. While this number is higher than for Arabic or Chinese, the performance of the model trained with XL-SUM is still better for the latter languages. No human evaluation was conducted for the Ukrainian language as the authors focus mainly on top 10 spoken languages. In spite of the need for further investigation of the Ukrainian corpora quality, we consider this dataset as a benchmark for comparison and evaluation in our study.

MassiveSumm (Varab and Schluter, 2021) is another multilingual dataset that contains 594,415 news articles in Ukrainian. The data is collected from the sources that follow OpenGraph standard (see Grusky et al., 2018). While the corpus is large, there is no profound analysis of its quality presented. The reported summarization results are less convincing than with XL-SUM for the same languages.

Concerning attempts to build automatic summarization model, most of research until recently focused on extractive summarization (see Shakhovska and Cherna, 2019). Abstractive summarization is mainly represented by finetuned multilingual models with XL-SUM[1] or extracted Ukrainian model from multilingual version[2]. Comparing to these works we present a sequence-to-sequence language model trained with a mixture of tasks for the newly developed dataset of Ukrainian news.

[1]see "mT5multilingualXLSum" at https://huggingface.co/csebuetnlp/mT5_multilingual_XLSum

[2]see "ukmt5base" at https://huggingface.co/kravchenko/uk-mt5base

2.3 Multilingual-T5 and Multitask Training

Text-to-Text Transfer Transformer, or simply T5, is a Transformer model with encoder-decoder architecture well suited for sequence-to-sequence tasks. The encoder comprises blocks with two main elements: a self-attention layer and a feed-forward network. The decoder has a slightly adjusted structure with standard attention added after each autoregressive self-attention layer.

No monolingual T5 model exists for Ukrainian. Hence multilingual version called mT5 is used. Similar to its original version, mT5 has been pre-trained on a large dataset cleaned with a set of heuristic rules (i.e., removal of all texts with less than three lines and 200 characters). The corpora cover more than 100 languages, and the Ukrainian part accounts for 1.51% with 41B tokens and 39M pages (see Xue et al., 2020).

We choose mT5 model as its training foresees transforming multi-task learning into finetuning on a mixture of datasets with the same text-to-text objective (see Raffel et al., 2020). "Prefix", i.e. some context provided to the model that is later used when making predictions, is added to the input text and helps model separate tasks. Thus, after pretraining, the model is further finetuned on a mixture of tasks in a sequence-to-sequence manner: the output is always a string, even in the case of quantitative values. This unified text-to-text approach in multi-task learning is a key element in our study as we mix Hromadske.ua data with summaries as target together with the same Hromadske.ua' articles and titles with "similar" as expected output.

3 Experimental setup

3.1 Methodology

The pre-trained mT5 checkpoint serves our experimentation as a baseline model. We considerate two downstream tasks for further training:

• *Summarization* with a respectful prefix that defines the task for the model. Here we use an article as input and a summary as a target.

• *Similarity* that learns the similarity between a text and its title. Here we use the same set of articles (sentence 1) together with the articles' titles (sentence 2) as an input and a string "similar" as a target.

This setup builds on the original idea of training T5 with a mixture of several tasks with the same text-to-text objective. Raffel et al., 2020 use independent datasets for each of the task. In contrast, we train the model with the same collection of texts adjusted for both tasks. Here, mT5 can see an article twice but with different target. This approach helps the model catch the gist of text usually reflected in its title and produce a more meaningful, topic-focused summary.

We concatenated adjusted versions of the dataset creating the mixed tasks for multi-task learning (see Figure 1). We refer to it as an extended dataset. Because of task mixing, the T5 approach does not require changes in model design for classification output on similarity as it is usually designed in multi-output settings (i.e., in Nan et al., 2021 supplementary classification head in the decoder of BART helped identify summary-worthy named entities to tackle hallucination problem).

Different checkpoints of mT5 are released: mT5-small, base, large and XL. Moreover, recently mT5 model fine-tuned on XL-SUM dataset made another step towards better summarization (see Hasan et al., 2021). We thus use mT5-small and mT5-large pretrained original checkpoints together with mT5-base model finetuned on a XL-SUM single task to assess empirically the presented hypothesis.

3.2 Training Dataset

In our experiment setup, we use the dataset of 36,488 articles collected and filtered from the website Hromadske.ua from September 2018 to June 2021. The total corpus shared by ***UberText***[3] initiative contains approximately 130K articles from Hromadske.ua, but this value decreased drastically after we applied several layers of heuristic rules.

Although the total Ubertext collection contains other news sources (Ukrainska Pravda, Unian, etc.), the task of automatic distinguishing of a summary from an article is quasi-impossible for most of them. In contrast, many articles from Hromadske.ua have consistent editorial structure:

Part 1: summary + Part 2: source of the news + Part 3: the article itself.

We observed a lexical pattern that helps define Part 2 in many texts : it tends to start with "Pro tse" (English translation: "This is") + a source. For example, "Про це повідомляє Маріупольська міська рада." (Transliteration: "Pro tse povidomlyaye Mariupolska miska rada", English translation: "This is reported by the Mariupol City Council").

[3]see details at https://lang.org.ua/en/.

INPUT	TARGET
До «червоної» зони карантинних обмежень 22 березня потрапила Сумська область.Загалом жорсткі обмеження запровадили вже у 8 регіонах. Translated: On March 22, the Sumy region entered the "red" zone of quarantine restrictions. In general, strict restrictions have already been introduced in 8 regions.	підсумувати: Тепер жорсткий карантин за розподілом МОЗ діє у Житомирській, Закарпатській, Івано-Франківській, Київській (потрапила туди 21 березня), Чернівецькій, Сумській, Одеській областях та Києві. Також напередодні в Миколаєві місцева влада самостійно запровадила «червону» зону в місті через критичну ситуацію з госпіталізацією пацієнтів. У «помаранчевій» зоні за розподілом МОЗ опинилися 11 регіонів: Вінницька, Дніпропетровська, Донецька, Луганська, Львівська, Миколаївська, Полтавська, Тернопільська, Хмельницька, Черкаська, Чернігівська областіРешта областей залишаються в «жовтій» зоні карантину. З 24 лютого Україна повернулася до адаптивного карантину. Translated: summarize: Now strict quarantine according to the Ministry of Health is in effect in Zhytomyr, Zakarpattia, Ivano-Frankivsk, Kyiv (from March 21), Chernivtsi, Sumy, Odesa regions and Kyiv. Also, the day before in Mykolaiv, local authorities independently introduced a "red" zone in the city due to a critical situation with hospitalization of patients. According to the Ministry of Health, 11 regions were in the "orange" zone: Vinnytsia, Dnipropetrovsk, Donetsk, Luhansk, Lviv, Mykolaiv, Poltava, Ternopil, Khmelnytskyi, Cherkasy, Chernihiv oblasts. The rest of the oblasts remain in the "yellow" quarantine zone. Since February 24, Ukraine has returned to adaptive quarantine
речення1 (sentence1): Тепер жорсткий карантин за розподілом МОЗ діє у Житомирській, Закарпатській, Івано-Франківській, Київській (потрапила туди 21 березня), Чернівецькій, Сумській, Одеській областях та Києві. Також напередодні... повернулася до адаптивного карантину речення2 (sentence2): У Сумській області запровадили «червону» зону карантину. Загалом в Україні вже 8 таких регіонів.	подібні / similar

Figure 1: Example of input for multi-task training with mixture of datasets having the same text-to-text objective. English translation provided alongside. Note sentence 1 is truncated to save the page space.

Recall from Section 3.1 that training employs the dataset comprising the following components:

- input: article –> target: summary;
- input: sentence 1: same article, sentence 2: title –> target: "similar"

Figure 1 displays an example of input-target used for training accompanied with English translation for non-Ukrainian speakers.

Occasionally, a summary repeats a title. To avoid these issues, we adopted an n-gram approach to discard title-summary near-duplicates. We followed the guidance from the original T5 paper (Raffel et al., 2020) and lowercased texts before using them. In addition, we deleted the titles that contain digits as the set-up does not foresee an assessment of numerical values consistency. Topic analysis classifies the filtered articles into four main categories: politics, sport, culture and science with a majority of texts falling in the first category. Human evaluation of datasets is expensive and time-consuming. Hence, automatic approaches serve to understand better and clean the dataset. The following metrics measure the quality of the training input:

Abstractivity: a metric based on the matched text spans between a text and a summary (Grusky et al.,

Dataset	ABS	SBert	Rouge-L
Hromadske.ua	82.30	0.52	39.4
XL-SUM	75.70	0.63	35.8

Table 1: Evaluation of the presented dataset (Hromadske.ua) comparing to XL-SUM.

2018).

SBertScore similarity between a summary and a first sentence of an article to avoid duplication of content by simple paraphrasing, as the model may learn to pay attention only to the first sentence.

ROUGE-L: the score reflects the longest sequence of words shared. In this case the lower score is preferable.

Not many datasets are available to train summarization model in Ukrainian. We find XL-SUM (Hasan et al., 2021) the most advanced and reliable benchmark for an intrinsic comparison with our dataset. Table 1 reports the comparison.

The evaluation proves a reasonable abstractiveness of the Hromadske.ua dataset, which is higher than XL-SUM. The Rouge-L score is also higher in our case, reflecting better originality of the benchmark summaries yet.

3.3 Metrics and evaluation

The benchmark metric for abstractive summarization tasks adopted by the research community is the ROUGE score. The metric compares a generated summary against a reference. We employ three sub-categories of the ROUGE score:

- ROUGE-1: unigram overlap
- ROUGE-2: bigram overlap
- ROUGE-L: Longest Common Subsequence

The evaluation strategy foresees a split of the available dataset into the training-validation-test set with the ratio 80:10:10. The validation and test comprise only summary-article pairs, as we do not tend to assess similarity task. Thus, the reported results include only summaries of previously non-seen articles ignoring the evaluation of titles' similarity.

4 Main Findings

4.1 Results

This section reports the results of training the following mT5 checkpoints:

1. mT5-small with 300M parameters pretrained ("mT5-small")

Checkpoint	Baseline	One task	Two tasks
mT5-small	Not tested	9.50/2.12/9.43	13.26/2.71/13.40
mT5-SUM	11.72/3.41/11.74	19.69/5.52/19.48	21.46/6.12/21.55
mT5-large	1.52/1.01/1.63	19.55/4.89/19.77	22.09/7.04/22.12

Table 2: ROUGE-1/2/L scores on test set

2. mT5-base with 580M fine-tuned only with XL-Sum dataset ("mT5-SUM")

3. mT5-large pretrained with 1.2B parameters ("mT5-large")

Each training includes tokenization with vocabulary given with mT5 checkpoint. The input is truncated to 1024 tokens with a maximum output length equal to 128. The constant learning rate of 0.001 mimics the original setup. No dropout is applied. The models have been trained with circa 10000 steps (compared to XL-SUM with 37000 steps).

Table 2 concludes the empirical findings on test split by comparing with the baseline (column 1), training with only articles-summary pairs (column 2), and training with article-summary and article-title similarity test (column 3). mT5 large one task[4] and mT5 large two tasks[5] model may be tested at HuggingFace hub with proposed text examples.

All setups show better performance of the models with two-task learning rather than fine-tuning on a sole summarization downstream objective. The values are usually more important with Rouge-1/2 scores than Rouge-L. The output for mT5-SUM baseline is lower than in the original paper. However, Hasan et al., 2021 adjust the Rouge score for the languages. It may explain the reported difference.

4.2 Discussion

The improvement of generative models' ability to produce better quality summaries and an introduction of the Ukrainian news dataset constitute two main objectives and contributions of the paper. An adjusted multi-task learning setup for mT5 models is employed to achieve the first goal. The heuristics and evaluation behind the Hromadske.ua dataset satisfy the second objective. Concerning further research, we plan to use BertScore (Zhang et al., 2019) to better assess a model's ability to grasp the gist of an article with contextual similarity. The proposed approach may especially benefit multi-text

[4]see mT5-large-one-task model at https://huggingface.co/SGaleshchuk/t5-large-ua-news

[5]see https://huggingface.co/SGaleshchuk/mT5-sum-news-ua

summarization. Testing with available multi-article datasets in English together with a construction of such source in Ukrainian create a basis for further research. Moreover, the presented training setup may be fully reproducible for other low-resource languages.

Limitations

This Section highlights the following limitations of the presented setup:

• Although we received satisfactory scores with the extended dataset of Hromadske.ua, more computational resources could allow longer training and thus better assessment of the model performance.

• Rouge score may penalize abstractiveness of generated summaries. Metrics that assess factuality could evaluate better the model results.

• Expert evaluation of the dataset's sample reveals summaries that sound like introduction rather than abstract of article.

References

Meng Cao, Yue Dong, and Jackie Chi Kit Cheung. 2022. Hallucinated but factual! inspecting the factuality of hallucinations in abstractive summarization. In *Proceedings of the 60th Annual Meeting of the Association for Computational Linguistics (Volume 1: Long Papers)*, pages 3340–3354.

Erkut Erdem, Menekse Kuyu, Semih Yagcioglu, Anette Frank, Letitia Parcalabescu, Barbara Plank, Andrii Babii, Oleksii Turuta, Aykut Erdem, Iacer Calixto, et al. 2022. Neural natural language generation: A survey on multilinguality, multimodality, controllability and learning. *Journal of Artificial Intelligence Research*, 73:1131–1207.

Max Grusky, Mor Naaman, and Yoav Artzi. 2018. Newsroom: A dataset of 1.3 million summaries with diverse extractive strategies. *arXiv preprint arXiv:1804.11283*.

Tahmid Hasan, Abhik Bhattacharjee, Md Saiful Islam, Kazi Samin, Yuan-Fang Li, Yong-Bin Kang, M Sohel Rahman, and Rifat Shahriyar. 2021. Xl-sum: Large-scale multilingual abstractive summarization for 44 languages. *arXiv preprint arXiv:2106.13822*.

Ziwei Ji, Nayeon Lee, Rita Frieske, Tiezheng Yu, Dan Su, Yan Xu, Etsuko Ishii, Ye Jin Bang, Andrea Madotto, and Pascale Fung. 2023. Survey of hallucination in natural language generation. *ACM Computing Surveys*, 55(12):1–38.

Feng Nan, Ramesh Nallapati, Zhiguo Wang, Cicero Nogueira dos Santos, Henghui Zhu, Dejiao Zhang, Kathleen McKeown, and Bing Xiang. 2021. Entity-level factual consistency of abstractive text summarization. *arXiv preprint arXiv:2102.09130*.

Colin Raffel, Noam Shazeer, Adam Roberts, Katherine Lee, Sharan Narang, Michael Matena, Yanqi Zhou, Wei Li, and Peter J Liu. 2020. Exploring the limits of transfer learning with a unified text-to-text transformer. *The Journal of Machine Learning Research*, 21(1):5485–5551.

Nataliya Shakhovska and Taras Cherna. 2019. The method of automatic summarization from different sources. *arXiv preprint arXiv:1905.02623*.

Daniel Varab and Natalie Schluter. 2021. Massivesumm: a very large-scale, very multilingual, news summarisation dataset. In *Proceedings of the 2021 Conference on Empirical Methods in Natural Language Processing*, pages 10150–10161.

Linting Xue, Noah Constant, Adam Roberts, Mihir Kale, Rami Al-Rfou, Aditya Siddhant, Aditya Barua, and Colin Raffel. 2020. mt5: A massively multilingual pre-trained text-to-text transformer. *arXiv preprint arXiv:2010.11934*.

Tianyi Zhang, Varsha Kishore, Felix Wu, Kilian Q Weinberger, and Yoav Artzi. 2019. Bertscore: Evaluating text generation with bert. *arXiv preprint arXiv:1904.09675*.

Extension Multi30K: Multimodal Dataset for Integrated Vision and Language Research in Ukrainian

Nataliia Saichyshyna, Daniil Maksymenko, Oleksii Turuta, Andriy Yerokhin, Olena Turuta and Andrii Babii
Kharkiv National University of Radio Electronics / Nauky Ave. 14, Kharkiv, Ukraine
{nataliia.saichyshyna, daniil.maksymenko, oleksii.turuta, andriy.yerokhin, olena.turuta, andrii.babii}@nure.ua

Abstract

We share the results of the project within the well-known Multi30k dataset dedicated to improving machine translation of text from English into Ukrainian. The main task was to manually prepare the dataset and improve the translation of texts. The importance of collecting such datasets for low-resource languages for improving the quality of machine translation has been discussed. We also studied the features of translations of words and sentences with ambiguous meanings.

The collection of multimodal datasets is essential for natural language processing tasks because it allows the development of more complex and comprehensive machine learning models that can understand and analyze different types of data. These models can learn from a variety of data types, including images, text, and audio, for more accurate and meaningful results.

1 Introduction

Creating and processing high-quality datasets for such low-resource languages as Ukrainian is incredibly important for solving machine learning tasks. The task of machine translation, like other tasks, requires large amounts of data to effectively learn and understand the nuances and complexities of language. However, for low-resource languages, the available data may be limited, which can make it difficult to develop accurate and efficient models. Datasets directly affect the performance of machine learning models. This can lead to higher accuracy and better generalization for tasks such as language translation, speech recognition, and natural language processing.

A multimodal dataset refers to a dataset that consists of various data types, each representing a different modality. These modalities can include images, text, audio, and other types of data, each with its own unique meaning. By including multiple domains, a dataset can collect a wider range of information, allowing the development of more complex machine learning models. For our task we decided to choose Multi30k (Elliott et al., 2016) dataset which consists of two modalities: images and their descriptions.

Multi30K is a modification of the Flickr30K dataset (Young et al., 2014) with 31,014 German translations of English annotations and more than 150,000 collected annotations in German. This dataset was edited by professional translators, and one picture corresponds to one annotation in English and German, which is the reason for choosing this dataset for further adaptation into Ukrainian.

The problem under consideration consists of three parts:

- **Task 1: Machine translation** involves translating a source language description of an image into a target language. The training data is made up of pairs of sentences in different languages. We published some results in our previous articles (Maksymenko et al., 2022) covering this topic. Here we want to extend some explanations and conclusions.
- **Task 2: Multilingual multimodal semantic search** is a task with great demand considering how much unstructured multimodal data is stored nowadays. We need methods to search it quickly not only for English but for other even low-resource languages. We wanted to check some available models with the support of Ukrainian language using samples from our translated version of Multi30k.
- **Task 3: Usage of multilingual text embedding models to measure translation quality** which should in theory allow us to check model performance without any target language ground truth text. Some hard cases like phrases with a figurative sense should be considered to either prove or disprove the efficiency of this approach.

Proceedings of the Second Ukrainian Natural Language Processing Workshop (UNLP), pages 54–61
May 5, 2023 ©2023 Association for Computational Linguistics

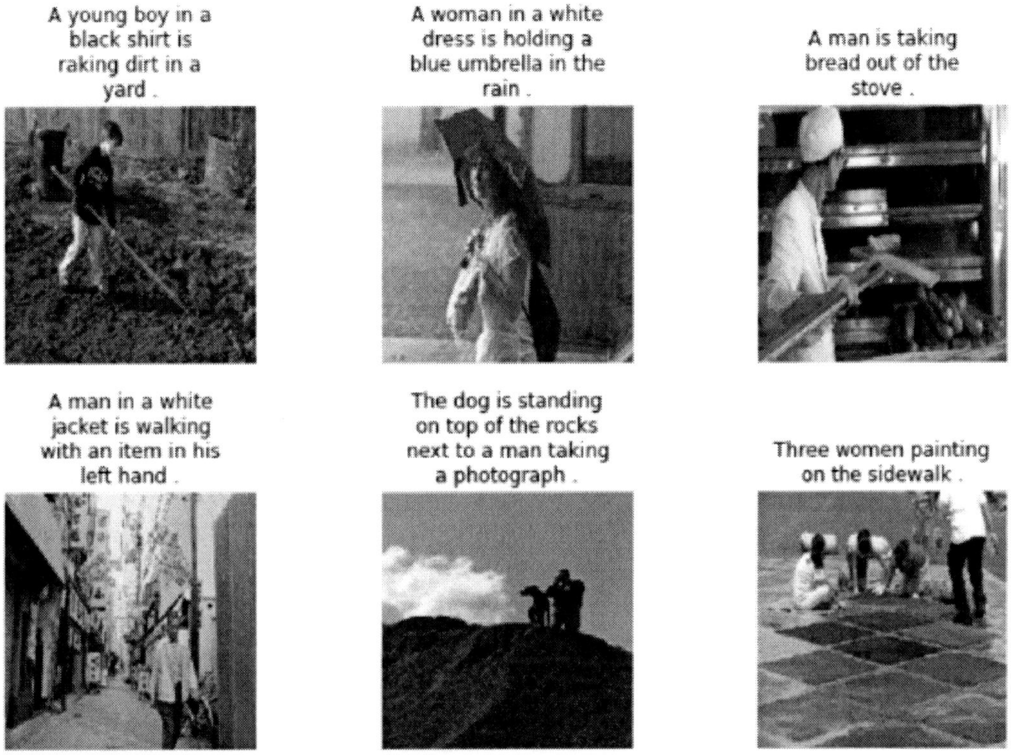

Figure 1: Annotations in English from Multi30k dataset

The first and main step of this research was to collect datasets for low-resource languages such as Ukrainian. We provided the necessary data to develop accurate and efficient machine-learning models. This may include datasets for tasks such as language translation, image captioning, text generation (Erdem et al., 2022), visual Q&A, sentiment analysis, and others.

2 Datasets and Tasks

The main dataset used for the tasks described above is the Multi30K dataset, which includes 31,000 images originally described in English. The presented dataset also includes translations created by professional German translators.

In the next iterations, this dataset was also translated into French (Elliott et al., 2017), Czech (Barrault et al., 2018) and Turkish (Citamak et al., 2020). Dataset overview is presented on Figure 1.

The dataset can be used to boost performance of some existing multilingual multimodal models for various machine learning tasks, such as multimodal machine translation, image captioning, image semantic search, cross-lingual transfer learning, and multilingual text summarization etc.

As a result, we managed to process 31,014 sentences for Ukrainian and English, and the number of words that are in this dataset was also counted. We prepared a Ukrainian version of Multi30k dataset with the following features. Comparison of the number of tokens for the languages from the original article (English and German) and Ukrainian can be seen in Table 1.

This number for the English language exceeds the given number for the Ukrainian language, due to its linguistic features, for example, there are no articles in Ukrainian.

Descriptions	Sentences	Tokens
English	31 014	357 172
German	31 014	333 833
Ukrainian	31 014	276 520

Table 1: Number of tokens in the dataset

3 Dataset preparation process

The first step was to load the selected dataset and conduct an initial inspection, determine the columns and data type, image format, count the number of sentences, words and images in order to select a further strategy for its processing.

At the next stage, we performed the translation of English descriptions of images into Ukrainian using Google Cloud Translator in order to provide a further basis for manual verification and correction of texts.

An example of the annotation we received after translation with the help of Google translator can be seen in Figure 2. This example clearly shows that the resulting translation is not accurate and correct in this case. Thus, here is an adjective that is incorrect in meaning and an incorrect declension, since the word dog is masculine in Ukrainian.

Further this translation was the basis on which our team, which was engaged in corrections, relied. Our team consisted of 8 people: students and teachers of our university. For this work, an English text, an image and a Ukrainian text translated by Google Cloud Translator were provided.

It is important to note that in the process of correcting the text, the person who did it had access to both the image and the pictures. Ukrainian translation turned out to be dependent on these two sources, sometimes the picture helped to recognize what exactly was meant by the English description.

During preparation for translations, the data set was cleaned of incorrect characters and punctuation

en: A white and tan dog runs through the tall green grass
uk: Біло-засмагла собака біжить крізь високу зелену траву

Figure 2: Sample from dataset

Cosine similarity value	Initial text	Manually translated text
0.9	1516	1546
0.8	3700	3763
0.7	4616	4675
0.6	4912	4919
0.5	4997	4977
0.4	4999	4999
0.3	5000	5000
0.2	5000	5000
0.1	5000	5000

Table 2: Cosine similarity count

in order to be able to be used for training.

The dataset is able on public repository `https://huggingface.co/datasets/turuta/Multi30k-uk` and `https://github.com/researchlabs/multi30k-uk`.

It is worth noting that the Google Cloud Translator translated simple sentences (which contain simple actions like "walk", "look", referring to a certain person) correctly and without comments. However, when faced with complex sentences and atypical actions, manual correction is required. Therefore, about 51% of the proposals were manually corrected.

4 Cosine similarity

The data obtained after translation were analyzed. We decided to calculate the cosine similarity using a multilingual model distiluse-base-multilingual-cased-v2 (Reimers and Gurevych, 2019) for the original translation using Google Cloud Translator and for the translation obtained after manual correction.

We got a high value of cosine similarity for all sentences for both languages. As a result, 4997 sentences have a high value, and 3 have a low value. Here, values above 0.4 are taken into account, which is considered sufficient for a general understanding of the meaning of a sentence or phrase.

Table 2 shows, using the example of 5000 records, the value of cosine similarity using the model described above.

The columns "Initial text" and "Manually translated text" indicate the number of sentences that exceed the corresponding cosine similarity value. Thus, as a result of our translation adjustment, an additional 30 values went out of range of 0.9, 63

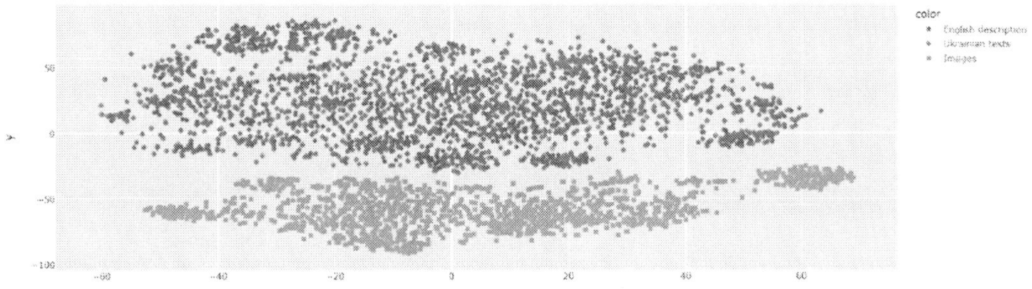

Figure 3: Texts and images embeddings projections

values went out of range 0.8, and so on.

This reflects the effectiveness of the work done on manual verification of the selected data.

5 Results

5.1 Machine translation

We published more detailed results of the machine translation task in our previous articles (Maksymenko et al., 2022). Those experiments involved not only obtained Multi30k translations, but also some other datasets, which we gathered like Ukrainian laws, scientific articles abstracts, programming documentation.

Machine translation was done using a fine-tuned MarianMT model, both on separate datasets and on all of them combined. We used Huggingface implementation, which is based on BART interface. This model was trained as a part of Helsinki NLP (Tiedemann and Thottingal, 2020) project with OPUS datasets.

Multi30k without any additional set did not drastically improve the performance of the MarianMT model (Junczys-Dowmunt et al., 2018), however it was able to improve generalization of previously tuned model as it provided some examples of new words and phrases, which were absent in the present checkpoint. Multi30k descriptions do not contain any domain specific words, the structure of sentences is easy to understand and capture. Such an effect was expected from it.

We used TATOEBA dataset with 5,000 texts to validate trained model and got METEOR score equal to 0.3810 and BERT F1 Score equal to 0.9232. METEOR was used as a classic token metric, which is more suitable for flexible languages as it uses synonyms matching and stemming to avoid extra penalties. BERT Score was used as an embedding metric to measure how well did the model capture meaning of the source text set.

5.2 Multilingual multimodal semantic search

We used a combination of CLIP and Siamese DistilBERT (Sanh et al., 2019) in our research as a multimodal semantic search model. "sentence-transformers/clip-ViT-B-32-multilingual-v1" model weights from Huggingface hub were used as an initial checkpoint for checked models. First of all, we tried to visualize embeddings of images, source English texts, and their manually fixed Ukrainian translations.

Models return vectors, which consist of 512 elements with values from -1 to 1. The first step here is to train a language embedding model, like original BERT, for a high-resource language like English. Then DistilBERT should try to replicate this embedding vector for translations of original texts to maximize cosine similarity between the same texts in different languages. The same process is applied to CLIP to replicate similar embedding space for corresponding images. So we encoded our images and texts in both languages and used TSNE to create 2D projections of original embedding vectors (figure 3). You can see how Ukrainian translations almost perfectly replicate the form of English text distribution, which proves that our fixed translations should be close to the original descriptions and can be further used for some real-world tasks. However, images fall into an absolutely different part of this embedding space. They try to replicate the form of those text clouds, but they are still far from texts and don't really correspond to their descriptions judging by embeddings. Only 44.5% of images correspond mostly to their real description. This value is equal to 29.55% for Ukrainian versions.

Here are some examples of errors made by the semantic search model. We have the following Ukrainian image description: "Молодий бородатий чоловік у білій безрукавці сидить

Figure 4: Original corresponding image and one proposed by model

за барабанною установкою" (Young bearded man wearing a white tank top sits behind a drum set.). The semantic search model returns a similar image, but with slightly different details. There is really a man with a beard who sits somewhere on figure 4, but he just draws something on his tablet and there are no drums.

Model finds subjects really well, as most errors we saw are related to the action or some environment details or background objects. We have some images where people swim by the river or some kind of lake using a canoe. These images can be distinguished by some small details like the number of people in the boat, the type of background (cave, rocks, some specific type of forest), description of the river. However, the algorithm usually catches only the most significant details like "people in a canoe". So it misses all those small details, like in a previous case with a bearded man.

So, we can not definitely recommend this model for some real-world tasks for Ukrainian language as it still makes some obvious mistakes, which can be fixed by further fine-tuning. That is where our proposed dataset can be useful, so we can try to drastically improve the performance of Ukrainian multimodal semantic search by using these combinations of images and their descriptions during further research.

5.3 Usage of multilingual text embedding models to measure translation quality

Every classic approach to measure the translation quality relies on some target language ground truth value. However, what if we need to check if translation is good to use and we do not have any previously checked sample? Modern multilingual language models can produce similar embeddings for the same text in multiple languages, so we can compare them in one shared space. We have shown it in the previous section of the article as Ukrainian texts distribute almost identically to English ones.

We calculated cosine similarity between English and Ukrainian embedding vectors to check how an external model (siamese DistilBERT in distiluse-base-multilingual-cased-v2 implementation) would score our fixed translations. On figure 5 is a histogram of cosine similarity scores distribution.

Most texts fall into 0.6 and higher bins, which is a really good result as it indicates that our translations capture original meaning. 98.38% of texts belong there. Such a result is a great achievement for this metric as it seems like it almost replicates human judgment. However, there are a few smaller beans, which are of interest to us. Let's start with the ones in the range [0.4, 0.6).

We checked texts which belong to these bins and mostly they consist of cases where an English phrase or word combination gets translated into a single Ukrainian word, which is also a rare and not commonly used word. Like for example phrase "horse shoes" gets translated into word "підковки", which is a correct translation, but it this word is not so common and can slightly misdirect the language model. Here is another similar example: English phrase "give high-fives" gets translated as "дає п'ять". Translation is correct and the phrase itself is similar to the English one, but the model gets confused a bit, because it does

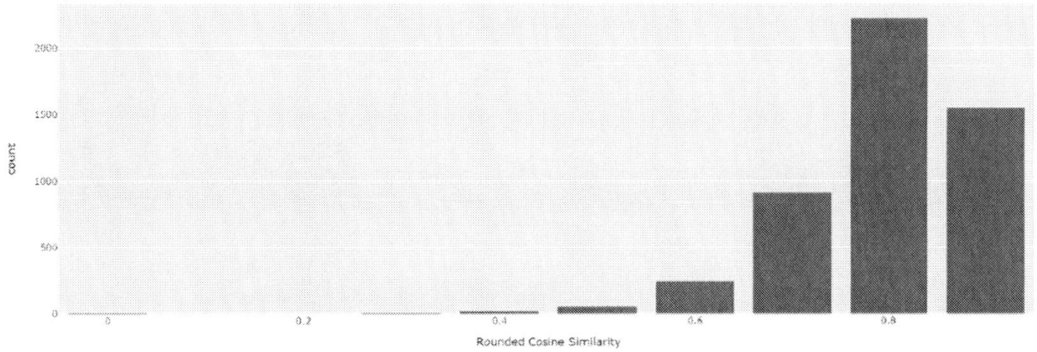

Figure 5: Histogram of cosine similarity scores distribution

not really understand the meaning of the phrase. That is an interesting case as it shows that even the correct translation of similar phrase in a figurative sense lowers the score.

Now let's move to some lower buckets in range [0, 0.4). There are only 3 texts in this buckets and all of them contain texts with some slangs or phrases with a figurative sense. For example a radio receiver was called "walkie talkie" in English description. Ukrainian version just used a word "рація". This text got a cosine similarity score 0.32 as model just was not able to capture this slang and connect it to Ukrainian analogue. Another example contains a rare word "волосінь", which stands for a fishing line. The model did not capture it as it probably did not encounter this word or some similar ones during the fit.

Also, we tried to do the same using a siamese DistilBERT aligned with image embeddings, which was used in task 2. We did not use images and just compared 2 texts. The results are drastically different as injection of visual information allowed neural network to better capture phrases like "high five" or "walkie talkey". It seems like an additional domain was able to give enough context for the network to compare these sentences in a more human-like way. Sentence which contained "walkie talkie" got 0.7456 score this time. There are no translations with a score lower than 0.5, if we measure the translation using this model. On figure 6 is the histogram we have built.

This area needs some further research, but from our tests and experiments it seems like such models can be used further to capture some figurative phrases or slangs in combination with some traditional metrics, like token-based ones. Usage of multidomain models to measure translation quality also has great potential as its results were much better than just text model. It fixed main problems, which we encountered in ordinary text model, but it definitely should be tested more before giving a recommendation to use it as a benchmark for machine translation.

We made some additional checks with some random phrases. English sources sound like "Murder will out" and "Keep the change". Here are Ukrainian translations: "Правди не сховаєш", "Здачі не треба". Only the textual model gave the following scores respectively: 0.2495 and 0.2599. Textual model tuned to resemble visual embeddings gave these scores: 0.9569 and 0.9497. Results are much better than we expected and outperform ones obtained from the only textual model. However, as we said before, the theory that visual embeddings were the main reason that boosted model performance still needs more proof and more research.

6 Conclusion

In conclusion, the importance of collecting high quality datasets for low-resource languages such as Ukrainian cannot be overestimated for machine learning tasks. An example of this was our project to improve the machine translation of text from English to Ukrainian by manually preparing the Multi30k dataset and examining translations of ambiguous words and sentences.

Collecting multimodal datasets that include different types of data such as images, text, and audio is especially important as they provide richer and more complex data for developing accurate and meaningful machine learning models. The results from our project demonstrate the impact of such datasets in improving the performance of machine

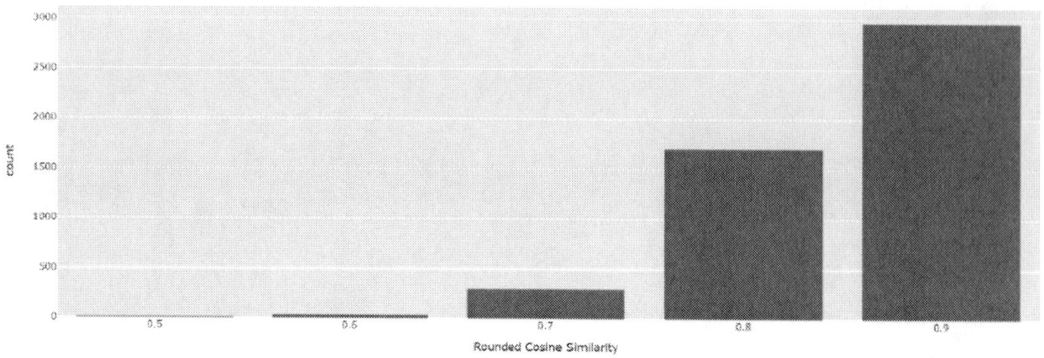

Figure 6: Histogram from a siamese DistilBERT aligned with CLIP image embeddings

learning models for tasks such as machine translation.

As a result, the creation and processing of such data sets will lead to a significant improvement in the solution of the problem of machine translation and many other tasks.

The project involved loading and validating a selected data set to determine the data type, image format, and word count. The data set was translated from English into Ukrainian using Google Translate, which served as the basis for manual verification and correction by a team of 8 people

As a further development we want to research siamese language models and cosine similarity of their embeddings even more to finally either prove or disprove that they can be used as benchmarks for machine translation. Also, we want to check how our gathered dataset will affect the performance of existing multimodal multilingual semantic search models by finetuning them using Ukrainian Multi30k. Another area for further research is to combine token metrics and text embeddings from a multilingual semantic search network to capture figurative meaning and some professional or just domain specific words and phrases.

Limitations

In the process of working on the study, we encountered a number of limitations and an unsuccessful experiment that did not give results. For example, different machine learning models sometimes showed different results, so it would be wise to explore more for our calculations. The images that are part of the considered datasets also require the necessary attention and refinement. We plan to integrate them more closely with textual information, thus improving the quality of the resulting machine translation. At some points in our study, we ran into a lack of computing power.

Ethics Statement

In creating this study, we are fully guided by generally accepted ethical principles towards the community of authors and organizers. We respect scientific developments and works and study them with interest for our further research and communication.

References

Loïc Barrault, Fethi Bougares, Lucia Specia, Chiraag Lala, Desmond Elliott, and Stella Frank. 2018. Findings of the third shared task on multimodal machine translation. In *Proceedings of the Third Conference on Machine Translation: Shared Task Papers*, pages 304–323, Belgium, Brussels. Association for Computational Linguistics.

Begum Citamak, Ozan Caglayan, Menekse Kuyu, Erkut Erdem, Aykut Erdem, Pranava Madhyastha, and Lucia Specia. 2020. Msvd-turkish: A comprehensive multimodal dataset for integrated vision and language research in turkish.

Desmond Elliott, Stella Frank, Loïc Barrault, Fethi Bougares, and Lucia Specia. 2017. Findings of the second shared task on multimodal machine translation and multilingual image description. In *Proceedings of the Second Conference on Machine Translation*, pages 215–233, Copenhagen, Denmark. Association for Computational Linguistics.

Desmond Elliott, Stella Frank, Khalil Sima'an, and Lucia Specia. 2016. Multi30K: Multilingual English-German image descriptions. In *Proceedings of the 5th Workshop on Vision and Language*, pages 70–74, Berlin, Germany. Association for Computational Linguistics.

Erkut Erdem, Menekse Kuyu, Semih Yagcioglu, Anette Frank, Letitia Parcalabescu, Barbara Plank, Andrii Babii, Oleksii Turuta, Aykut Erdem, Iacer

Calixto, Elena Lloret, Elena-Simona Apostol, Ciprian-Octavian Truică, Branislava Šandrih, Sanda Martinčić-Ipšić, Gábor Berend, Albert Gatt, and Grăzina Korvel. 2022. Neural natural language generation: A survey on multilinguality, multimodality, controllability and learning. *J. Artif. Int. Res.*, 73.

Marcin Junczys-Dowmunt, Roman Grundkiewicz, Tomasz Dwojak, Hieu Hoang, Kenneth Heafield, Tom Neckermann, Frank Seide, Ulrich Germann, Alham Fikri Aji, Nikolay Bogoychev, André F. T. Martins, and Alexandra Birch. 2018. Marian: Fast neural machine translation in C++. In *Proceedings of ACL 2018, System Demonstrations*, pages 116–121, Melbourne, Australia. Association for Computational Linguistics.

Daniil Maksymenko, Nataliia Saichyshyna, Oleksii Turuta, Olena Turuta, Andriy Yerokhin, and Andrii Babii. 2022. Improving the machine translation model in specific domains for the ukrainian language. In *2022 IEEE 17th International Conference on Computer Sciences and Information Technologies (CSIT)*, pages 123–129.

Nils Reimers and Iryna Gurevych. 2019. Sentence-BERT: Sentence embeddings using Siamese BERT-networks. In *Proceedings of the 2019 Conference on Empirical Methods in Natural Language Processing and the 9th International Joint Conference on Natural Language Processing (EMNLP-IJCNLP)*, pages 3982–3992, Hong Kong, China. Association for Computational Linguistics.

Victor Sanh, Lysandre Debut, Julien Chaumond, and Thomas Wolf. 2019. Distilbert, a distilled version of bert: smaller, faster, cheaper and lighter. *ArXiv*, abs/1910.01108.

Jörg Tiedemann and Santhosh Thottingal. 2020. OPUS-MT – building open translation services for the world. In *Proceedings of the 22nd Annual Conference of the European Association for Machine Translation*, pages 479–480, Lisboa, Portugal. European Association for Machine Translation.

Peter Young, Alice Lai, Micah Hodosh, and Julia Hockenmaier. 2014. From image descriptions to visual denotations: New similarity metrics for semantic inference over event descriptions. *Transactions of the Association for Computational Linguistics*, 2:67–78.

Silver Data for Coreference Resolution in Ukrainian: Translation, Alignment, and Projection

Pavlo Kuchmiichuk
University of Rochester
pavlo.kuchmiichuk@rochester.edu

Abstract

Low-resource languages continue to present challenges for current NLP methods, and multilingual NLP is gaining attention in the research community. One of the main issues is the lack of sufficient high-quality annotated data for low-resource languages. In this paper, we show how labeled data for high-resource languages such as English can be used in low-resource NLP. We present two silver datasets for coreference resolution in Ukrainian, adapted from existing English data by manual translation and machine translation in combination with automatic alignment and annotation projection. The code is made publicly available[1].

1 Introduction

Coreference resolution is a task that requires clustering the mentions in text that refer to the same underlying entity (Poesio and Artstein, 2008). For example, in a sentence "John asked Dan to drive him to work because his car was broken.", "John", "him", and "his" belong to the same cluster. In the past few years, significant progress has been achieved for English coreference resolution. To compare, in 2017 the average F_1 score of the model with the best performance in the CoNLL-2012 shared task (Pradhan et al., 2012) was 67.2 (Lee et al., 2017), and in 2021 the score of the best model increased to 81.0 (Dobrovolskii, 2021).

While the task of entity coreference resolution is relatively well-researched in English, it remains uncharted territory for many other languages. Models developed with English in mind often fail to perform on the same level if used for a different language (Joshi et al., 2020).

One of the prevalent issues when working with low-resource languages is the lack of annotated data. It is often complicated to find or compile high-quality datasets even for English, and labeled data for complex tasks in other languages is much rarer. Such data scarcity hinders NLP progress, as many state-of-the-art models require large amounts of labeled texts for training which are not available for low-resource languages (Ruder, 2020; Fincke et al., 2022). Building new high-quality datasets is essential for expanding NLP research to the low-resource setting.

One way of mitigating the data scarcity issue is adapting the data collected for high-resource languages. In this paper, we present two silver datasets annotated for coreference resolution in Ukrainian, both of which are built using existing English labeled data as a basis. First, we manually translated the Winograd Schema Challenge Dataset (Levesque et al., 2012) into the Ukrainian language. This dataset contains pairs of sentences with an ambiguous anaphor that can only be resolved using world knowledge and reasoning. Second, we used a machine translation model to translate texts from OntoNotes 5.0 (Weischedel et al., 2011) into Ukrainian, followed by automatically aligning and projecting annotations based on the cross-attention layer of an encoder-decoder model. Our approach allows efficiently creating silver datasets based on existing high-quality data, which can then be used to extend language model training to low-resource languages.

2 Related Work

In this section, we analyze different techniques commonly utilized to help with data scarcity issues in multilingual NLP.

2.1 Cross-lingual Transfer Learning

Methods such as cross-lingual transfer learning make it possible for the models to learn meanings of words across different languages simultaneously. Large pre-trained multilingual language models can transfer the knowledge learned from labeled data available in abundance for high-resource languages to low-resource ones.

[1] https://github.com/pkuchmiichuk/ua-coref

Proceedings of the Second Ukrainian Natural Language Processing Workshop (UNLP), pages 62–72
May 5, 2023 ©2023 Association for Computational Linguistics

Cross-lingual transfer learning relies on finding a shared cross-lingual space for languages in the system. Aligning the source and target embedding spaces is one of the methods commonly used for this. Recently, pre-trained multilingual encoders have also been shown to yield good performance on various NLP tasks (Xu and Murray, 2022).

Pires et al. (2019) demonstrate how mBERT, a language model pre-trained on 104 languages, is able to generalize quite well for NLP tasks in different languages. The authors perform NER and POS tagging experiments to show that mBERT performs the cross-lingual transfer quite well, considering the model does not see any markers that denote the input language on the pre-training stage. Instead, mBERT is able to capture multilingual representations of words. The representations capture useful linguistic information in a language-agnostic way, which allows the model to handle knowledge transfer even across languages with different scripts.

Wu and Dredze (2019) reaffirm this conclusion after exploring the performance of mBERT on tasks such as document classification, natural language inference, named entity recognition, POS tagging, and dependency parsing. While learning multilingual representations, the model also retains language-specific information which contributes to its capabilities.

Models that capture multilingual representations of words can be especially useful for word alignment, showing robust performance on different language pairs (Dou and Neubig, 2021). Researchers have also explored cross-lingual learning for coreference resolution in particular. Cruz et al. (2018) use a large Spanish corpora to create a model for Portuguese, leveraging FastText multilingual embeddings. Urbizu et al. (2019) work on coreference resolution for Basque, relying on English data from OntoNotes to train a cross-lingual model.

2.2 Domain Adaptation

Domain adaptation involves training a language model for a task in a specific domain without having enough data to train the model directly on in-domain data. As domain adaptation specifically aims to overcome lack of in-domain data issues, it is especially useful when working with low-resource languages. For example, one can consider data in a high-resource language such as English out-of-domain, and train language models for a target low-resource language using domain adaptation techniques.

Xu et al. (2021) introduce a gradual fine-tuning approach for domain adaptation. This contrasts with the common approaches to the task, using which the model is pre-trained on out-of-domain data and fine-tuned on in-domain data in one stage. Instead, the authors propose an iterative multi-stage fine-tuning method: the model is gradually fine-tuned on datasets composed both of out-of-domain and in-domain data. On each subsequent iteration, the percentage of in-domain data in the dataset increases. In training, this steers the model into target domain direction gently instead of using it as-is in zero-shot setting or directly performing one-stage fine-tuning on the whole target dataset. The gradual fine-tuning approach shows promising results for NLP tasks like dialogue state tracking and event extraction, outperforming both the pre-trained models and models fine-tuned using one-stage method. The authors conduct event extraction experiments on English and Arabic datasets, which highlights how the method can be utilized for working with low-resource languages. It is shown that gradual fine-tuning significantly improves results in comparison with baseline models.

Maurya et al. (2021) suggest using an additional pre-training step before fine-tuning the language model for solving natural language generation tasks in the target low-resource language. This allows the model to overcome the problem of mismatch between pre-training and fine-tuning objectives. Introducing an auxiliary task as an additional pre-training step improves the multilingual word representation and helps warm-start the model for performing a specific task in target language.

Xu and Murray (2022) use mixed fine-tuning to overcome the deficiencies of the common approach to target domain adaptation. Instead of focusing at one language at a time, mixed fine-tuning allows to use one multilingual model to handle many target languages at once and avoid overly language-specific models. A stochastic gradient surgery technique is used to mitigate the issue of conflicting gradients among different languages. The significant performance increase is specifically important for languages linguistically distant from English. This affirms that abruptly shifting to the target domain by one-stage fine-tuning can hinder the model, while mixed fine-tuning helps it to learn the representations more smoothly.

Knowledge transfer is also important for coreference resolution specifically. Xia and Van Durme (2021) demonstrate the effectiveness of continued training for multilingual coreference resolution, which involves first training a model on a source dataset until convergence, and then using it to train a second model on a target dataset. Yuan et al. (2022) use active learning for situations where no substantial in-domain, labeled data is available; this approach explores different sampling strategies for further labeling and continued training.

Domain adaptation methods such as gradual or mixed fine-tuning can be especially useful when using silver target datasets for training, helping to overcome the inherent noise problem.

2.3 Annotation Projection

Manual annotation for coreference resolution is a particularly challenging task because of the variety of coreference phenomena and the lack of standardized annotation guidelines. Automatic projection approach allows using the annotated data in the source language to transfer the linguistic annotation to unlabeled target data.

As outlined by Nateras (2022), common approaches to annotation projection usually utilize sentence-aligned parallel corpora or neural machine translation systems. Correct word alignment is crucial for the quality of the projected annotations; both automated and manual alignment methods have been proposed. As opposed to training the models exclusively on labeled data in the source language, target data with projected labels, while noisy, allows directly leveraging linguistic features of the target language.

Grishina (2019) provides a comprehensive overview of annotation projection methods applied to coreference resolution specifically. The discussed studies range from experimenting with manual projection of coreference chains (Harabagiu and Maiorano, 2000) to fully relying on translation-based approaches (Ogrodniczuk, 2013). In most of the works, English has been used as a source language; however, projecting from multiple other languages at the same time has been shown to improve the quality of the projected annotations. Grishina (2019) also conducts three annotation projection experiments using statistical word alignment with GIZA++ (Och and Ney, 2003) as well as mention extractors for the source and target languages.

Yarmohammadi et al. (2021) explore data projection and the use of silver data in zero-shot cross-lingual information extraction. The authors conduct experiments on English-Arabic annotation projection. Specifically, they translate the source text to the target language using a machine translation system, obtain word alignments using publicly available automatic tools, and directly project the annotations along the word alignments. The created silver data is then used to augment the training set.

Our approach to annotation projection presented in this work is similar to that of Yarmohammadi et al. (2021), with some important differences. First, we aligned the words based on cross-attention of the machine translation model rather than relying on statistical or embedding-based alignment. Second, when projecting a multi-token span, our approach allows multiple projected spans in the target text, while Yarmohammadi et al. (2021) decided to form a contiguous span containing all aligned tokens from the same source span, potentially including tokens not aligned to the source span in the middle.

3 Ukrainian Coreference Resolution

In this section, we present a survey of existing research for coreference resolution in Ukrainian.

Hlybovets (2018) focuses on building complex information processing systems using a concept of agent-based modeling. A coreference resolution module is presented as part of the bigger system. For detecting mentions, the author uses a rule-based NER system based on a generalized left-to-right (GLR) parser; the system can detect PER, ORG and LOC entities. A manually annotated news corpus is used for NER testing; the system achieves 0.48 F_1 score. To determine if the mentions are coreferent, methods from Soon et al. (2001) and Raghunathan et al. (2010) are adapted: the resulting system uses a multi-pass filtering sieve together with a decision tree classifier. The author does not report accuracy scores for this part of the system.

Pogorilyy and Kramov (2019) attempt to create a coreference resolution system for Ukrainian using a convolutional neural network. Following Clark and Manning (2016), coreference resolution is presented as a clustering task. Every entity in the text is considered a separate cluster at the initialization step. The task of the model is then to go over pairs of clusters and merge the ones that refer to the same entity.

For creating the clusters, the system proposed in Pogorilyy and Kramov (2019) uses a rule-based filtering sieves module and a multichannel CNN module. The rules are mostly based on direct string comparison with regular expressions, although some of them incorporate dictionaries of entity names scraped from Wikipedia. Then, pairs of clusters are given as an input to a convolutional neural network. Clusters are represented by averaging the word2vec embeddings of the corresponding entity words. The CNN module works as a binary classifier; to train it, the authors use the SEARN method adapted from Clark and Manning (2016). A dataset of Ukrainian news articles is used for training, testing, and evaluation. The model achieves 92.11 F_1 score for the B^3 coreference evaluation metric.

In Telenyk et al. (2021) the authors continue the work presented previously, now making some important changes. First, BiLSTM is trained instead of a CNN. Second, they perform feature analysis and conclude that word embeddings used for mention representation contribute a lot to the result, so they turn to ELMo embeddings instead of word2vec used previously. As for the results, the proposed model achieves 92.21 F_1 score for the B^3 coreference evaluation metric. Another important contribution is that both the pre-trained model and the dataset are made available to the public, which allows using them as a baseline for continuing research in this direction (Kramov, 2021).

The model can be used for different tasks; three endpoints are available to extract mentions, estimate coherence of the text and extract coreferent pairs. It also attempts to perform POS tagging and extract other grammatical features described in the previous checkpoint of the evaluated texts.

The Coreferent Clusters dataset presented by Kramov (2021) is, to our knowledge, the only publicly available dataset for coreference resolution in Ukrainian. It is distributed via Mendeley as a MYSQL database. The database contains a single table *word* with the texts and relevant information about the tokens: their parts of speech, case, animacy, gender, number, aspect, and mood. All mentions are labeled, including singletons, which are potentially coreferent but appear only once in a document. Each non-singleton mention belongs to a coreferent cluster. It is unclear whether the dataset was annotated manually or automatically, as the authors provide no specifics about the corpus creation process. Table 1 demonstrates the detailed statistics of Coreferent Clusters as well as the silver Ukrainian OntoNotes dataset presented in Section 5.

Overall, the task of coreference resolution in Ukrainian remains underresearched. High-quality annotated datasets are needed to appropriately evaluate the performance of existing models as well as train new ones using state-of-the-art NLP methods.

4 Data

In this section, we describe the base English datasets used to form the silver Ukrainian datasets. We explore a total of two source datasets: a smaller test dataset that allows for testing coreference resolution systems ability to deal with complicated anaphora ambiguity cases, as well as a large dataset commonly used for training coreference resolution models.

4.1 Winograd Schema Challenge Dataset

A Winograd schema is a pair of sentences that have only a slight difference in words, but contain an anaphora ambiguity that can only be resolved with world knowledge and reasoning. Such sentences can be quite complicated for coreference resolution models to solve, while human readers usually easily deal with them. An example of a Winograd schema are sentences such as:

1. The man couldn't lift his son because he was so weak.
2. The man couldn't lift his son because he was so heavy.

The pronoun "he" corefers with "the man" in the first sentence, and with "son" in the second.

The English Winograd Schema Challenge dataset contains 285 Winograd schema sentences that cover a wide range of linguistic features and world knowledge (Levesque et al., 2012). The size of the collection is understandably limited, as creating a large and diverse set of high-quality Winograd schemas is quite difficult. The goal of the Winograd Schema Challenge dataset is then not to provide a training dataset, but rather test language models that claim to have solved the problem of coreference resolution and pronoun disambiguation.

Translations of the WSC dataset are available in Chinese, Japanese, French, Portuguese, and Hebrew. Authors of French and Portuguese transla-

Dataset	Documents	Sentences	Tokens	Mentions	Clusters
Coreferent Clusters (Kramov, 2021)	2,528	17,122	361,534	24,257	8,538
Ukrainian OntoNotes	3,493	94,269	1,456,717	201,700	44,071

Table 1: The statistics of Ukrainian coreference resolution corpora. The counts for mentions do not include singletons.

tions made a few changes to the schemas in order to avoid unintended cues such as grammatical gender.

In a quite extensive survey of WSC, Kocijan et al. (2022) highlight three main methods commonly used to solve the Winograd Schema Challenge. Feature-based approaches rely on extracting relevant information in the form of sentence or word features and are usually rule-based. Neural approaches take advantage of semantic similarities between word embeddings or use RNNs for encoding the local context. Finally, the third group includes approaches that use large language models pre-trained on huge text corpora.

While the Winograd Schema Challenge has been largely overcome as originally formulated, the problem of commonsense reasoning still stands as one of the major NLP challenges. The low-resource setting makes solving the task even harder: having annotated collections such as the WSC dataset in other languages is vital to exploring different aspects of commonsense reasoning. We decided to manually translate the WSC dataset to Ukrainian, attempting to preserve the ambiguity of the schemas.

4.2 OntoNotes 5.0

OntoNotes 5.0 (Weischedel et al., 2011) is a large dataset containing annotations of syntactic parse trees, named entities, semantic roles, and coreference. The dataset contains texts of multiple genres such as telephone conversations, newswire, broadcast news, broadcast conversation, web text, and religious text. OntoNotes 5.0 is also multilingual, as it contains English, Chinese, and Arabic subsets.

The coreference annotation in OntoNotes connects coreferring instances of specific referring expressions, primarily noun phrases that introduce or access a discourse entity. Notably, the annotation does not include singletons–clusters containing only one entity. OntoNotes 5.0 is the primary dataset for experiments on coreference resolution, as it is used as a standard in CoNLL-2012 shared task (Pradhan et al., 2012).

We use OntoNotes 5.0 as a basis for automatically translating, aligning, and projecting annotations to create a silver Ukrainian version of it.

5 Silver Data Creation

In this section, we describe the methods and the process of creating silver Ukrainian coreference resolution datasets on the basis of high-quality English data.

5.1 Manual Translation

For the Ukrainian version of the Winograd Schema Challenge dataset, we manually translated the English schemas. In the process of translation, English proper names were replaced with Ukrainian ones. The resulting corpus contains 263 Winograd schema sentences. 22 sentences were excluded from the dataset, as no equivalent translation was found that would preserve the ambiguity. This is mostly due to specific ambiguous phrases used in English that would not retain their features when translated into Ukrainian. The resulting dataset can be used as a complex challenge for a coreference resolution system.

5.2 Machine Translation

While the WSC dataset translation in Ukrainian is tailored for complex cases of coreference resolution, it contains few sentences and can't be reliably used for training. Hence, we decided to build on OntoNotes 5.0 to compile a sufficient amount of data for further model training and evaluation. In particular, our approach is to take an annotated English dataset, translate it with a machine translation model, align the corresponding mentions in original and translated parallel texts, and project the annotations using the obtained alignment.

As the translation and alignment needs to be done automatically, we relied on using a high-quality machine translation model to bear this task. Specifically, we chose one of OpusMT models, as they are easily accessible through the *huggingface* library, work with Ukrainian and English, and are generally of high quality (Tiedemann and Thottingal, 2020). The *Helsinki-NLP/opus-mt-en-*

uk model was used to translate from English to Ukrainian; this model achieves 50.2 BLEU score on Tatoeba.en.uk test set.

5.3 Alignment

After translating the sentences with the chosen model, different methods can be used to align the words in source and target sentences. This allows matching the spans corresponding to entity mentions in source and target sentences in order to project the annotations later.

Attention-based Alignment The attention-based approach used in Transformer models can help interpret how the model functions (Bahdanau et al., 2015; Belinkov and Glass, 2019). Attention shows how the model assigns weight to different input elements; in case of sequence-to-sequence machine translation models, it is possible to use this advantage to see which source tokens the model attends to when producing a target translation. The interpretability of attention weights has been the subject of various experiments, and while the saliency methods have been proven to work better, cross-attention can still provide important information about the functionality of the models (Vashishth et al., 2019; Jain and Wallace, 2019; Wiegreffe and Pinter, 2019; Bastings and Filippova, 2020).

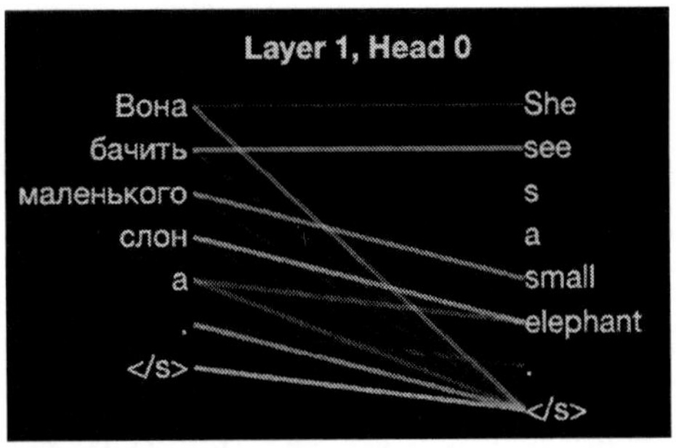

Figure 1: Cross-attention weight graph for one of the heads of the model.

For this approach, we used a visualization tool to determine if cross-attention of the machine translation model is enough for aligning the words. Using the *bertviz* package, we created attention weight graphs of all the layers and heads of the chosen model (Vig, 2019). The resulting visualization showed that for many layers, most of the attention is concentrated on the end token rather than other source words. Therefore, we decided to use only the cross-attention from the 0-th head of the 1-st layer, as it correlated the most with the intuitive judgment of how the words should be aligned.

Embedding-based Alignment Another method to align source and target sentences after machine translation relies on large pre-trained multilingual models that find a shared cross-lingual space for all the languages in the system.

The AWESOME aligner presented in Dou and Neubig (2021) is an example of this approach. Such method allows extracting the embeddings from multilingual models such as mBERT and using it to predict the alignment. Contrary to the attention-based alignment, aligning with AWESOME does not ensure every target word gets aligned with a corresponding source word.

Alignment based on Data Modification One more approach that can be utilized for this task is based in modifying the existing data to mark the specific entities in the source text. The marks then need to be preserved after translation, so that the entities can be recognised in the target text, For example, one could enclose the specific mentions in the source sentence in brackets or XML tags, then translate them, and look for marked words in translation, as the machine learning model often correctly reproduces the marks used. This makes it possible to locate the translated mention in the target text and align it with the corresponding one in the source.

This can be done using an iterative method. However, the machine translation model output can change quite drastically depending on which part of the input is marked. This also means that at each iteration, the translated sentence could be different, so it is unclear which of them to use as a "golden" translation.

For the final dataset, we decided to use the attention-based approach. We extracted the cross-attention weights for a specific translated sentence from the model, produced correct tokens from subtokens returned by the model, and aligned the relevant mentions. If most of the attention from the target token was concentrated on the *</s>* tag, we used the second highest-weighted source token for the alignment.

5.4 Projection

Projection is the next stage after aligning the source and target texts. This part depends significantly on the format the base corpus is presented in. OntoNotes 5.0 follows the standard format of CoNLL-2012 shared task, in which the coreference clusters contain the entities for each text. For projecting, only some information is necessary: namely, *cased_words*, which contains the tokenized document, *sent_id*, which contains ids of sentences the tokens appear in, and *clusters*, which contains the clusters of coreferring entities.

The attention-based alignment approach we have chosen relies on automatically translating texts from English into Ukrainian with a machine translation model. However, the model can only translate sentences rather than full texts. This makes the alignment and projection process non-trivial, as the whole text cannot be translated at once. Instead, every single sentence needs to undergo the process separately.

The general algorithm follows these stages:

1. Split the document into sentences.
2. For each span mentioned in a coreference cluster, find the specific sentence it appears in.
3. Modify the span indices so that they correspond to the sentence rather than the whole document.
4. Modify the new span representation so that it includes all the tokens in the span rather than only start and end word.

After that, the source sentences can be translated via a machine translation model. Since we now know the mentions present in each source sentence, the overall task amounts to aligning the sentences, extracting the specific target tokens aligned with source mentions tokens, producing the mapping between source and target mentions, and reconstructing the coreference clusters based on this mapping.

The main complications lie in the fact spans are often not equivalent in two languages. Alignment is done on the token level, and it is quite possible that words that form a continuous span in the source sentence will not form one in the target sentence. A few different alignment situations can happen: one source word may correspond to multiple target words, multiple source words may correspond to one target word, or source/target words may not align with a separate word at all.

Keeping the possible issues in mind, we wrote the alignment and projection scripts, which can then be used to form a mapping from source to target mentions. According to this mapping, we compile target coreference clusters for the silver Ukrainian version of OntoNotes 5.0. While somewhat noisy, the attention-based alignment usually correctly matches the entities and allows to properly project the annotations and form coreference clusters.

Detailed statistics of the created Ukrainian OntoNotes corpus are shown in Table 1. The OntoNotes dataset is significantly larger than Coreferent Clusters (Kramov, 2021), as the documents in OntoNotes generally contain longer sentences with more mentions.

6 Error analysis

In this section, we provide an analysis of the formed silver Ukrainian datasets.

6.1 Ukrainian WSC Dataset

Manually translating the schemas into Ukrainian does not only allow using the dataset as a complex challenge for a coreference resolution system, but also clearly illustrates the coreference differences in Ukrainian and English.

For some sentences, no equivalent existed that would preserve the ambiguity while keeping the content intact. Particular words or phrases that appear ambiguous in English may not retain those properties when translated into Ukrainian. To use such schemas properly, new pairs of sentences should be written with differing content. When translating, we attempted to keep the original content of the sentence unchanged when possible.

Manual translations can also be subpar sometimes. This approach to creating a dataset requires finding the middle ground between preserving as much original source content as possible and maintaining the overall schema form. While some of the Winograd Challenge Schema dataset pairs are grammatically correct in Ukrainian, native speakers may regard such sentences as less fluent than possible. The reason for that is the ambiguity itself: in fluent Ukrainian sentences, different devices would be used by speakers to remove the ambiguity and make the coreference resolution task easier.

For example, for the Winograd schema presented before, it would be more fluent to say "The man couldn't lift his son because $\emptyset$ was so weak" in Ukrainian. This requires omitting the subject in the subordinate clause– a grammatically correct way of expressing the same content that will clearly resolve the ambiguity. The subject of "was" would be understood to correspond to the subject of the main clause.

The use of pronouns could be another example of the differences between two languages. It is grammatically correct and fluent to use demonstrative pronouns in Ukrainian where English can only use personal ones. Using the same example, "The man couldn't lift his son because *that was so heavy." can be used in Ukrainian, and "that" in this case will clearly point to the "son". Hence, in order to preserve both the ambiguity of the schema and its fluency in the target language, the content of the sentence must often be altered.

Similarly, other issues arise when resorting to literal translations of the schemas. Ukrainian nouns and pronouns all have grammatical gender, and personal pronouns are as such used for both proper and common nouns; in the sentences where English can use "it" for something denoting an object, eliminating the option for a coreference link from a pronoun like "he", Ukrainian may use "he" in place of both words, resulting in more ambiguities. Overall, literally translating the schemas does not work in many cases; other schemas should be presented to deal with this issue.

In sum, the error analysis shows that main complications in manual translation of complex datasets such as WSC arise when trying to relay the content perfectly in a different language. The distinct features of the source and target language may not allow for a trivial conversion; in this case, new original examples must be created for the resulting dataset.

6.2 Ukrainian OntoNotes Dataset

In the Ukrainian OntoNotes Dataset, the most prevalent errors are connected with the reliance on the machine translation model.

The quality of the English-Ukrainian translations produced by the OpusMT model used are sometimes below average. In some cases, the model produces the target text in a different language, which supposedly comes from incorrectly labeled data it was trained on. In addition, the task is made more complicated because of the nature of the English OntoNotes 5.0 dataset: its genre diversity presents a lot of problems for the machine translation model. As the model has not been trained on the text of some specific genres such as telephone conversations, the translation for such documents is of poor quality. For future work in this direction, we suggest choosing a different machine translation model to get translations that would be less noisy.

The alignment approach we chose also relies on the machine translation model, so naturally, its quality may be lower than expected for the same reasons. The alignment fully depends on the cross-attention layer of the encoder-decoder model. This may lead to mistakenly aligning unrelated words and then including them in the coreference clusters. Pruning the resulting clusters to get rid of such noise seems to be a promising future direction. In addition, other alignment methods such as statistical alignment or embedding-based alignment should be explored.

7 Conclusion

Creating new datasets is crucial in order to extend NLP research to the low-resource setting. Labeled data for languages such as English can be effectively utilized for this task. We present an approach to efficiently create silver data corpora for low-resource languages based on existing annotated data for high-resource languages such a English with machine translation, alignment, and annotation projection. We demonstrate how the suggested methods can be used to create two corpora for training and testing coreference resolution models for Ukrainian. The scripts for automatic translation, alignment, and projection, as well as the Ukrainian WSC dataset are made publicly available[2].

Future work will involve training and evaluating a baseline model using the created silver Ukrainian datasets. The suggested approaches may be improved by using different machine translation models or trying out better alignment methods.

Limitations

Our approach to creating silver data for Ukrainian on the basis of English annotated corpora is based on manual and machine translation. As the quality of the resulting translations is of utmost importance, the method has a few important limitations.

For manual translation of small sophisticated test datasets, the approach requires enrolling professional annotators with relevant experience. For an intricate corpus such as the WSC dataset, the annotation process may involve creating new content and altering the source documents significantly to

[2] `https://github.com/pkuchmiichuk/ua-coref`

preserve the specific features of the text required for the task.

For automatic translation, alignment, and annotation projection, a machine translation model from high-resource source language into the low-resource target language should be present. Such models may not exist whatsoever for many low-resource languages or exhibit poor quality, which limits the potential use of our approach.

References

Dzmitry Bahdanau, Kyunghyun Cho, and Yoshua Bengio. 2015. Neural machine translation by jointly learning to align and translate. In *3rd International Conference on Learning Representations, ICLR 2015, San Diego, CA, USA, May 7-9, 2015, Conference Track Proceedings*.

Jasmijn Bastings and Katja Filippova. 2020. The elephant in the interpretability room: Why use attention as explanation when we have saliency methods? In *Proceedings of the Third BlackboxNLP Workshop on Analyzing and Interpreting Neural Networks for NLP*, pages 149–155, Online. Association for Computational Linguistics.

Yonatan Belinkov and James Glass. 2019. Analysis methods in neural language processing: A survey. *Transactions of the Association for Computational Linguistics*, 7:49–72.

Kevin Clark and Christopher D. Manning. 2016. Improving coreference resolution by learning entity-level distributed representations. In *Proceedings of the 54th Annual Meeting of the Association for Computational Linguistics (Volume 1: Long Papers)*, pages 643–653, Berlin, Germany. Association for Computational Linguistics.

André Ferreira Cruz, Gil Rocha, and Henrique Lopes Cardoso. 2018. Exploring spanish corpora for portuguese coreference resolution. In *2018 Fifth International Conference on Social Networks Analysis, Management and Security (SNAMS)*, pages 290–295.

Vladimir Dobrovolskii. 2021. Word-level coreference resolution. In *Proceedings of the 2021 Conference on Empirical Methods in Natural Language Processing*, pages 7670–7675, Online and Punta Cana, Dominican Republic. Association for Computational Linguistics.

Zi-Yi Dou and Graham Neubig. 2021. Word alignment by fine-tuning embeddings on parallel corpora. In *Proceedings of the 16th Conference of the European Chapter of the Association for Computational Linguistics: Main Volume*, pages 2112–2128, Online. Association for Computational Linguistics.

Steven Fincke, Shantanu Agarwal, Scott Miller, and Elizabeth Boschee. 2022. Language model priming for cross-lingual event extraction. *Proceedings of the AAAI Conference on Artificial Intelligence*, 36(10):10627–10635.

Yulia Grishina. 2019. *Assessing the applicability of annotation projection methods for coreference relations*. Doctoral thesis, Universität Potsdam.

Sanda M. Harabagiu and Steven J. Maiorano. 2000. Multilingual coreference resolution. In *Sixth Applied Natural Language Processing Conference*, pages 142–149, Seattle, Washington, USA. Association for Computational Linguistics.

Andrii Hlybovets. 2018. Agent-based software systems for the search and analysis of information. *Doctor of Technical Sciences, Taras Shevchenko National University of Kyiv*.

Sarthak Jain and Byron C. Wallace. 2019. Attention is not Explanation. In *Proceedings of the 2019 Conference of the North American Chapter of the Association for Computational Linguistics: Human Language Technologies, Volume 1 (Long and Short Papers)*, pages 3543–3556, Minneapolis, Minnesota. Association for Computational Linguistics.

Pratik Joshi, Sebastin Santy, Amar Budhiraja, Kalika Bali, and Monojit Choudhury. 2020. The state and fate of linguistic diversity and inclusion in the NLP world. In *Proceedings of the 58th Annual Meeting of the Association for Computational Linguistics*, pages 6282–6293, Online. Association for Computational Linguistics.

Vid Kocijan, Ernest Davis, Thomas Lukasiewicz, Gary Marcus, and Leora Morgenstern. 2022. The defeat of the winograd schema challenge.

Artem Kramov. 2021. Coreferent clusters (dataset and a pre-trained model).

Kenton Lee, Luheng He, Mike Lewis, and Luke Zettlemoyer. 2017. End-to-end neural coreference resolution. In *Proceedings of the 2017 Conference on Empirical Methods in Natural Language Processing*, pages 188–197, Copenhagen, Denmark. Association for Computational Linguistics.

Hector J. Levesque, Ernest Davis, and Leora Morgenstern. 2012. The Winograd Schema Challenge. In *13th International Conference on the Principles of Knowledge Representation and Reasoning, KR 2012*, Proceedings of the International Conference on Knowledge Representation and Reasoning, pages 552–561. Institute of Electrical and Electronics Engineers Inc.

Kaushal Kumar Maurya, Maunendra Sankar Desarkar, Yoshinobu Kano, and Kumari Deepshikha. 2021. ZmBART: An unsupervised cross-lingual transfer framework for language generation. In *Findings of the Association for Computational Linguistics: ACL-IJCNLP 2021*, pages 2804–2818, Online. Association for Computational Linguistics.

Luis Fernando Guzman Nateras. 2022. Modern cross-lingual information extraction. Area exam, University of Oregon, Computer and Information Sciences Department.

Franz Josef Och and Hermann Ney. 2003. A systematic comparison of various statistical alignment models. *Computational Linguistics*, 29(1):19–51.

Maciej Ogrodniczuk. 2013. Translation- and projection-based unsupervised coreference resolution for polish. In *Language Processing and Intelligent Information Systems*, pages 125–130, Berlin, Heidelberg. Springer Berlin Heidelberg.

Telmo Pires, Eva Schlinger, and Dan Garrette. 2019. How multilingual is multilingual BERT? In *Proceedings of the 57th Annual Meeting of the Association for Computational Linguistics*, pages 4996–5001, Florence, Italy. Association for Computational Linguistics.

Massimo Poesio and Ron Artstein. 2008. Anaphoric annotation in the ARRAU corpus. In *Proceedings of the Sixth International Conference on Language Resources and Evaluation (LREC'08)*, Marrakech, Morocco. European Language Resources Association (ELRA).

Sergiy Pogorilyy and Artem Kramov. 2019. Coreferent pairs detection in Ukrainian texts using a convolutional neural network. *Visnyk Universytetu "Ukraina"*.

Sameer Pradhan, Alessandro Moschitti, Nianwen Xue, Olga Uryupina, and Yuchen Zhang. 2012. CoNLL-2012 shared task: Modeling multilingual unrestricted coreference in OntoNotes. In *Joint Conference on EMNLP and CoNLL - Shared Task*, pages 1–40, Jeju Island, Korea. Association for Computational Linguistics.

Karthik Raghunathan, Heeyoung Lee, Sudarshan Rangarajan, Nathanael Chambers, Mihai Surdeanu, Dan Jurafsky, and Christopher Manning. 2010. A multi-pass sieve for coreference resolution. In *Proceedings of the 2010 Conference on Empirical Methods in Natural Language Processing*, pages 492–501, Cambridge, MA. Association for Computational Linguistics.

Sebastian Ruder. 2020. Why You Should Do NLP Beyond English. `http://ruder.io/nlp-beyond-english`.

Wee Meng Soon, Hwee Tou Ng, and Daniel Chung Yong Lim. 2001. A machine learning approach to coreference resolution of noun phrases. *Computational Linguistics*, 27(4):521–544.

Sergii Telenyk, Sergiy Pogorilyy, and Artem Kramov. 2021. The complex method of coreferent pairs detection in a Ukrainian-language text based on a BiLSTM neural network. In *2021 IEEE 3rd International Conference on Advanced Trends in Information Theory (ATIT)*, pages 205–210.

Jörg Tiedemann and Santhosh Thottingal. 2020. OPUS-MT – building open translation services for the world. In *Proceedings of the 22nd Annual Conference of the European Association for Machine Translation*, pages 479–480, Lisboa, Portugal. European Association for Machine Translation.

Gorka Urbizu, Ander Soraluze, and Olatz Arregi. 2019. Deep cross-lingual coreference resolution for less-resourced languages: The case of Basque. In *Proceedings of the Second Workshop on Computational Models of Reference, Anaphora and Coreference*, pages 35–41, Minneapolis, USA. Association for Computational Linguistics.

Shikhar Vashishth, Shyam Upadhyay, Gaurav Singh Tomar, and Manaal Faruqui. 2019. Attention interpretability across nlp tasks.

Jesse Vig. 2019. A multiscale visualization of attention in the transformer model. In *Proceedings of the 57th Annual Meeting of the Association for Computational Linguistics: System Demonstrations*, pages 37–42, Florence, Italy. Association for Computational Linguistics.

Ralph Weischedel, Eduard Hovy, Mitchell Marcus, Martha Palmer, Robert Belvin, Sameer Pradhan, Lance Ramshaw, and Nianwen Xue. 2011. *OntoNotes: A Large Training Corpus for Enhanced Processing*.

Sarah Wiegreffe and Yuval Pinter. 2019. Attention is not not explanation. In *Proceedings of the 2019 Conference on Empirical Methods in Natural Language Processing and the 9th International Joint Conference on Natural Language Processing (EMNLP-IJCNLP)*, pages 11–20, Hong Kong, China. Association for Computational Linguistics.

Shijie Wu and Mark Dredze. 2019. Beto, bentz, becas: The surprising cross-lingual effectiveness of BERT. In *Proceedings of the 2019 Conference on Empirical Methods in Natural Language Processing and the 9th International Joint Conference on Natural Language Processing (EMNLP-IJCNLP)*, pages 833–844, Hong Kong, China. Association for Computational Linguistics.

Patrick Xia and Benjamin Van Durme. 2021. Moving on from OntoNotes: Coreference resolution model transfer. In *Proceedings of the 2021 Conference on Empirical Methods in Natural Language Processing*, pages 5241–5256, Online and Punta Cana, Dominican Republic. Association for Computational Linguistics.

Haoran Xu, Seth Ebner, Mahsa Yarmohammadi, Aaron Steven White, Benjamin Van Durme, and Kenton Murray. 2021. Gradual fine-tuning for low-resource domain adaptation. In *Proceedings of the Second Workshop on Domain Adaptation for NLP*, pages 214–221, Kyiv, Ukraine. Association for Computational Linguistics.

Haoran Xu and Kenton Murray. 2022. Por qué não utiliser alla språk? mixed training with gradient optimization in few-shot cross-lingual transfer. In *Findings of the Association for Computational Linguistics: NAACL 2022*, pages 2043–2059, Seattle, United States. Association for Computational Linguistics.

Mahsa Yarmohammadi, Shijie Wu, Marc Marone, Haoran Xu, Seth Ebner, Guanghui Qin, Yunmo Chen, Jialiang Guo, Craig Harman, Kenton Murray, Aaron Steven White, Mark Dredze, and Benjamin Van Durme. 2021. Everything is all it takes: A multipronged strategy for zero-shot cross-lingual information extraction. In *Proceedings of the 2021 Conference on Empirical Methods in Natural Language Processing*, pages 1950–1967, Online and Punta Cana, Dominican Republic. Association for Computational Linguistics.

Michelle Yuan, Patrick Xia, Chandler May, Benjamin Van Durme, and Jordan Boyd-Graber. 2022. Adapting coreference resolution models through active learning. In *Proceedings of the 60th Annual Meeting of the Association for Computational Linguistics (Volume 1: Long Papers)*, pages 7533–7549, Dublin, Ireland. Association for Computational Linguistics.

Exploring Word Sense Distribution in Ukrainian with a Semantic Vector Space Model

Nataliia Cheilytko and **Ruprecht von Waldenfels**
Friedrich Schiller University Jena
natalia.cheilytko@gmail.com, ruprecht.waldenfels@uni-jena.de

Abstract

The paper discusses a Semantic Vector Space Model targeted at revealing how Ukrainian word senses vary and relate to each other. One of the benefits of the proposed semantic model is that it considers second-order collocates of the words and, thus, has more potential to distinguish word senses observed in a unique concordance line, compared to the models that take into account only immediate collocates. Combined with the Multidimensional Scaling technique, this model allows for a lexicographer to explore the Ukrainian word senses distribution on a large scale. The paper describes the first research results and the following steps of the initiative.

1 Introduction

Word Vector Space Model (VSM) is a distributional semantic technique initially developed in statistical natural language processing and is a principal tool in Computational Linguistics (Turney and Pantel, 2010). Such models treat text as multidimensional vector space, where a word, a combination of words, or a sentence are represented as a vector so that it is possible to apply various vector algebra operations: calculate distance between them, apply dimensionality reduction to the vector space, and cluster.

Among VSMs, a group of models targets semantic items with more precise attention. According to Hilpert and Saavedra (2020), a semantic vector is a statistically processed frequency list of all collocates of a particular word in a given corpus, which expresses the idea that one can distinguish the meaning of a word by its context. For example, compare: *"I have a great fan of rock among my friends"* (fan as a person) to *"I have a great fan with several heating options"* (fan as a device).

The representatives of the Leuven variationist school have been advocates for Semantic Vector Space Models as statistical state-of-art for lexicographers to identify semantic patterns in big unstructured corpora, helping linguists to avoid unfeasible manual data exploration (Heylen et al., 2015).

2 Approach

There are many techniques to build and examine a Semantic VSM. The proposed approach is based on a specific kind of Semantic Vector Space Model that, in addition to considering immediate collocates of words, also accounts for the second-order collocates – typical collocates of words found in concordance lines built for a given word of interest. In such a way, a word is represented not only by friends but also by friends of a friend if to follow a social network metaphor.

Heylen et al. (2012) and Montes and Geeraerts (2022) used the second-order collocate vectors to examine semantic variations of the pluricentric Dutch. Hilpert and Saavedra (2020) applied this technique to English to investigate boundaries among various senses of a polysemic word and between different lexemes. The authors showed that Semantic VSM and visual analytics could provide a solid support for lexicological analysis of polysemy in large corpora. In our research, we reproduce and expand this methodology to explore Ukrainian word sense distribution to identify how words belonging to a particular synonymous set are related and contrasted.

The experiment performed contains the following steps:

1) build Semantic Vector Space Model for the given Ukrainian corpora, including a vocabulary of the most frequent words and their co-occurrence matrix;
2) from the corpora, extract concordance lines, and calculate second-order collocate vectors for them;
3) apply dimensionality reduction with the multidimensional scaling technique, as Wheeler (2005) proposed, to the vectors and visualize them on a scatterplot for particular words from the validation

Proceedings of the Second Ukrainian Natural Language Processing Workshop (UNLP), pages 73–78
May 5, 2023 ©2023 Association for Computational Linguistics

set;
4) perform the pairwise calculation of cosine similarity to the vectors in question.

3 Data

Given that we are interested in identifying regional variation of Ukrainian over time, we performed our initial set of experiments on the corpus with texts published in the Kyiv region within 1940–1969. The texts in the corpus are fiction and periodic publications. The corpus size is relatively small for the word-sense exploration tasks (30 mln tokens total) but sufficient for the proof-of-concept. The source of the textual data investigated is the General Annotated Corpus of the Ukrainian[1] (Shvedova, 2020).

4 Implementation

For the experiment, a set of Python data science and natural language processing libraries have been used (scikit-learn, pandas, numpy, matplotlib, beautiful soap, NLTK).
The morphological tagger and lemmatizer of the Ukrainian[2] preprocessed the input texts. Specific high-frequency words were removed from the texts. Then a vocabulary model was created based on the word frequency across the corpus. The chosen size of the vocabulary for the experiment is 3,000 words so that the most frequent 3,000 lemmas (with the exclusion of highly-frequent grammatical words) comprised the vocabulary.
As the next step, for each pair of words from the vocabulary, we calculated the amount of time they co-occur in the same 4-token-window context in each corpus. As a result, we obtained a sparse co-occurrence matrix of collocates for the vocabulary elements and then normalized it with the PMI (Pointwise Mutual Information) index. To make the co-occurrence matrix less sparse, we kept only those columns and rows that contain at least one value with a PMI > 1.0.
In the next step, we extracted concordance lines for particular words of interest (with 5+5 and 10+10 words windows), shortened the lines to include only the words from the vocabulary, and calculated second-order collocate vectors for the lines. We consider only concordance lines with five or more vocabulary words for further processing.
The second-order collocate vector calculation is the following: for each word in a shortened concordance line, get its vector representation in the co-occurrence matrix initially built (*i. e.* a corresponding column in the co-occurrence matrix). Then average those word vectors for a particular concordance line. Therefore, each word of interest obtained concordance lines with the corresponding second-order collocate vectors[3].
For the sake of assessing the quality of the model, the multidimensional scaling technique and calculation of cosine distance were applied to the averaged second-order collocate vectors.

5 Model Assessment

Despite a relatively small input corpus, the proposed model turned out sensitive enough to distinguish different words and word senses and see commonalities among them.
The PMI co-occurrence matrix with first-order collocates already gives some understanding of word senses. Let us consider the top 10 collocates for *dvygun* ('an engine'; 'a driving force') with their PMI values (*dvygun* ('an engine') 4.53, *potužnyj* ('powerful') 3.64, *atomnyj* ('nuclear') 3.45, *polit* ('a process of flying') 3.38, *vičnyj* ('eternal') 3.27, *švydkist'* ('speed') 3.15, *raketa* ('a rocket') 3.10, *zamovknuty* ('to become silent') 3.05, *korabel'* ('a ship') 2.97.
And for its synonym *motor* ('a motor', 'an engine'): *gurkit* ('roar') 3.88, *motor* ('a motor') 3.33, *gudity* ('to buzz') 3.16, *kabina* ('a cabin') 3.16, *zavesty* ('to start an engine') 2.996, *litak* ('an airplane') 2.991, *potužnyj* ('powerful') 2.78, *traktor* ('a tractor') 2.77, *avtomašyna* ('a car') 2.73, *avtomobil'* ('an automobile') 2.64.
From these collocates, we can already see the difference between the two synonyms. In the Kyiv corpus 1940-1969, *motor* often denotes common-life vehicles (autos, boats, tractors). In contrast, *dvygun* is associated with "serious" topics like space travel, nuclear power, and metaphorically a driving force and a cause of activities and events.
Trying to distinguish word senses only by immediate collocates may not capture sense similarity if words in the context do not overlap. That is why the second-order collocate approach gives better sensitivity to similar word senses even if direct collocates in the concordance lines differ. To evaluate

[1] `http://uacorpus.org/Kyiv/en`
[2] `https://github.com/brown-uk/nlp_uk`
[3] The source code for building the model and data samples are stored at `https://github.com/NataliaChey/unlp_2nd_order_vectors`

the model's ability to capture word sense commonalities and differences, we have compared the cosine semantic similarity measure calculated for the second-order collocate vectors and an alternative VSM – the 200k Ukrainian floret vectors available via the spaCy framework[4]. For example, for *dvygun* in the two concordance lines:

1) *"Nočamy v tumani gorily svitliačky, i vytt'a zviriv inodi zaglušalo šum dvyguna v tabori."* (*"At night, fireflies burned in the fog, and the howling of the animals sometimes drowned out the noise of the engine in the camp."*)

2) *„Kolia prysluhavsia. Ni, dvyguny dyryzablia gudut' tak samo monotonno j nevpynno."* (*"Kolia listened. No, the airship's engines were buzzing just as monotonously and incessantly."*)

the semantic similarity measure by the second-order collocates is 0.9976, and by the Ukrainian floret vectors – 0.7508.

In this example, the different context words in both lines express the same idea that an engine creates noise, represented with different context words, which the model was able to capture with the help of information about the second-order vectors.

Currently, the vocabulary of the model accounts for 3,000 lemmas. For the first concordance line, the following vocabulary words contributed to the calculation: *zvir* ('an animal'), *inodi* ('sometimes'), *šum* ('noise'), *tabir* ('a camp'), *soldat* ('a soldier'). And for the second line, those collocates are *Kolia* (a person name), *prysluhatysia* ('to listen up'), *gudity* ('to buzz').

Let us consider another example with the pair of synonyms *dvygun* and motor in the following contexts:

1) *"Zarevly dvyguny, dribnyi drižˇ projšov po mašyni."* (*"The engines roared to life, and a small shudder went through the car."*)

2) *"Do jogo čujnogo vucha doletilo poforkuvann'a motora, srkyp galm. Prybuv komendant taboru – Bil'ava Bestija."* (*"A light engine whirring and brakes screeching reached his sensitive ears. The camp commandant, the Blonde Beast, had arrived."*)

The semantic similarity measure by the second-order collocates is 0.9799, and by the Ukrainian floret vectors – 0.6416.

The vocabulary elements for the former concordance line are *smuga* ('a lane'), *myt'* ('a momemnt'), *zupynytys'a* ('to stop'), *dribnyj* ('small'), *projty* ('to pass through'), *mašyna* ('a machine'). And for the latter: *vuho* ('an ear'), *legkyi* ('light'), *prybuty* ('to arrive'), *komendant* ('commander'), *tabir* ('camp').

The first results are promising. However, the initial version of the model has limitations due to a relatively small vocabulary size. It works well with the concordance lines with at least five collocates from the vocabulary. Therefore, we will significantly increase the model's vocabulary to 20–50k lemmas on the project's next iteration to make it comprehend a wider range of words in more versatile contexts.

It is also important to mention that we calculated the semantic similarity for vectors with already reduced dimensionality and only for the target words instead of the entire vocabulary. Thus, the provided comparison to the alternative language model is made solely to show that the model can find commonalities in non-overlapping concordance lines.

In addition to the cosine similarity metric, the multidimensional scaling technique made it possible to explore the model outputs visually. Figures 1–5 demonstrate the scatterplots for several synonymous word pairs. Multidimensional scaling was applied separately to the second-order collocate vectors of a particular group of words or a single word per each test case.

The dots on the plot are the reduced vectors. For a word or a pair of words, one can investigate close and remote dots to validate whether they denote similar or distinct occurrences. Such vector-space-based visual representations of word concordances bring additional insights for lexicographers targeted at exploring polysemy, various semantic relations, and semantic variation in language.

Figure 1 contains 97 vectors built from the 5+5

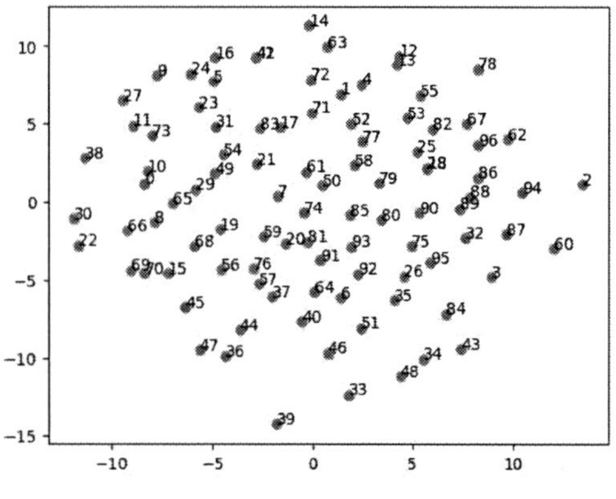

Figure 1: The Second-order Collocate Vectors: *dvygun*

[4] https://spacy.io/models/uk#uk_core_news_lg

concordance lines for *dvygun*. This word has two senses: 'engine as a mechanical device', and an abstract metaphoric sense, 'something that pushes, causes things to happen'. In the corpus, the first sense dominates. However, several vectors on the plot represent the second sense. Let us consider vector d on the right of the plot with the following collocates: *vplyv* ('influence'), *rozym* ('intelligence'), *istoria* ('history'), *rid* ('lineage'), *svitogl'ad* ('a world view').

If to compare vector 2 to vector 10 having the vocabulary collocates: *dokaz* ('a proof'), *Kolia* (a person name), *prysluhatysia* ('to listen up'), *gudity* ('to buzz'), the cosine similarity for these vectors is negative -0.7647, which indicates different senses.

Figure 2 shows 183 vectors built from the 5+5 con-

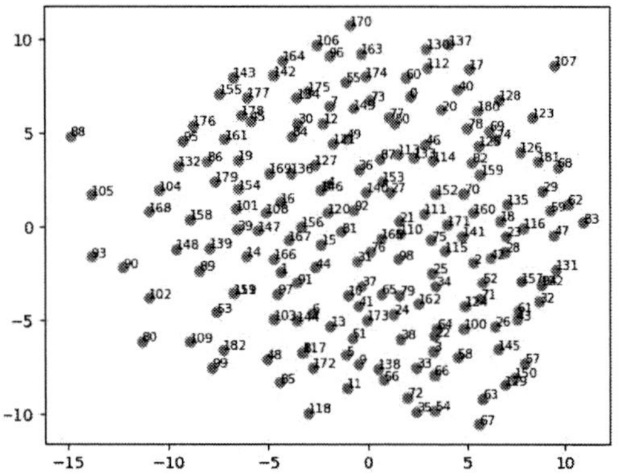

Figure 2: The Second-order Collocate Vectors: *motor*

cordance lines for *motor* ('engine'). The following two vectors demonstrate again that the model is able to capture sense similarity despite non-overlapping collocates. Consider vector 69 with the vocabulary collocates: *prosto* ('easily'), *znyknuty* ('to dissapear'), *prolunaty* ('to resound'), *signal* ('a signal'), *zakryčaty* ('to scream') and vector 74 with the vocabulary collocates: *mašyna* ('a machine'), *movčaty* ('to be silent'), *rušyty* ('to move'), *pravoruč* ('to the right'). For these two vectors, the semantic similarity by the second-order collocates is 0.99, and by the Ukrainian floret vectors is 1.0.

The model has captured the concordance lines with another sense of motor, usually occurring as an exclamation during a movie production: *"Motor!"* as *"Action!"*. The vectors 86, 176–179 are located quite close to each other on the plot. The corresponding concordance lines contain a word denoting exclamation and attention (*kruknuty, kryčaty* ('to cry out'), *vyguknyty* ('to exclaim') and *uvaga* ('attention')), as well as nouns denoting movie production – *režyser* ('director') and the likes.

Vector 107 (with the vocabulary collocates *vidro* ('a bucket'), *krutyty* ('to spin'), *kriz'* ('through'), *dirka* ('a hole')) stays apart on the left for a reason. The context is atypical – a humorous story from a humoristic magazine *Perets, 1961* on how to construct an engine from a bucket: *"Vkladajete v take vidro vyprany bilyznu, motor krutyt' vidro, voda kriz' dirky vylitaje, bilyzna sohne na očah!.."* (*"Put the laundry in the bucket, the motor spins the bucket, the water flies out through the holes, and the laundry dries before your eyes!"*)

Figure 3 shows that *motor* and *dvygun* have over-

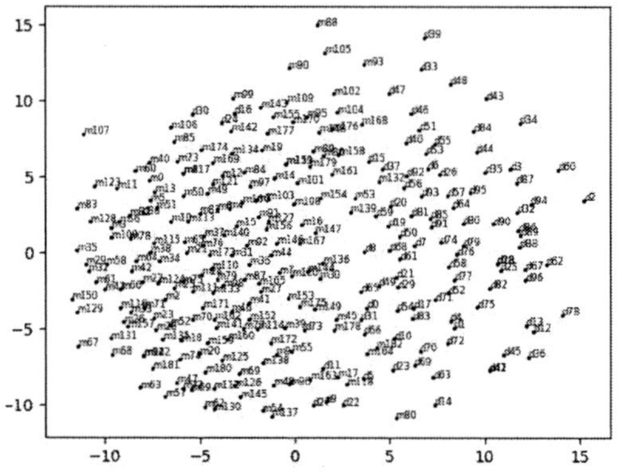

Figure 3: The Second-order Collocate Vectors: *motor* (m) and *dvygun* (d)

lapping areas but also quite distinct ones, which proves the above observation that these two synonyms have separate areas of usage: *motor* for common everyday-life vehicles and devices, whereas *dvygun* is for large industrial machinery.

Figure 4 shows how the items of another synset

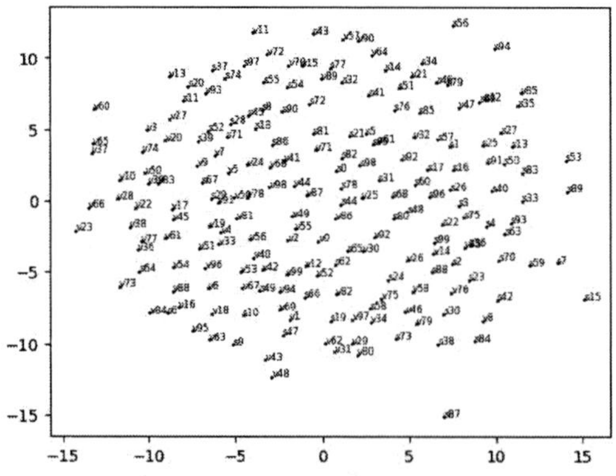

Figure 4: The Second-order Collocate Vectors: *volia* (v) and *svoboda* (s)

volia ('freedom', 'a will') and *svoboda* ('freedom')

are distributed. This time, we calculated the second-order collocate vectors for 10+10 concordance lines.

The top PMI collocates for *svoboda* are *svoboda* ('freedom') 3.58, *borec'* ('a fighter') 3.43, *demokratia* ('democracy') 3.28, *carstvo* ('a kingdom') 2.52, *myr* ('peace') 2.46, *demokratyčnyi* ('democratic') 2.45, *poniatt'a* ('a concept') 2.4, *ideal* ('an ideal') 2.37, *borot'ba* ('a fight') 2.34.

And for *volia*, the top collocates are *pamjataty* ('to remember') 4.16, *odynyca* 2.42 ('a unit'), *volia* ('freedom') 2.37, *nevolia* ('captivity') 2.31, *nacia* ('a nation') 2.26, *zusyll'a* ('an effort') 2.24, *vlada* ('power', 'authorities') 1.99, *borec'* ('a fighter') 1.94, *rozum* ('intelligence') 1.94, *bažann'a* ('a desire') 1.88.

Since both words are relatively frequent ((*volia*5k, *svoboda* 1.6k occurrences in the corpus), we plotted 100 random concordance lines per synonym.

On the plot, the vectors for both words overlap significantly, which indicates that *volia* tends to denote the concept of freedom more often than the idea of will in the texts published in Kyiv in 1940-1969.

Figure 5 provides an example with two semantically unrelated words (*svoboda* and *dvygun*) – to demonstrate how the model distinguishes them.

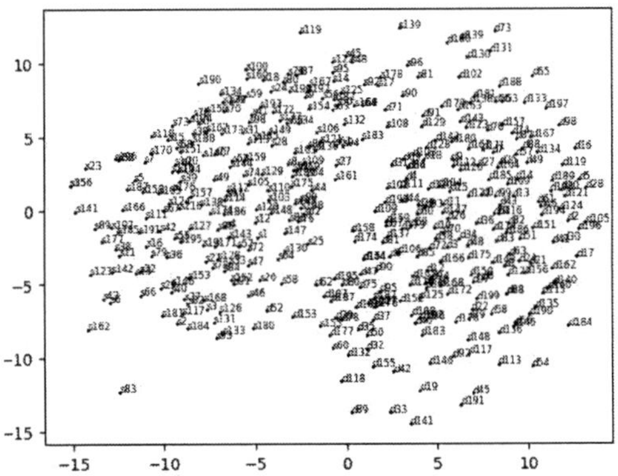

Figure 5: The Second-order Collocate Vectors: *dvygun* (d) and *svoboda* (s)

The plot contains two completely separate clusters. The provided observations for the test cases make us believe in the potential of the Semantic Vector Space Model with second-order collocate vectors for various semantic explorations of Ukrainian, including but not limited to word-sense disambiguation problems, regional variation investigation, and diachronic semantics.

Combined with profound lexicological analysis, such formal semantic representation applied to large-scale corpora would make it possible to reveal hidden trends and model dynamics of language over time and across different regions.

6 Further Work

The initial set of experiments with the proposed semantic model has opened several directions for the subsequent research and development to enhance and extend this approach. The ambition is to reveal Ukrainian word variation over regions, time, and registers following the prior work of von Waldenfels (2014).

Therefore, we have to deal with the problem of a semantic model being generic enough to represent the Ukrainian language as a whole and simultaneously being sensitive to regional and time-wise peculiarities. The open question that requires further exploration is building time-and-region-specific models vs. a single semantic model.

In addition, certain steps of the current data processing pipeline and analytic modeling require enrichment. We aim to continue experimenting with pipeline configuration decisions, vectorizer algorithms, and dimensionality reduction algorithms, utilizing clustering techniques, and various visualization approaches, including building semantic graphs.

Moreover, to properly represent a wide range of word senses, the model must be trained on significantly larger corpora (ideally, billions of tokens) and consider a vocabulary of greater size (at least 20,000 words).

Another challenge is to make the semantic model able to deal with high-frequency words, like prepositions, since their semantic variation is of high research interest for many lexicographers. Traditionally, such words are excluded from a vector space model as stop words, but we would like to treat them as another valuable target of semantic modeling.

Last but not least, there is a need to tackle several language standards of Ukrainian in specific periods of its history, which requires both additional data normalization and model sensitivity to different standards.

7 Limitations

During this initial phase of the research, we needed more digital textual data, especially for the period before WWII, and a poor representation of various

regions of Ukraine. Therefore, we had to limit our exploration to the texts published in 1940–1969 for the most represented region in the General Annotated Corpus of Ukrainian.
Apart from that, we had to simplify some of the data processing steps to avoid using extensive GPU resources, which, however, is unavoidable in the further stages of the project.

8 Ethics Statement

The broader value of the research is grounded on exploring and showing the versatility and growth of the Ukrainian language with the help of advanced NLP techniques combined with solid linguistic analysis.

References

Kris Heylen, Dirk Speelman, and Dirk Geeraerts. 2012. Looking at word meaning. an interactive visualization of semantic vector spaces for dutch synsets. *Proceedings of the EACL-2012 joint workshop of LINGVIS UNCLH: Visualization of Language Patterns and Uncovering Language History from Multilingual Resources*, pages 16–24.

Kris Heylen, Thomas Wielfaert, Dirk Speelman, and Dirk Geeraerts. 2015. Monitoring polysemy: Word space models as a tool for large-scale lexical semantic analysis. *Lingua*, 157:153–172.

Martin Hilpert and David Correia Saavedra. 2020. Using token-based semantic vector spaces for corpus-linguistic analyses: From practical applications to tests of theoretical claims. *Corpus Linguistics and Linguistic Theory 2020*, 16(2):393–424.

Mariana Montes and Dirk Geeraerts. 2022. How vector space models disambiguate adjectives: A perilous but valid enterprise. *Yearbook of the German Cognitive Linguistics Association*, 10(1):7–32.

Maria Shvedova. 2020. The general regionally annotated corpus of ukrainian (grac, uacorpus.org): Architecture and functionality. *Proceedings of the 4th International Conference on Computational Linguistics and Intelligent Systems (COLINS 2020)*, I:489–506.

Peter D. Turney and Patrick Pantel. 2010. From frequency to meaning: Vector space models of semantics. *Journal of Artificial Intelligence Research*, 37:141–188.

Ruprecht von Waldenfels. 2014. Explorations into variation across slavic: Taking a bottom-up approach. *Aggregating Dialectology, Typology, and Register Analysis*, pages 290–323.

Eric S. Wheeler. 2005. Multidimensional scaling for linguistics. *Quantitative linguistics. An international handbook*, pages 548–553.

The Parliamentary Code-Switching Corpus: Bilingualism in the Ukrainian Parliament in the 1990s-2020s

Olha Kanishcheva
University of Jena
kanichshevaolga@gmail.com

Maria Shvedova
University of Jena
National University "Lviv Polytechnic"
mariia.o.shvedova@lpnu.ua

Tetiana Kovalova
University of Jena
V. N. Karazin Kharkiv National University
tvkovalova@karazin.ua

Ruprecht von Waldenfels
University of Jena
ruprecht.waldenfels@uni-jena.de

Abstract

We describe a Ukrainian-Russian code-switching corpus of Ukrainian Parliamentary Session Transcripts. The corpus includes speeches entirely in Ukrainian, Russian, or various types of mixed speech and allows us to see how speakers switch between these languages depending on the communicative situation. The paper describes the process of creating this corpus from the official multilingual transcripts using automatic language detecting and publicly available metadata on the speakers. On this basis, we consider possible reasons for the change in the number of Ukrainian speakers in the parliament and present the most common patterns of bilingual Ukrainian and Russian code-switching in parliamentarians' speeches.

1 Introduction

As a result of Ukraine's long history of political dependence on Russia, first as part of the empire, then throughout its Soviet history, a significant number of people in Ukraine are bilingual in Ukrainian and Russian. Since Ukraine's independence (after 1991), the share of the use of the Ukrainian language in society has gradually increased and the share of Russian has decreased; the war of 2022 has significantly accelerated this process (Kulyk, 2023).

In the 20th century, the issue of Ukrainian-Russian bilingualism was the subject of many studies by Ukrainian linguists with a focus on deviations from Russian normative use and interference from Ukrainian. In the 21st century, the focus was mainly on sociolinguistic studies concerning the distribution of both languages and the tasks of supporting the Ukrainian language and pushing back stigmatized mixed Ukrainian-Russian speech known as Surzhyk. The main research methods applied to Ukrainian-Russian bilingualism were interviews and questionnaires, as well as analysis of individual texts, dictionaries, and normative sources.

Corpus-based studies of Ukrainian-Russian bilingualism have not yet become widespread. An exception is the Oldenburg Surzhyk corpus, which consists of mixed speech recordings made by researchers in different regions of Ukraine, and the studies based on it that examine the distribution of different variants within mixed Ukrainian-Russian speech depending on the region and the characteristics of speakers (Hentschel and Reuther, 2020; Palinska and Hentschel, 2022).

Creating a corpus is a promising method of studying code-switching, as it allows us to see code-switching in a broader linguistic context and quantify language use. Dedicated corpora of code-switching have been created for English and Hindi (Dey and Fung, 2014), English and Welsh (Deuchar et al., 2018), German and Turkish (Özlem Çetinoğlu, 2016), Estonian and Russian (Zabrodskaja, 2009), and many more.

This study aims to create a corpus of Ukrainian-Russian code-switching based on transcripts of Ukrainian parliamentary sessions. These transcripts include not only parliamentary speeches, but also discussions between the speakers. This presents a rich bilingual discourse with speakers using Ukrainian, Russian, or different kinds of mixed speech and switching between these languages depending on the communicative situation. This corpus will allow us to improve our understanding of common switching patterns found in Ukrainian parliamentary speeches.

The remainder of this paper is organized as fol-

Proceedings of the Second Ukrainian Natural Language Processing Workshop (UNLP), pages 79–90
May 5, 2023 ©2023 Association for Computational Linguistics

lows: Section 2 discusses related work. specifically existing code-switching corpora, their features, and research related to these corpora, and presents a selection of the most important recent work in this domain. In Section 3 we present the code-switching corpus of Ukrainian parliamentary session transcripts and go into detail describing the main features of this corpus. The pre-processing, normalization, and processing steps during corpus compilation are given in Section 4. Here, we present the results of the separation of transcript into speakers and language identification. In Section 5, we present an analysis of the transcripts regarding the speaker's language, as it relates to normative documents and political events, showing possible reasons affecting the use of Ukrainian in parliament. Here we also present some typical cases of code-switching. The last Section 6 finalizes the paper and suggests some future works and improvements.

1.1 Research Tasks on Ukrainian Code-Switching Corpus

The transcripts of parliamentary sessions have become the material for numerous linguistic corpora. The CLARIN[1] collection contains 31 such corpora for different languages. (Kryvenko, 2018) reports the creation of a corpus of Ukrainian parliamentary texts for discourse analysis. The corpus does not have language annotation and consists of 1.26 million tokens of different types of parliamentary texts from 2002-2017 (parliamentary news, minutes of plenary sittings, hearings and committees' meetings, Speaker's addresses, committee agendas, reports, announcements, etc.). In 2021, a corpus of about 70 million tokens of Verkhovna Rada plenary session transcripts from 1990-2020 was added to GRAC.v.12[2], with the text in non-Ukrainian languages automatically removed (Starko et al., 2021). The parliamentary transcripts are a ready-to-research record of spoken language, which is of considerable size and available for download from an open source. An important advantage of such texts is also the publicity of information about the speakers, which allows for the most detailed annotation of the corpus and free access to their biographies in the process of deeper linguistic research. Parliamentary corpora can be used not only in the field of linguistic research but also in the social sciences, for various studies of parliamentary discourse. Since the Verkhovna Rada transcripts corpus contains texts in Ukrainian, Russian, and bilingual mixed speech, this corpus can be used to study code-switching, both from a sociolinguistic and psycholinguistic perspective.

[1] https://www.clarin.eu/resource-families/parliamentary-corpora

[2] http://uacorpus.org/

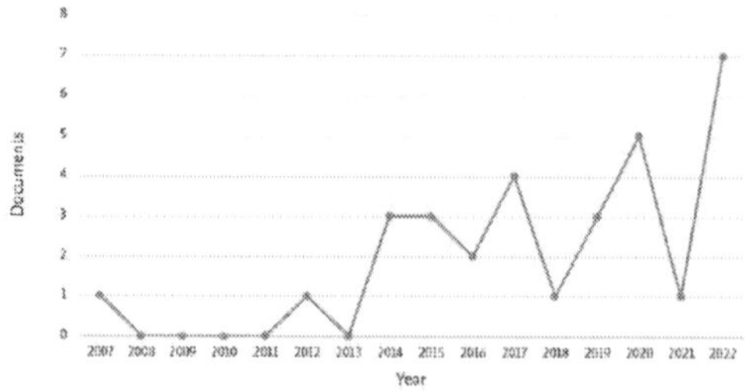

Figure 1: The number of publications related to code-switching corpora in the Scopus database.

2 Related Work

Over the past few years, research in the field of code-switching corpora has increasingly attracted the attention of researchers. Figure 1 shows the number of publications related to code-switching corpora in the Scopus database with overall dynamics increasing every year.

A lot of research is devoted to corpora with audio tracks, and these corpora are used to improve the quality of speech recognition with mixed corpora. Modipa and Davel (2022) present two reference corpora for the analysis of Sepedi-English code-switched speech in the context of automatic speech recognition. Sreeram et al. (2019) describe the collection of a Hinglish (Hindi-English) code-switching database at the Indian Institute of Technology Guwahati (IITG) which is referred to as the IITG-HingCoS corpus. Dau-Cheng et al. (2015) introduce the South East Asia Mandarin-English corpus, a 63-h spontaneous Mandarin-English code-switching transcribed speech corpus suitable for LVCSR and language change detection/identification research. The corpus consists of recordings of unscripted interviews and free conversations by 157 Singaporean and Malaysian speakers who speak a mixture of Mandarin and English switching within sentences.

Some researchers consider code-switching corpora from the point of view of psycholinguistics and investigate the reasons for switching from one language to another. Beatty-Martínez et al. (2020)

show that code-switching does not always involve additional effort and resources. Deuchar (2020) presents the differentiation of code-switching from borrowing, the methods for evaluating competing models of grammaticality in code-switching, and the importance of studying variables as well as uniform patterns in code-switching.

Thus, researchers use code-switching corpora for various tasks, investigating different aspects from speech recognition to psycholinguistic reasons for switching between languages.

In our work, we study a code-switching corpus of parliamentary speech. Several such code-switching corpora based on parliamentary texts already exist, including the bilingual Dutch-French speeches from the Belgium Federal texts (Marx and Schuth, 2010) and the Bilingual Corpus of Basque Parliamentary Transcriptions (Escribano et al., 2022). The DutchParl corpus (the Parliamentary Documents in Dutch) contains the Belgian Federal documents, bilingual French-Dutch texts which are presented in the original French or Dutch and contain an aligned translation in the second language. The BasqueParl corpus contains only original bilingual transcripts in Basque and Spanish and represents the bilingual discourse of the Basque Parliament. It is designed for the automatic analysis of political discourse, including the use of languages and their correlation with entities. BasqueParl shows that there has been no significant change in the amount of bilingualism in parliament over the period 2012-2020, which is covered by the corpus [p. 3387].

A specific feature of the Ukrainian corpus of parliamentary transcripts from 1990-2020 is that the proportions and use of the two languages in it change noticeably and unevenly over the years, gradually reaching 100% Ukrainian in the second half of the 2010s. The language policy in the Ukrainian parliament has been a hot political issue for all these years, and the actual use of languages has varied depending on the political situation. The corpus shows the history of the existence and decline of postcolonial bilingualism in parliamentary discourse.

3 Corpus Description

The corpus of the Verkhovna Rada (the Ukrainian unicameral parliament) proceedings contains texts recorded from 1990 until 2020, downloaded from the official website of the Verkhovna Rada[3]. The timespan starts even before Ukrainian independence when Verkhovna Rada was an institution of a Soviet republic. The size of the initial data is about 70 million tokens. A specific feature of the corpus is that it represents a bilingual Ukrainian-Russian discourse with different shares of Ukrainian, Russian, and bilingual speech in different years. The Ukrainian language prevails in the corpus, and its share was increasing over the years: from a minimum of 76% in 1995 to 100% in 2018-2020.

The parliamentary speeches and remarks are recorded literally, in the language actually spoken, and language mixing is also accurately reproduced in the transcript. This accuracy allows us to analyze the use of a particular language in dialog and its correlation with other interlocutors' language and the session's topic.

The corpus consists of text files ("txt" format), organized by speaker, that is, text files that contain all the utterances of each member of parliament for the year made both in speeches and in the discussion; this is not unlike the Hansard website of British parliamentary discussions. This form allows us to analyze the use of Ukrainian and Russian by each speaker. The corpus is being annotated by age and the political party of a given speaker, as well as by the administrative region of Ukraine (or by another country if applicable) where they were born and educated.

4 Corpus Preparation

The transcript of parliamentary sessions is a single file that contains all parliamentary sessions for the whole year. An example excerpt from the 2013 transcript is given in Appendix A.

From this fragment, it can be seen that the speakers are written in capital letters with initials. Sometimes this is the name and middle name, i.e. two initials, and sometimes only one initial, only the name is given. At the beginning of each session, the Chairman or *head* is announced who is in charge of the meeting, and further in the text he is referred to merely as "HOLOVUJUČYJ" (Presiding).

Also, the text may contain timestamps (16:11:06), quotations (for example, "...In accordance with Article 13 of the Law of Ukraine "On the Status of People's Deputy of Ukraine..."), and remarks (for example, "Splashes", "Noise in the hall").

[3] https://iportal.rada.gov.ua/meeting/stenogr

Number of files	Number of sentences	Number of tokens
1957	826 471	16 657 948

Table 1: The quantitative data of our corpus.

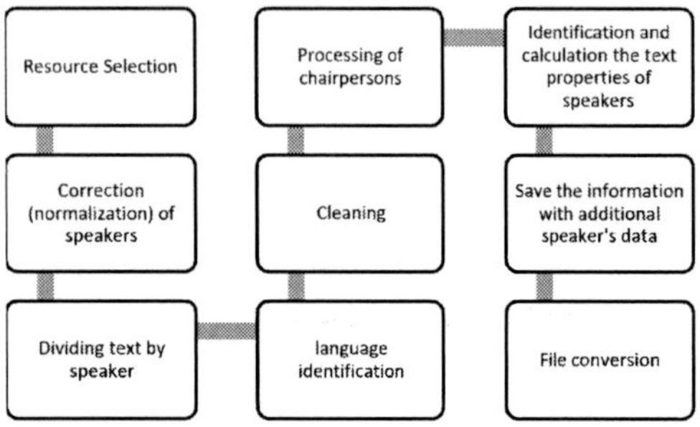

Figure 2: A general pipeline of parliament transcripts processing.

In this work, transcripts from 2010 to 2019 were processed. General information on these files is presented in Table 1.

As a result of the transcript analysis, a general approach to the processing of parliamentary transcripts was formed, which has the stages presented in Figure 2.

Due to the fact that the stenographer allows for variations in the spelling of the names and surnames of speakers, such as a large number of spaces, or spaces between initials, before processing the entire file, we normalize all speakers, i.e. we bring them to the form Surname N.P. This helps to further significantly reduce the number of incorrect files for each incoming.

Then we divide the entire transcript by speakers, namely members of parliament, invited ministers, etc. As a result, a separate file was generated for each speaker. An example of such a file is given in Appendix B.

Speaker separation is done automatically on the basis of the transcription. Sometimes the transcriber makes mistakes in spelling the last name or initials, which results in the software recording several speakers instead of one. Such mistakes have been corrected manually. For example, the surname «Arzhevityn» can be misspelt as «Azhevityn» and without manual verification, it is quite difficult to understand whether this is a real surname or whether it is a mistake. This could be automated if only members of parliament were present in the transcript, but since there are invited people, this cannot be implemented.

Next, we carry out the identification of the head at a meeting in parliament. He/She is mentioned once at the beginning of the meeting. He/She can also change within one convocation. Therefore, the statements of head for one convocation may refer to different people.

We then clean up the speakers' lines of timestamps and remarks.

At the next stage, we determine the language(s) of each speaker on the sentence level. To this end, tried out different modules for determining the language: CLDv3: Compact Language Detector v3 (Google company)[4], LangDetect[5], Spacy-langdetect[6], fastText[7], Lingua-py[8] were tested, and none of these modules showed the desired accuracy. For example, let's consider sentences for which the language was specified as Ukrainian, but they are written in Russian.

- "Davajte slovo" ("Give us the floor ")
- "No ved' tak že nespravedlivo!" ("But it's just as unfair!")
- "Davajte vernem!" ("Let's return!")
- "No ja vam skažu tak." ("But I'll tell you this.")
- "Ja choču poblagodarit' gospodina Grojsmana." ("I want to thank Mr. Hroysman.")

The sentence *"Davajte slovo"* can be both in Russian and in Ukrainian, it is really difficult for the system to determine the language of the sentence based only on the spelling, and in this case, it completely matched. Only phonetic notation can help here. The remaining examples are written in Russian but identified as Ukrainian.

We chose the Lingua-py library, as it made fewer identification errors than the rest of the tested libraries. All experiments to evaluated the accuracy of language detection were carried out manually. However, this library was also making mistakes.

To determine to what extent a speaker uses both languages, we first identified the language used in each sentence using the above-mentioned module and then summed up the number of tokens for

[4]https://github.com/google/cld3

[5]https://pypi.org/project/langdetect/

[6]https://pypi.org/project/spacy-langdetect/

[7]https://fasttext.cc/docs/en/language-identification.html

[8]https://github.com/pemistahl/lingua-py

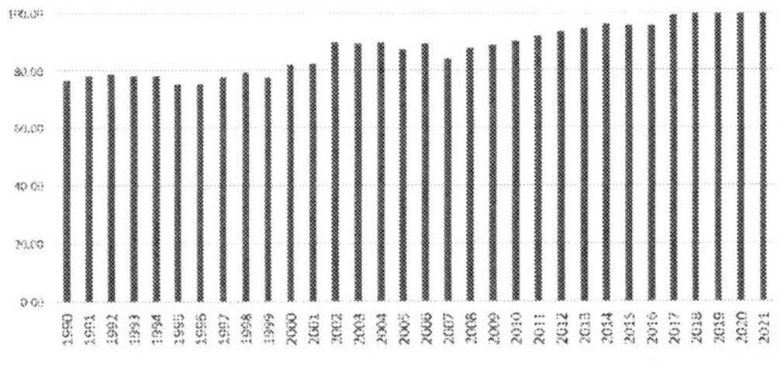

Figure 3: A quantitative report of parliament speeches by language for each year (1990-2021).

each language per speaker. Then the percentage of Ukrainian in the speaker's speech was determined in tokens. Sentences shorter than 5 tokens were not considered, since language recognition modules often make mistakes in short sentences.

Next, we determined which party the representative belongs to, as well as some statistical characteristics of the text, such as the number of tokens offered, etc. In the future, we also plan to add the year and place of birth of the parliament members, in order to check whether the age and region of birth influence language preferences and switching between languages.

5 Data Analysis

5.1 Research Tasks on Ukrainian Code-Switching Corpus

To analyze the use of languages in the Ukrainian parliament, we divided the texts into separate files by the speaker and the year of the three sessions of the parliament. The data are grouped by convocations:

- Verkhovna Rada of Ukraine of the 6th convocation (2007-2012) (II half).
- Verkhovna Rada of Ukraine of the 7th convocation (2012-2014).
- Verkhovna Rada of Ukraine of the 8th convocation (2014-2019).

For each convocation, the number of speakers using Ukrainian, Russian, or both languages was counted.

A quantitative report of parliament speech by language for each year (1990-2021) is given in Figure 3. The diagram shows that the share of the Ukrainian language in the corpus is gradually increasing and reached 100% in 2018.

This has been influenced by a combination of policy changes and relevant legislation passed

	6 conv.	**7 conv.**	**8 conv.**
Ukrainian	67,4%	70,1%	68,1%
Russian	2,9%	2,5%	2,5%
Bilingual	29,7%	27,4%	29,4%

Table 2: The proportional ratio of Russian-speaking, Ukrainian-speaking, and bilingual speakers in the work of the Parliament of the 6th, 7th, and 8th convocations.

over the years. Thus, the 1989 Law "On Languages in the Ukrainian SSR" determined that in the Ukrainian SSR the language of work, record keeping, and documentation, as well as relations between state, party, public bodies, enterprises, institutions, and organizations is the Ukrainian language (Law, 1989). The Regulations of the Verkhovna Rada of Ukraine adopted in 2010 defined the state language as the working language of the Verkhovna Rada, its bodies, and officials. Speeches in other languages were allowed only to foreigners and stateless persons (Regulations, 2010).

In 2012, the Kivalov-Kolesnichenko law was adopted, which allowed the use of not only Ukrainian but also other working languages in the parliament (Law, 2013). This law caused significant public resonance and was revoked in February 2014 after the Russian invasion. In February 2018, this law was declared unconstitutional.

In 2019, a new Law "On Ensuring the Functioning of the Ukrainian Language as the State Language" was adopted, which established the mandatory use of Ukrainian in the official sphere (Law, 2019).

As can be seen from Figure 3, in 2007, the smallest share of the use of the Ukrainian language by speakers of the parliament was found. The increase in the use of the Russian language in the parliament in 2007 may be related, on the one hand, to the campaign in the Verkhovna Rada against President Viktor Yushchenko, who supported a pro-Western course and derussification, and on the other hand, to Ukraine's ratification of the European Charter for Regional and Minority Languages. After the adoption of the Charter, the so-called "parade of linguistic sovereignty" took place in Ukraine, when a number of local councils of the eastern and southern regions of Ukraine, violating the Constitution of Ukraine and the Law of Ukraine "On Local Self-Government", declared Russian the regional language in their respective territories.

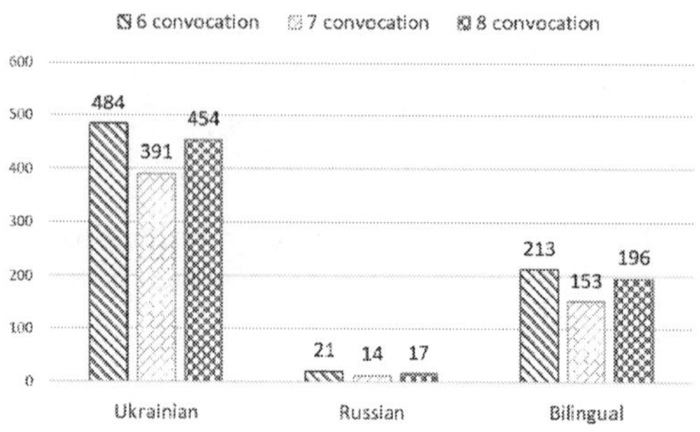

Figure 4: A quantitative report of parliament speakers by language for each convocation (6, 7, and 8 convocations).

Researchers note that the struggle between the pro-Ukrainian and the pro-Russian approach to state language policy intensified after the March 2006 parliamentary elections won by the pro-Russian Party of Regions and gradually entered a heated phase. The efforts of the pro-Ukrainian wing in the executive authorities to support the Ukrainian language encountered opposition from the deputies of the Party of Regions in the parliament and some local councils. In parallel with this, political actions were taking place to give the Russian language the status of the second state language (Marusyk, 2015; Masenko, 2018; Shumlyanskyi, 2007; Skvirska, 2008).

The language distribution by political parties is presented in Appendix C. This appendix provides a table that shows to which extent using a particular language goes along party lines and how often representatives of different parties use both languages.

We assumed that the proportions of Ukrainian speakers, Russian speakers, and switchers in each convocation would depend on the composition of the parties in it; moreover, we hypothesized that the pro-government parties would speak Ukrainian more than others. The largest parties in the parliament of the 6th convocation were the Party of Regions and Yulia Timoshenko's Bloc, of the 7th convocation, Party of Regions and the All-Ukrainian Association "Batkivshchyna", of the 8th convocation, People's Front and Petro Poroshenko's Bloc (Protocol, 2007; Protokol, 2012; Protocol, 2014). A quantitative report of parliament speakers by language for each convocation (6, 7, and 8 convocations) is given in Figure 4, the proportion practically does not change (Table 2).

It should be noted that among the members of the Party of Regions that openly proposed the status of Russian as the second state language the share of language switchers compared to Ukrainian speakers in all convocations was significant. Thus, in the Regions' fraction within the Parliament of the 6th convocation, the number of code-switchers is higher than the number of Ukrainian-speakers (77 and 63 respectively). In the 7th convocation the respective numbers are close: 50 and 53.

The absolute leader among language switchers in the work of the 6th and 7th convocations of the Parliament, as can be seen from the data presented in the appendices, is the Communist Party of Ukraine, known for its pro-Russian political platform (in the 8th convocation, the party was actually legally banned).

The rather large share of code-switchers in comparison with Ukrainian speakers in the Petro Poroshenko Bloc of the 8th convocation is noteworthy. Most likely, this is due to the fact that the head of the bloc and its members advocated for the regional status of the Russian language, distinguishing it from other national minority languages. See, for example, draft law No. 4178a of 26 June 2014, where Petro Poroshenko proposed to amend Article 143 of the Constitution of Ukraine, which would allow local authorities to change the status of a language with a special emphasis on Russian (DraftLaw, 2014). Petro Poroshenko later changed his position on the state language as reflected in his speech at the Verkhovna Rada on 20 September 2018, where he expresses strong support for the Ukrainian language. This corresponds to the achievement of monolingualism in the Ukrainian parliamentary discourse in general, as shown in Figure 3.

5.2 Cases of Code-Switching

In this section, we describe the most common types of combined use of Ukrainian and Russian we found in parliamentarians' speeches; note that at this point, we adduce data only from 2003, which has been manually annotated. Below, each type is illustrated with examples from the transcripts. Ukrainian text is given in standard font, and Russian text is in cursive font. All examples have been translated into English.

- Ukrainian speakers insert phraseology or quotations in Russian.

Šanovni kolehy, u mene pislja toho jak u nas vidbuvajet'sja ce obhovorennja, skladajet'sja take vražennja, jake možna oxarakteryzuvaty vidomym vyslovom: *"Šumim, bratcy, šumim!"* (Jurij Solomatin, 2003)[9].

Dear colleagues, after this discussion, I have an impression that can be characterized by a well-known phrase: *"We make noise, friends, we make noise!"* (Yuriy Solomatin, 2003. The phrase is based on a quotation from *Woe from Wit*, the classical 19th-century Russian play by A. Griboyedov. Here and below we italicize the text that appears in the original Russian).

- Russian speakers insert the names of laws and documents in Ukrainian.

Na vaše rassmotrenie vnositsja proekt zakona Ukrainy pro vnesennja zmin do dejakyx zakonodavčyx aktiv Ukraïny ščodo bankrutstva hirnyčnyx pidpryjemstv (Viktor Turmanov, 2003).

We are submitting for your consideration a draft law of Ukraine on amendments to certain legislative acts of Ukraine regarding the bankruptcy of mining enterprises (Victor Turmanov, 2003).

- Russian speakers insert Ukrainian legalese technical terms and clichés.

Predlagaju v cilomu. *Mnogo golosov "za". Vse* zauvažennja *učteny* (2003).

I propose [to adopt the draft law] as a whole. *Many votes in favor. All* the comments *have been taken into account* (2003).

- Ukrainian speakers insert words in Russian.

Ce ne prjamyj zv'jazok, a ce poserednij... *kosvennyj*... poserednij zv'jazok (Mykola Poliščuk, 2003).

This is not a direct connection, but an indirect... *intermediate*... indirect connection (Mykola Polishchuk, 2003).

- Unmotivated heavy mixing of Russian and Ukrainian.

My, do reči, peredbačajemo značne zbil'šennja vytrat na medycynu, *ja ob ètom uže govoril. Sovokupnye raschody konsolidirovannogo bjudžeta na medicinu vozrastajut u nas v poltora raza.* Krim toho, cilyj rjad cil'ovyx prohram *pravitel'stvo* peredbačaje, *predusmatrivaet na finansirovanie, v tom čisle, kstati, i na* možlyve pidvyščennja likars'kyx zasobiv v cini (Mykola Azarov, 2003).

By our way, we expect a significant increase in healthcare costs, *as I have already mentioned. The total consolidated budget expenditures on healthcare are going to increase by one and a half times.* In addition, a number of targeted programs *the government* envisages, *provides to finance, including, by the way,* a possible increase in the price of medicines (Mykola Azarov, 2003).

- The speaker switches languages for stylistic purposes, distinguishing between the official position proclaimed in Ukrainian and personal opinions added in Russian.

Šanovnye *narodnye deputaty*! Urjad Ukraïny pidtrymuje sxvalennja Verxovnoju Radoju proektu Zakonu Ukraïny pro obov'jazkove straxuvannja cyvil'no-pravovoï vidpovidal'nosti vlasnykiv transportnyx zasobiv v peršomu čytanni. Ce oficijna pozycija.

No kak narodnyj deputat dvuch predyduščich sozyvov, ja choču dobavit', čto vpervye podobnyj proekt ja sam dokladyval zdes' ešče v 1996 godu. S tech por dva našich sozyva proveli vremja v diskussijach vokrug ètogo proekta, tak skazat', v poiskach soveršenstva. I ja sejčas slyšu, čto vidvigajutsja vnov' te že samye argumenty, primerno (Viktor Suslov, 2003).

Dear *Members of Parliament*! The Government of Ukraine supports the adoption by the Verkhovna Rada of the draft Law of Ukraine on compulsory insurance of civil liability of vehicle owners in the first reading. This is the official position.

But as a representative of two previous convocations, I would like to add that I first presented a similar draft law here myself back in 1996. Since then, our two convocations have spent time in discussions around this project, so to speak, in search of perfection. And I hear now that the same arguments are being put forward again, roughly (Victor Suslov, 2003).

- Triggered code-switching. In the first example, the speaker switches from Russian to Ukrainian after pronouncing the name of an official document in Ukrainian. The second speaker switches from Ukrainian to Russian after using Russian phraseology.

Uvažaemyj Vladimir Michajlovič, Gennadij Borisovič! Ja chotel by prosit' vključit' do **pereliku ob'jektiv** šče misto *Kremenčug* ta misto

[9] The text is presented in transliterated form according to the original transcript, without typographical or other corrections.

Zolotonošu. Cyx dvox mist nemaje v pereliku, a problema duže hostra v cyx dvux mistax je. Djakuju (Vasyl' Havryljuk, 2003).

Dear Vladimir Mikhailovich, Gennady Borisovich! I would like to ask you to include in the **list of objects** the city of *Kremenchug* and the city of Zolotonosha. These two cities are not on the list, and the problem is very acute in these two cities. Thank you (Vasyl Havryluk, 2003).

I ja xoču šče raz spytaty, čy rozhljadalasja možlyvist' Ministerstvom finansiv skasuvaty okremi podatkovi pil'hy, jaki b daly dodatkovi doxody bjudžetu. Ale vynykaje taka sytuacija, ščo u nas palyvno-enerhetyčnyj kompleks, znajete, jak ***dojnaja korova****, kotoraja v principe i obespečivaet segodnja opredelennye resursy, kogda my rassmatrivaem uveličenie dochodom, ne dumaja o tom, čto byla mnogie gody ta nedoimka, kotoraja po suti dela absoljutno ne rešala absoljutno nikakich finansovych voprosov i v bjudžete v dal'nejšem. Spasibo* (Valerij Konovaljuk, 2003).

And I want to ask again whether the Ministry of Finance has considered the possibility of canceling certain tax privileges that would bring additional budget revenue. But there is a situation where we have the fuel and energy complex, you know, *as a* ***milk cow****, which basically provides certain resources today when we consider increasing revenues, without thinking about the fact that there was a debt for many years, which in fact did not solve any financial issues in the budget in the future. Thank you* (Valeriy Konovaluk, 2003).

- Code-switching in a dialog under the influence of the interlocutor's speech.

HOLOVA. (...) Propozycija komitetu jaka? Bud' laska, Vasyl' Petrovyč.

CUŠKO V. P. [mostly Russian-speaking]. Propozicija *komiteta – podderžat' v pervom čtenii* (2003).

CHAIR. (...) What is the Committee's proposal? Please, Vasyl Petrovych.

TSUSHKO V. P. The Committee's proposal *is to support it in the first reading* (2003).

- Language switching is used to mark quoted speech.

Vony vzjaly mene u take kil'ce - ce robitnyky, masa ljudej, (...) a ty, deputat, stoïš pered nymy odyn na odyn. I vony na tebe tysnut': *čto ty tam ničego ne delaeš', den'gi nam ne dajut, vy tam vse sobiraetes' i sidite!* A ja kažu: ty pidoždy, ty pidoždy, ja v jakij frakciï naxodžusja, vsi zaraz v opozyciï do Prezydenta, a xto ja taka? (Ol'ha Hinzburh, 2003).

They encircled me, they are workers, a lot of people, (...) and here you are, a representative, standing in front of them face to face. And they put pressure on you: *why don't you do anything there, they don't give us any money, you all just gather and sit there!* And I say: hold on, hold on, what deputy group am I in, everyone is in opposition to the President now, and who am I?" (Olha Hinzburh, 2003).

- Switching to another language to illustrate a tolerant attitude to linguistic diversity.

A ščo stosujet'sja ridnoï movy, ja tak vvažaju, ščo ridna mova – ce mova rodyny, v jakij vyxovuvalasja ljudyna. *I voobšče davajte tolerantno otnositsja, čto kasaetsja i russkogo i ukrainskogo jazyka. Ne sleduet politizirovat' ètot vopros* (Henadij Vasyl'jev, holovujučyj, 2003).

As for the mother tongue, I believe that the mother tongue is the language of the family in which a person was brought up. *And in general, let's be tolerant when it comes to both Russian and Ukrainian. We should not politicize this issue* (Hennady Vasilyev, Chairman, 2003).

The examples presented were taken from the 2003 transcript not yet included in the corpus, however, we think the same types are also to be found in the data from 2010 to 2019. Still, the identification of new types of language switching requires a more detailed analysis and is planned to be carried out in future studies.

6 Conclusions and Future Plans

In this paper, we present the Ukrainian-Russian Code-Switching Corpus of Ukrainian Parliamentary Session Transcripts (1990-2020), its composition, annotation, and research possibilities. The language markup in the corpus is carried out at the sentence level.

The corpus represents bilingual Ukrainian-Russian parliamentary discourse, which has been changing over the years and became monolingual Ukrainian in the second half of the 2010s. We tried to analyze whether laws and the general political situation affect the actual use of languages in the Council. It turned out that laws are a deterrent to increasing the use of the Russian language in parliament. In some cases, the influence of political trends on the use of languages can be assumed (for example, 2007, when the increase in the share of the Russian language coincided with the pro-Russian campaign in Ukraine), but this requires additional research.

In the future, we plan to process the entire corpus of parliamentary transcripts for 1990-2020 and consistently trace the manifestations of Ukrainian-Russian bilingualism over 30 years and the history of its fading. We found some typical cases of bilingual speeches on the material of 2003 texts, and we want to look for similar cases automatically and trace the trends of different cases (language mixing and language switching) in the Rada over the years. In the future, additional corpus labeling is planned, such as part of speech, and entities will make it possible to identify additional connections between speakers. It would be interesting also to apply thematic modeling and trace the correlation between the discussion of the language issue in parliament and the actual use of languages.

Besides, in the future, it is planned to connect the interface and change the corpus storage format in order to store dialog information and all the necessary metadata.

Limitations

We see the following main limitations at this point in time:

- The error rate in distinguishing Russian and Ukrainian and its impact is not known.
- Due to variations in the input data, the automatic speaker identification needs extensive manual post-editing.
- Different types of code-switching are extremely hard to automatically distinguish.
- In our data collection approach, we combine all utterances of each speaker in a single file. Right now, we therefore cannot automatically distinguish between speakers who use both Russian or Ukrainian alternatively, without mixing within a unit of discourse (bilingual speakers) and speakers who mix languages (code-switching speakers). This will be addressed in later work.
- Right now, we do not take the amount of data of speakers into account. Naturally, speakers with a lot of data are more probable to have text in both languages; this is disregarded right now and its impact is unclear.

Ethics Statement

Our scientific work complies with the ACL Ethics Policy[10]. The corpus was created on the basis of publicly available data.

Acknowledgements

We would like to thank Reviewers for taking the time and effort necessary to review the manuscript. We sincerely appreciate all valuable comments and suggestions, which helped us to improve the quality of the manuscript.

We would like to thank Kyrylo Zakharov for downloading the plenary session transcripts from the Verkhovna Rada website.

This research was partially funded by the Humboldt Foundation and the Volkswagen Foundation.

References

Anne L. Beatty-Martínez, Christian A. Navarro-Torres, and Paola E. Dussias. 2020. Codeswitching: A Bilingual Toolkit for Opportunistic Speech Planning. *Frontiers in Psychology*, 11.

Lyu Dau-Cheng, Tan Tien-Ping, Chng Eng-Siong, and Li Haizhou. 2015. Mandarin-English code-switching speech corpus in South-East Asia: SEAME. *Language resources and evaluation*, 49(3):581–600.

Margaret Deuchar. 2020. Code-Switching in Linguistics: A Position Paper. *Languages*, 5(2):22.

Margaret Deuchar, Peredur Davies, and Kevin Donnelly. 2018. *Building and Using the Siarad Corpus: Bilingual conversations in Welsh and English (Studies in Corpus Linguistics (SCL), 81, Band 81)*. John Benjamins Publishing Co.

Anik Dey and Pascale Fung. 2014. A Hindi-English Code-Switching Corpus. In *Proceedings of the Ninth International Conference on Language Resources and Evaluation (LREC'14)*, pages 2410–2413, Reykjavik, Iceland. European Language Resources Association (ELRA).

DraftLaw. 2014. Draft Law on Amendments to the Constitution of Ukraine (regarding the powers of state authorities and local self-government bodies) of 26.06.2014 No. 4178a.

[10]https://www.aclweb.org/portal/content/acl-code-ethics

Nayla Escribano, Jon Ander González, Julen Orbegozo-Terradillos, Ainara Larrondo-Ureta, Simón Peña-Fernández, Olatz Perez de Viñaspre, and Rodrigo Agerri. 2022. BasqueParl: A Bilingual Corpus of Basque Parliamentary Transcriptions. In *Proceedings of the Thirteenth Language Resources and Evaluation Conference*, page 3382–3390, Marseille, France. European Language Resources Association (ELRA).

Gerd Hentschel and Tilmann Reuther. 2020. Ukrainisch-russisches und russisch-ukrainisches Code-Mixing. Untersuchungen in drei Regionen im Süden der Ukraine. *Colloquium: New Philologies*, 5:105–132.

Anna Kryvenko. 2018. Constructing a Narrative of European Integration in the Verkhovna Rada of Ukraine: A Corpus-Based Discourse Analysis. *Cognition, communication, discourse*, 17:56–74.

Volodymyr Kulyk. 2023. Language and identity in Ukraine at the end of 2022. *Zbruch*.

Law. 1989. On languages in the Ukrainian SSR: Law of the Ukrainian Soviet Socialist Republic of October 28, N 8312-11.

Law. 2013. On the principles of state language policy: Law of Ukraine dated july 3, 2012 No. 5029-vi. *Information of the Verkhovna Rada of Ukraine*, No. 23. Art. 218.

Law. 2019. On ensuring the functioning of the Ukrainian language as a state language: Law of Ukraine dated April 25, 2019 No. 2704-viii. *Information of the Verkhovna Rada of Ukraine*, No. 21, Article 81.

Taras Marusyk. 2015. State language policy in Ukraine in the last decade. *Universe*, 3-4:257–258.

Maarten Marx and Anne Schuth. 2010. DutchParl. The parliamentary documents in Dutch. In *Proceedings of the Seventh International Conference on Language Resources and Evaluation (LREC'10)*, Valletta, Malta.

Larisa Masenko. 2018. Language conflict in Ukraine: ways of solution. *Ukrainian Language*, 2:20–35.

Thipe I. Modipa and Marelie H. Davel. 2022. Two sepedi-english code-switched speech corpora. *Lang Resources & Evaluation*, 56:703–727.

Olesya Palinska and Gerd Hentschel. 2022. Regional'ny'e osobennosti ispol'zovaniya ukrainsko-russkoj smeshannoj rechi (surzhika) i vliyanie dialektov: pristavki i predlogi VID / OT. *LingVaria*, 34(2):229–253.

Protocol. 2007. Protocol of the Central Election Commission "On the results of the elections of people's representatives of Ukraine".

Protocol. 2014. Protocol of the Central Election Commission "On the results of the elections of the national deputy of Ukraine in the general state multimandate electoral district".

Protokol. 2012. Protocol of the Central Election Commission "On the results of the elections of the national deputy of Ukraine in the general state multimandate electoral district".

Regulations. 2010. About the Regulations of the Verkhovna Rada of Ukraine. *Information of the Verkhovna Rada of Ukraine*, 14-15, 16-17.

Stanislav Shumlyanskyi. 2007. Bilingual threats and chances of bilingualism. *Criticism*, 1-2:5–7.

Vira Skvirska. 2008. "Language is a weapon of politics", or about language problems in post-Soviet Odesa. page 167–195.

Ganji Sreeram, Dhawan Kunal, and Sinha Rohit. 2019. Iitg-HingCoS corpus: A Hinglish code-switching database for automatic speech recognition. *Speech communication*, 110:76–89.

Vasyl Starko, Andriy Rysin, and Maria Shvedova. 2021. Ukrainian Text Preprocessing in GRAC. In *Proceedings of the 16th International Conference on Computer Sciences and Information Technologies (CSIT)*, volume 2, pages 101–104, Lviv, Ukraine.

Anastassia Zabrodskaja. 2009. Evaluating the Matrix Language Frame model on the basis of a Russian-Estonian codeswitching corpus. *International Journal of Bilingualism*, 13(3):357–377.

Özlem Çetinoğlu. 2016. A Turkish-German Code-Switching Corpus. In *Proceedings of the Tenth International Conference on Language Resources and Evaluation (LREC'16)*, page 4215–4220, Portorož, Slovenia. European Language Resources Association (ELRA).

A Sample transcript of a parliamentary session

HOLOVUJUČYJ. Prošu. Narodnyj deputat Klyčko.

16:11:06

KLYČKO V.V.

Dobryj den', dorohi kolehy, xoču šče raz zvernuty uvahu, ščo Verxovna Rada, na žal', prodovžuje ne vykonuvaty svoix funkcij i ne pracjuje jak vona povynna pracjuvaty.

Holova Verxovnoi Rady neodnorazovo nahološuvav na tomu, ščo povynno buty personal'ne holosuvannja. Šče raz xoču nahadaty, ščob my znovu ne povertalysja do praktyky holosuvannja, tak zvane fortepiano čy pianino, koly deputaty bihajut' ta holosujut' za ljudej, jaki ne prysutni v zali. Ce perše. Po-druhe, ja vpevnenyj, ščo s'ohodnišnij den' my povynni proholosuvaty zakon pro spivpracju Ukraïny ta... jevropejs'koï intehraciï i obov'jazkovo rozhljanuty zakonoproekt pro vybory, miscevi vybory...

HOLOVUJUČYJ. Prošu, dajte zakinčyty.

(Translation:

CHAIR. Please. People's deputy Klitschko.

16:11:06

KLYCHKO V.V.

Good afternoon, dear colleagues, I would like to point out once again that the Verkhovna Rada, unfortunately, continues to not perform its functions and does not work as it should.

The Chairman of the Verkhovna Rada repeatedly emphasized that there should be personal voting. I want to remind once again that we should not return to the so-called piano voting practice, when deputies run and vote for people who are not present in the hall. This is the first.

Secondly, I am sure that today we must vote on the law on cooperation of Ukraine and... European integration and must consider the draft law on elections, local elections...

CHAIR. Please let me finish.

B The example of a file for one parliament speaker

<lang = "uk">Šanovni kolehy, s'ohodni važlyvyj den' dlja Ukraïny.</lang>

<lang = "uk">S'ohodni v Mins'ku vidbudet'sja zasidannja tr'oxstoronn'oï kontaktnoï hrupy.</lang>

<lang = "uk">I my očikujemo vid neï serjoznyx rezul'tativ, može, navit' i proryvu v spravi vrehuljuvannja konfliktu na Donbasi.</lang>

<lang = "uk">Takož s'ohodni v Jevropejs'komu parlamenti vidbudet'sja special'ni sluxannja ščodo vykonannja Mins'kyx domovlenostej.</lang>

<lang = "uk">Cóho domohlasja Ukraïna.</lang>

<lang = "uk">I dlja nas je duže važlyvoju reakcija jevropejs'koï spil'noty na ti hrubi porušennja Mins'kyx domovlenostej, na jaki jdut' rosijs'koterorystyčni vijs'ka na Donbasi.</lang>

<lang = "uk">S'ohodni Mins'ki domovlenosti – ce jedynyj zapobižnyk vid velykoï vijny na Donbasi.</lang>

<lang = "uk">I tomu tak važlyvo nam vsima zasobamy pidtrymaty ïxnje vykonannj.</lang>

<lang = "uk">Takož xoču zvernuty vašu uvahu na te, ščo ljudy na Donbasi vže vtomleni vid toho, ščo tam vidbuvajet'sja.</lang>

<lang = "uk">Včorašni podiï, koly 500 ljudej vyjšly i pišly neozbrojenymy na bandytiv Zaxarčenka z avtomatamy, i skazaly ïm, ščo treba zupynyty te, ščo vidbuvajet'sja tam, zabraty harmaty z ïxnij dvoriv, prypynyty vbyvaty ljudej, prypynyty vijnu, – ce peršyj pryznak toho, ščo vidbuvajet'sja protverezinnja vsjudy, v tomu čysli i na Donbasi.</lang>

<lang = "uk">I my spodivajemosja, duže skoro ukraïnci pokažut' vsim cym najmancjam i bandytam na dveri.</lang>

<lang = "uk">I ešče.[11]</lang>

<lang = "ru">Kak odessit choču obratit' vaše vnimanie na očen' važnyj moment.</lang>

<lang = "ru">Segodnja u nas planiruetsja privatizacija, v tom čisle obsuždaetsja privatizacija "Odesskogo priportovogo zavoda".</lang>

<lang = "ru">Bezuslovno, podderživaja neobchodimost' poiska ėffektivnych sobstvennikov dlja gosudarstvennogo imuščestva, choču obratit' vnimanie, čto my ne možem narušat' zakon.</lang>

<lang = "ru">A u nas est' Zakon "Ob ėkologičeskom audite", kotoryj preduprеždaet, čto ljubye dejstvija s takim krajne opasnym predprijatiem kak "Odesskij priportovyj zavod", v sostav kotorogo vchodit krupnejšee v Evrope ammiakochranilišče emkost'ju 120 tysjač tonn.</lang>

<lang = "ru">Vdumajtes' v ėtu cifru – 120 tysjač tonn ammiaka – ne mogut byt' sdelany bez objazatel'nogo ėkologičeskogo audita, k sožaleniju on do sich por ne vypolnen, a v tože vremja predstaviteli pravitel'stva dokladyvajut o planach privatizacii OPZ.</lang>

<lang = "ru">Choču obratit' vnimanie Kabineta Ministrov na neobchodimost' neukosnitel'nogo vypolnenija zakonodatel'stva Ukrainy v sfere ėkologii dlja togo čtoby obespečit' bezopasnost' žitelej Odessy millionnoj i gorodov vokrug nee.</lang>

<lang = "ru">Ved' Odesskij priportovoj zavod nachodit'sja vsego liš' v 15 kilometrach ot pervych mnogokvartirnych domov Odessy i bezopasnost' na nem ėto zalog žizni i zdorov'ja bolee milliona čelovek.</lang>

<lang = "ru">Spasibo.</lang>

C Language picture by political parties in parliament

[11]A typical example of incorrect automatic language detection of a short sentence.

Party	Convocation								
	6 (2007-2012)			7 (2012-2014)			8 (2014-2019)		
	UKR	RUS	Bilingual	UKR	RUS	Bilingual	UKR	RUS	Bilingual
Our Ukraine–People's Self-Defense Bloc / Блок «Наша Україна — Народна самооборона»	38	0	21						
Lytvyn Bloc / Блок Литвина	11	1	4						
Petro Poroshenko Bloc / Блок Петра Порошенка							74	1	46
Yulia Tymoshenko Bloc / Блок Юлії Тимошенко	66	2	40						
All-Ukrainian Agrarian Association "Spade" / ВАО «ЗАСТУП»							1	0	0
All-Ukrainian Union "Fatherland" / ВО «Батьківщина»				62	0	23	2	0	3
All-Ukrainian Union "Freedom" / ВО «Свобода»				24	0	9	2	0	3
Communist Party of Ukraine / Комуністична партія України	2	2	20	12	0	16			
People's Party / Народна партія				0	0	1			
People's Front / Народний фронт							53	0	22
Our Land / Наш край							1	0	0
Self Reliance / Об'єднання «Самопоміч»							13	0	15
Opposition Bloc / Опозиційний блок							4	4	12
Ukrainian Democratic Alliance for Reform of Vitali Klitschko / Партія «УДАР» Віталія Кличка				25	0	8			
Party of Regions / Партія регіонів	63	9	77	53	7	50			
Right Sector / Правий сектор							1	0	0
Radical Party of Oleh Liashko / Радикальна партія Олега Ляшка				0	0	1	10	0	12
Self-nomination				20	1	8	33	4	32
Union / Союз				0	0	1			
Ukrainian Association of Patriots / Українське об'єднання патріотів — УКРОП							3	0	0

Creating a POS Gold Standard Corpus of Modern Ukrainian

Vasyl Starko
Ukrainian Catholic University
Ukraine
vstarko@gmail.com

Andriy Rysin
Independent researcher
USA
arysin@gmail.com

Abstract

This paper presents an ongoing project to create the Ukrainian Brown Corpus (BRUK), a disambiguated corpus of Modern Ukrainian. Inspired by and loosely based on the original Brown University corpus, BRUK contains one million words, spans 11 years (2010–2020), and represents edited written Ukrainian. Using stratified random sampling, we have selected fragments of texts from multiple sources to ensure maximum variety, fill nine predefined categories, and produce a balanced corpus. BRUK has been automatically POS-tagged with the help of our tools (a large morphological dictionary of Ukrainian and a tagger). A manually disambiguated and validated subset of BRUK (450,000 words) has been made available online. This gold standard, the biggest of its kind for Ukrainian, fills a critical need in the NLP ecosystem for this language. The ultimate goal is to produce a fully disambiguated one-million corpus of Modern Ukrainian.

1 Introduction

Ukrainian has a growing ecosystem of NLP datasets and tools. Still, it falls into the category of low-resource languages, despite increasing interest in the language and the development of multiple resources and tools over the past couple of years. Most general-purpose corpora that are available for Ukrainian, such as the General Regionally Annotated Corpus of Ukrainian (GRAC) by Shvedova et al. (2017-2023), Zvidusil by Kotsyba et al. (2018), and the Ukrainian Language Corpus (KUM) by Darchuk (2003-2023) and her team, are only accessible via a web user interface. Among downloadable Ukrainian corpora, one project that stands out here thanks to its size and thoroughness is UberText 2.0 by Chaplynskyi (2023). However, one of the missing resources is a reliable, balanced, and disambiguated corpus of sufficient size.

Until recently, the only such resource was the treebank created within the Universal Dependencies project by Natalia Kotsyba, Bohdan Moskalevskyi, and Mykhailo Romanenko.[1] With the overall size of some 120,000 tokens, it is comprised of fiction (24%), essays (8%), legal acts (7%), fairytales (7%), analytical articles (6.5%), news (6%), commentary (5%), textbooks (5%), Wikipedia articles (5%), scholarly works (4%), letters (3%), and some other types.[2] The creators made a laudable effort to include a wide variety of texts, and their resource has been invaluable for Ukrainian NLP. Nevertheless, some aspects require improvement. For one thing, the texts in the UD Ukrainian treebank come both from modern sources (past 15–20 years) and the first half of the 20th century, which does not make the entire treebank representative of any one period. Second, the proportions of text types are far from reflecting either the production or the consumption of texts in modern Ukrainian society. For example, news is significantly more popular than its share in this treebank would suggest. Third, a bigger corpus would help achieve better quality of NLP models. Furthermore, the small proportions of all types, except fiction, in the treebank complicate the task of training or fine-tuning models for a specific type. Finally, the development of this treebank seems to have come to a halt several years ago.

2 Corpus Design

Perceiving the need for a more balanced and larger disambiguated corpus, we have developed the Ukrainian Brown Corpus (BRUK)[3] modeled on the original Brown University corpus. The Brown University Standard Corpus of Present-Day American English (Francis and Kucera, 1979) has been an indispensable resource for the development of computational linguistics. It has given rise to

[1] https://universaldependencies.org/treebanks/uk_iu/index.html
[2] https://mova.institute/
[3] https://github.com/brown-uk/corpus

Proceedings of the Second Ukrainian Natural Language Processing Workshop (UNLP), pages 91–95
May 5, 2023

an entire family of Brown corpora, including the Lancaster-Oslo/Bergen Corpus (LOB) (Johansson, 1978), the Freiburg-Brown Corpus of American English (FROWN) (Hundt et al., 1998) and Freiburg-LOB Corpus of British English (FLOB) (Hinrichs et al., 2007) (Leech and Smith, 2005). Similar corpora have also been constructed for other languages (Koeva et al., 2006) and successfully used for training NLP models.

In order to establish the categorial structure of BRUK, we have used the same method of an expert poll with averaged results as did Henry Kucera and W. Nelson Francis and kept the overall split into informative and imaginative types. However, further subdivision into categories is different as it is aimed at reflecting the prevalence of each category of texts in modern Ukrainian society. This is in line with the established practice as corpora derived from the Brown University corpus include modifications on the original design and adjustments to account for the specific features of the language and country in question. The categories thus established for BRUK are as follows (percentages represent proportions of the total size):

A. Press, 25%. While BRUK has no formal subdivision into reportage, editorials, and reviews, a special effort has been made to represent these subcategories and ensure topical diversity (politics, society, finances, sports, culture, and environment). This category includes texts selected from national, regional, and local (city or district-level) mass media outlets in both printed and electronic form.

B. Religion, 3%. Importantly, texts representing different religions have been included.

C. Skills and Hobbies, 7%. Popular topics, such as household, crafts, farming, gardening, and construction, are represented.

D. Essays, Biography, Memoirs, etc., 7%. This is a catch-all category for informative texts that do not fit elsewhere, including forewords, personal letters, and literary and art criticism.

E. Administrative Documents, 3%. Laws, government regulations, reports, and official letters comprise this category.

F. Popular Science, 5%. Experts agreed that these texts required a separate category due to their linguistic characteristics.

G. Science, 10%. A balanced selection of texts in natural sciences and the humanities has been made.

H. Textbooks, 15%. This sizable category reflects the important role such texts play in Ukraine, where a wide audience of students reads them.

I. Fiction, 25%. While no formal subdivision has been adopted, variety is ensured by selecting works of different lengths (from short stories to novels) and genres.

In filling each category in the corpus with texts, we employed random sampling through crowdsourcing: more than a hundred individuals were involved in sample selection. Submitted samples were verified and filtered by corpus creators, for example, to remove duplicates and avoid overrepresentation of a particular newspaper, author, or topic.

Each text fragment in the corpus is supplied with metadata identifying the author(s), title, book/journal title (if applicable), place and year of publication, publisher, page range, length in tokens, orthography (official or alternative), and detected errors. Metadata information is stored separately from texts in a .csv file available for download and processing. Each file containing a text fragment is given a name that begins with a letter (A–I) for the respective category, enabling users to quickly separate the necessary category from the entire corpus.

3 Text Requirements

Texts in BRUK must meet a set of requirements, some of which mirror those for the original Brown University Corpus, while others represent a conscious departure from its model to match the realities of modern Ukrainian better:

1 Original (not translated) and human-written texts. The primary challenge here was to weed out texts surreptitiously translated from Russian (a common practice among some publishers and mass media outlets in Ukraine) and products of machine translation. In doubtful cases, we opted to err on the side of exclusion.

2 Edited prose only. Non-prose works, e.g., poems and drama pieces, are excluded, as are non-edited texts. In dubious cases, we rejected texts that clearly needed editing.

3 Written, rather than spoken, texts. BRUK generally represents written Ukrainian with only a sprinkle of "quasi-spoken" texts. Fiction may include dialogue, and some news articles contain interviews. Several texts selected for the corpus

were first spoken and then written down, such as public speeches and sermons.

4 Texts first published in 2010–2020. We excluded texts with the publication date within this period but written much earlier. The original Brown corpus represents one year. This narrow focus led to certain entities and topics being overrepresented, such as U.S. President John F. Kennedy and the tense U.S. relations with the Soviet Union before the Cuban Missile Crisis. For BRUK, we decided to draw samples from a longer period (11 years) in an effort to overcome this issue and ensure a better topical balance.

5 Texts published in mainland Ukraine. While diaspora texts are essential for the Ukrainian language, they are characterized by a number of divergencies in spelling, grammar, and lexis. They need to be collected in a separate corpus, which would make a valuable complement to BRUK.

6 Up to 2,000 words in total from one source. While the original Brown Corpus contained 500 continuous samples of text, each around 2,000 words long, BRUK is more fragmented as it is comprised of more fragments that are smaller in size. Most fragments contain less than 1,000 words of running text, and just a handful reach the 2,000-word mark. This approach has made it possible to include a greater variety of sources.

Detailed annotation guidelines[4] have been used by all contributors to BRUK.

4 POS tagging

4.1 Tools

BRUK has been automatically part-of-speech tagged using VESUM[5], a Large Electronic Dictionary of Ukrainian, and the TagText tagger for Ukrainian, part of the NLP UK toolkit for Ukrainian[6]. For proofreading the disambiguated part of BRUK, we used a modified Ukrainian module of LanguageTool[7], particularly its token agreement and case government rules. This allowed us to automatically detect a number of POS tagging errors that are hard to catch for human annotators. One of the determining factors in favor of these tools is that VESUM is the largest machine-readable morphological dictionary of Ukrainian. Its current version (6.1.1) comprises over 418,000 lemmas from which more than 6.5 million wordforms are generated. The dictionary achieves 97–99% word coverage on non-encyclopedic texts. Moreover, the TagText tagger includes a dynamic tagging component to recognize and tag words not found in VESUM, reaching 95% accuracy on these out-of-vocabulary items (Starko and Rysin, 2022). This combination of tools has been successfully utilized to tag successive iterations of GRAC, a large reference corpus of Ukrainian (Shvedova, 2020) (Starko et al., 2021). Second, unlike other morphological dictionaries of Ukrainian, VESUM includes numerous proper nouns and nonstandard lemmas, such as alternative spellings, slang, deprecated lexical items, dialectal words, and substandard wordforms, which are not to be found in other lexicographic resources. These linguistic items occur in modern texts and need to be duly recognized.

4.2 POS Tagset

BRUK has been tagged using the POS tagset of 21 tags, some of which are supplied by the VESUM dictionary and others assigned by TagText dynamically as it processes texts:

1 Inflection classes from VESUM: noun, verb, adj(ective), adv(erb), advp (adverbial participle), numr (numeral), conj(unction), prep(osition), part(icle), int(erjection), onomat(opoeic word), foreign (transliteration into Ukrainian), and noninfl(ected word that does not fit elsewhere).

2 Dynamic tags: number, date, time, hashtag, punct(uation), symb(ol), unknown (word written in Ukrainian letters but not recognized), and unclass (word that cannot belong to the Ukrainian lexicon, e.g., alphanumeric abbreviations, words in Latin script, non-Ukrainian words in Cyrillic, etc.).

Additional tags found in BRUK that describe, among other things, specific morphological features of Ukrainian words, such as case, number, and gender for nouns, can be looked up online[8].

[4] https://github.com/brown-uk/corpus/blob/master/doc/vymohy_do_frahmentiv.md

[5] https://github.com/brown-uk/dict_uk

[6] https://github.com/brown-uk/nlp_uk

[7] https://github.com/languagetool-org/languagetool/tree/master/languagetool-language-modules/uk

[8] https://github.com/brown-uk/dict_uk/blob/master/doc/tags.txt

Texts tagged with the tools described above will contain part-of-speech ambiguity, with merely several hundred cases of ambiguity resolved automatically (Starko and Rysin, 2022). Thus, the next step in preparing BRUK was the manual disambiguation of automatically POS-tagged texts.

5 Disambiguation

Ukrainian is a highly inflected language with ubiquitous lexical and morphological ambiguity. In BRUK, an ambiguous word may have from 2 to over 30 homonymic readings.

As of this writing, ambiguity has been resolved for 450,000 Ukrainian words (560,000 tokens), making the disambiguated subset of BRUK the biggest such resource for Ukrainian. This part comprises 80,000 Ukrainian types and over 37,000 lemmas. Morphological ambiguity (58% of the words in the disambiguated subset of BRUK) is much more prevalent in Ukrainian than lexical ambiguity (13%), and a Ukrainian word has 2.88 homonym interpretations on average.

After automatic tokenization, lemmatization, and POS tagging (all performed by TagText), BRUK texts were subjected to a two-stage (in some cases, three-stage) disambiguation process. Initially, ambiguity was resolved by trained individuals (students), and these results were then verified by an expert linguist. Another expert was consulted in difficult cases. The nuances of tagging were communicated to students during training, and a number of challenging cases are explained in tagging guidelines[9]. The outcome of this process is a set of disambiguated texts in which each token has one correct and verified reading.

6 Conclusions and Future Work

The Ukrainian Brown Corpus (BRUK) is a one-million balanced corpus of modern Ukrainian covering 2010–2020. It is loosely modeled on the original Brown University corpus and consists of small fragments (mostly up to 1,000 but no longer than 2,000 words of running text) divided between 9 categories. The creators have made a concerted effort to ensure variety in the corpus along different dimensions. The corpus has been automatically tokenized, lemmatized, and POS-tagged. A subset of BRUK (450,000 words) has been manually disambiguated, validated through a multi-stage process, and made available for download.

Several factors make BRUK a unique resource compared to other Ukrainian corpora: it is a balanced downloadable corpus comprised of Modern Ukrainian text samples that vary along several dimensions and is currently the largest corpus representing a POS gold standard for Ukrainian. BRUK has the potential to become a key resource in solving the foundational problem of POS disambiguation for a wide variety of practical projects. Other applications are also possible, such as testing spellchecking systems, NER models, and so on. BRUK has been used to build a stochastic model for POS tagging, generating a strong baseline. On the theoretical side, BRUK provides insights into Ukrainian morphology that have already helped us improve its formal description for the purposes of NLP and computational linguistics research.

Our immediate plans include the semiautomatic disambiguation of the rest of BRUK (550,000 words). It is desirable to complement BRUK with later publications to cover a rapidly growing number of texts about the unprovoked war Russia unleashed against Ukraine on 24 February 2022. Further plans include adding a dependency annotation layer to the corpus.

Another line of activity is training language models. Even if trained on the released subset of BRUK rather than the entire corpus, they can be instrumental in solving various computational linguistics and NLP tasks, bringing the Ukrainian language a step closer to the status of a mid-resource language.

Limitations

No corpus is fully representative of the language in question. By design, BRUK represents only modern written Ukrainian focusing on edited texts. Even though BRUK includes texts referring to the COVID-19 pandemic, a separate collection may need to be added to better represent this widely discussed topic. Furthermore, new official orthographic rules for Ukrainian were introduced in mid-2019. The spelling novelties are reflected in BRUK texts published in 2019–2020, but their proportion is relatively small compared to the pre-2019 texts. Even though the orthographic changes are not drastic, it might be advisable to complement the corpus with more after-reform texts.

[9]https://github.com/brown-uk/corpus/blob/master/doc/skladni_momenty_tegiv.md

Ethics Statement

Our work aims to enrich the ecosystem of NLP resources and tools for the Ukrainian language. By making the BRUK corpus downloadable, we hope to stimulate research into Ukrainian both inside Ukraine and worldwide. The broader impact of our project lies in the fact that BRUK can be used to train Ukrainian language models and utilize them in various other NLP projects, specifically to tag and disambiguate much larger Ukrainian corpora.

Acknowledgements

This research has been supported by a grant from the Humanities Faculty of the Ukrainian Catholic University and a private donation. We thank Olha Havura, Nastia Osidach, Natalia Olishkevych, Natalia Cheilytko, Mariana Romanyshyn, and many other colleagues and UCU students who have contributed to BRUK.

References

Dmytro Chaplynskyi. 2023. Introducing UberText 2.0: a corpus of modern Ukrainian at scale. In *Proceedings of the Second Ukrainian Natural Language Processing Workshop*, pages 1–10, Dubrovnik, Croatia. Association for Computational Linguistics.

Nataliia Darchuk. 2003-2023. Korpus ukrayinskoyi movy.

Nelson W. Francis and Henry Kucera. 1979. BROWN CORPUS MANUAL MANUAL OF INFORMATION to accompany A Standard Corpus of Present-Day Edited American English, for use with Digital Computers.

Lars Hinrichs, Nicholas Smith, and Birgit Waibel. 2007. The part-of-speech-tagged 'Brown' corpora: a manual of information, including pointers for successful use.

Marianne Hundt, Andrea Sand, and Rainer Siemund. 1998. Manual of Information to Accompany the Freiburg-Brown Corpus of American English (FROWN).

Stig Johansson. 1978. Manual of Information to Accompany the Lancaster- Oslo/Bergen Corpus of British English (FROWN).

Svetla Koeva, Svetlozara Leseva, Ivelina Stoyanova, Ekaterina Tarpomanova, and Maria Todorova. 2006. Bulgarian Tagged Corpora. *In Proceedings of the Fifth International Conference Formal Approaches to South Slavic and Balkan Languages*, pages 78–86.

Natalia Kotsyba, Bohdan Moskalevskyi, and Mykhailo Romanenko et al. 2018. Laboratoriya ukrayins'koyi.

Geoffrey Leech and Nicholas Smith. 2005. Extending the possibilities of corpus-based research on English in the twentieth century: A prequel to LOB and FLOB. *ICAME Journal*, 29:83–98.

Maria Shvedova. 2020. The General Regionally Annotated Corpus of Ukrainian (GRAC, uacorpus.org): Architecture and Functionality. In *International Conference on Computational Linguistics and Intelligent Systems*, pages 489–506, Lviv.

Maria Shvedova, Ruprecht von Waldenfels, Serhii Yaryhin, Andriy Rysin, Vasyl Starko, and Tymofij Nikolajenko et al. 2017-2023. GRAC: General Regionally Annotated Corpus of Ukrainian.

Vasyl Starko and Andriy Rysin. 2022. VESUM: A Large Morphological Dictionary of Ukrainian As a Dynamic Tool. In *Computational Linguistics and Intelligent Systems.*, volume 6th Int. Conf, pages 71–80, Gliwice. COLINS.

Vasyl Starko, Andriy Rysin, and Maria Shvedova. 2021. Ukrainian Text Preprocessing in GRAC. In *IEEE 16th International Conference on Computer Sciences and Information Technologies (CSIT)*, pages 101–104, Lviv.

UA-GEC: Grammatical Error Correction and Fluency Corpus for the Ukrainian Language

Oleksiy Syvokon
oleksiy.syvokon@gmail.com

Olena Nahorna
Grammarly
olena.nahorna@grammarly.com

Pavlo Kuchmiichuk
pavlo.kuchmiichuk@gmail.com

Nastasiia Osidach
Grammarly
nastasiya.osidach@grammarly.com

Abstract

We present a corpus professionally annotated for grammatical error correction (GEC) and fluency edits in the Ukrainian language. We have built two versions of the corpus – GEC+Fluency and GEC-only – to differentiate the corpus application. We collected texts with errors (33,735 sentences) from a diverse pool of contributors, including both native and non-native speakers. The data cover a wide variety of writing domains, from text chats and essays to formal writing. Professional proofreaders corrected and annotated the corpus for errors relating to fluency, grammar, punctuation, and spelling. This corpus can be used for developing and evaluating GEC systems in Ukrainian. More generally, it can be used for researching multilingual and low-resource NLP, morphologically rich languages, document-level GEC, and fluency correction. To test the effectiveness of our corpus, we trained a basic but reasonable baseline model. The corpus is publicly available at `https://github.com/grammarly/ua-gec`.

1 Introduction

Grammatical error correction (GEC) is a task of automatically detecting and correcting grammatical errors in written text. GEC is typically limited to making a minimal set of grammar, spelling, and punctuation edits so that the text becomes free of such errors. Fluency correction is an extension of GEC that allows for broader sentence rewrites to make a text more fluent—i.e., sounding natural to a native speaker (Sakaguchi et al., 2016).

Over the past decade, NLP researchers have been primarily focused on English GEC, where they indeed made substantial progress: $F_{0.5}$ score of the best-performing model in the CoNLL-2014 shared task has increased from 37.33 in 2014 to 68.75 in 2022 (Ng et al., 2014; Rothe et al., 2021). Multiple available datasets and shared tasks were a major contributing factor to that success.

However, languages other than English still present a set of challenges for current NLP methods. Mainstream models developed with English in mind are suboptimal for morphologically rich languages as well as languages with differing grammar (Tsarfaty et al., 2020; Ravfogel et al., 2018; Hu et al., 2020; Ahmad et al., 2019). The common issue is a scarcity of data—particularly high-quality annotated data that could be used for evaluation and fine-tuning.

More recently, the NLP community has started to pay more attention to non-English NLP (Ruder, 2020). This positive recent trend manifests itself in the creation of new GEC corpora for mid- and low-resource languages: German, Czech, and Spanish, to name a few (Boyd, 2018; Náplava and Straka, 2019; Davidson et al., 2020). These datasets are important to expand NLP research to new languages and to explore new ways of training models in a low-resource setting.

Furthering that trend, we present a corpus annotated for grammatical errors and fluency in the Ukrainian language: UA-GEC. We first collected texts from a diverse pool of writers, both native and non-native speakers. The corpus covers a wide variety of domains: essays, social media posts, chats, formal writing, and more. We recruited professional proofreaders to correct errors related to grammar, spelling, punctuation, and fluency. Our corpus is open source for the community[2] under the CC-BY 4.0 license.

To summarize, our contributions are as follows:

- For the first time, diverse texts in Ukrainian are collected and annotated for grammatical, punctuation, spelling, and fluency errors.
- The corpus is released for public use under the CC-BY 4.0 licence.
- A baseline model is trained.

[2] `https://github.com/grammarly/ua-gec`

Proceedings of the Second Ukrainian Natural Language Processing Workshop (UNLP), pages 96–102
May 5, 2023 ©2023 Association for Computational Linguistics

Split	Writers	Texts	Sentences	Tokens	Annotations	Error rate
Train	752	1,706	31,038	457,017	38,383	8.1%
Test	76	166	2,697	43,601	7,865	9.0%
TOTAL	828	1,872	33,735	500,618	46,248	8.2%

Table 1: The GEC+Fluency corpus statistics. Test split is independently annotated by two annotators (*Error rate* is the average of the two in this case)

Split	Writers	Texts	Sentences	Tokens	Annotations	Error rate
Train	752	1,706	31,046	457,004	29,390	6.1%
Test	76	166	2,704	43,605	5,931	6.8%
TOTAL	828	1,872	33,750	500,609	35,321	6.3%

Table 2: The GEC-only corpus statistics. Test split is independently annotated by two annotators (*Error rate* is the average of the two in this case)

2 Data collection

In this section, we describe the collection of texts with errors in the Ukrainian language. Section 3 will explain the annotation details.

2.1 Statistics

Parameter		Writers	Sent.
Native	Yes	600	27,646
	No	238	6,072
Gender	Female	537	18,520
	Male	288	14,212
	Other	9	986
Background	Technical	291	13,654
	Humanities	356	12,819
	Natural sci.	39	1,389
	Other	168	5,856

Table 3: Profile of respondents

We have collected 1,872 texts (33,735 sentences) written by 492 unique contributors. The average length of a text snippet is 18 sentences.

We partition the corpus into training and test sets. Each split consists of texts written by a randomly chosen disjoint set of people: all of a particular person's writing goes to exactly one of the splits. To better account for alternative corrections, we annotated the test set two times (Bryant and Ng, 2015). The resulting statistics are shown in Table 2.

In order to collect the data, we created an online form for text submission. All respondents who contributed to the data collection were volunteers. To attract a socially diverse pool of authors, we shared the form on social media. It contained a list of questions related to gender, native tongue, region of birth, and occupation, making it possible to further balance subcorpora and tailor them so they meet the purpose of various NLP tasks. Table 3 illustrates the profile of respondents based on some of these parameters.

2.2 Collection tasks

The online form offered a choice of three tasks: 1) writing an essay; 2) translating a fictional text fragment into Ukrainian; 3) submitting a personal text. Our goal was to collect a corpus of texts that would reflect errors typically made by native and non-native speakers of Ukrainian. Therefore, before performing a task, the respondents were asked not to proofread their texts as well as to refrain from making intentional errors. Each task varied in the number of requirements.

Write an essay on the topic "What's your favorite animal?" Genre: fictional. In the essay, state: what your favorite animal is; what it looks like; why you like this particular animal; whether you would like to keep it at home. Volume: about 15 sentences.
Write a letter of complaint. Recipient: a restaurant administrator. Genre: formal. In the letter, state: the date of your visit to the restaurant; the reason for your complaint; your suggestions about how the restaurant could improve its service. Volume: about 15 sentences.

Table 4: Examples of the essay prompts. In total, there were 20 prompts in the *Essay* task.

Essays. Respondents were offered one of twenty essay topics, each stipulating the genre, length, and structure of the essay. We chose from among the most common topics for essays (e.g., "What was your childhood dream?") not requiring a profound knowledge of a certain subject, which made it easy for the respondents to produce texts. Each essay was supposed to be written in accordance with one of four genres: formal, informal, fictional, or journalistic. The scientific genre was excluded as a potential writing blocker due to its inherent complexity. Specification of the genre allowed us to moderate the heterogeneity of the corpus. Besides topic and genre requirements, each task description contained prompts—i.e., prearranged points to cover in the text that facilitated text production. Refer Table 4 for essay prompts examples.

Translation of fictional texts. Fictional text fragments were taken from public domain books written by classic authors in five languages: English, French, German, Polish, and Russian. The rationale behind suggesting translation from a range of foreign languages was to diversify the errors made by respondents as a result of L1 interference.

Personal texts. Unlike the aforementioned tasks, personal text submission was not explicitly regulated: respondents could submit texts of any genre, length, or structure. However, no more than 300 sentences submitted by a unique person were added to the corpus. This was done to balance the corpus from an idiolect perspective.

UA-GEC is mostly composed of personal texts (62%); fictional texts translations rank second (35%), and essays are the least numerous (3%).

3 Data annotation

We enrolled two annotators on the project, both native speakers of Ukrainian with a degree in Ukrainian linguistics. One of them was a freelance editor, and the other was a teacher of Ukrainian.

In order to diversify the type of tasks one can perform using the corpus, we released two versions of UA-GEC: GEC+Fluency and GEC-only. The former surfaces spelling, punctuation, grammar errors as well as errors associated with unnatural-sounding sentence elements. The latter captures only GEC errors, which makes it possible to perform tasks that are narrower and more objective in scope.

GEC+Fluency. The annotation process encompassed two sequential subtasks: error correction followed by error labeling. We found that the given annotation design was more efficient than performing error correction and labeling in a combined mode as it would increase the cognitive load of the task.

GEC-only. After having the data fully edited and labeled, we programmatically removed edits labeled as Fluency and had annotators review the remaining annotations to make sure Fluency-dependent edits were still valid and correct suggestions that no longer made sense.

3.1 Annotation format

The categorized errors in the processed data are marked by the following in-text notations: `{error=>edit:::Tag}`, where `error` and `edit` stand for the text item before and after correction, respectively, and `Tag` denotes an error category. Table 5 lists example sentences annotated for each high-level category.

Besides error correction and labeling, the annotators were asked to identify sensitive content—i.e., sentences containing pejorative lexis or perpetuating bias related to race, gender, age, etc. Such sentences are marked in the metadata, which enables simple data filtering to debias it by the stated criteria. The GitHub repository contains a detailed description of the annotation scheme along with a Python library to process the corpora.

3.2 Error categories

Our label set includes four high-level categories: punctuation, spelling, grammar and fluency. Additionally, grammar and fluency suggestions are further divided into fine-grained categories. Table 6 provides a detailed description of error categories and Table 7 demonstrates the error distribution by category.

`Spelling` accounts for 19% of all corrections. This is similar to RULEC-GEC (Rozovskaya and Roth, 2019), where the portion of spelling errors is 21.7%. `Punctuation` edits (43%) are more frequent than in other corpora (for example, in the W&I corpus (Bryant et al., 2019), `Punctuation` is 17%). We explain this by the fact that in the Ukrainian language, punctuation rules are sharply defined; thus, a lot of punctuation marks are frequently misused, especially commas. Also, there were a large number of typographical fixes, like replacing a dash ("-") with an em-dash ("—") where appropriate. Grammatical errors (`G/`) accounts for 14.4% of all errors.

Fluency. The fluency category (`F/`) embraces error types that have to do with the inaccurate use of lexical or structural units. Specifically, such edits relate to the correction of miscollocations and

Error type	Example
Grammar	Він {ходимо=>ходить:::G/Number} до школи. `He {go=>goes:::Grammar} to school.`
Spelling	Він {хотв=>хотів:::Spelling} поговорити. `He {wnted=>wanted:::Spelling} to talk.`
Punctuation	Ти будеш завтра вдома {=>?:::Punctuation} `Are you going to be home tomorrow {=>?:::Punctuation}`
Fluency	{Існуючі =>Теперішні:::F/Style} ціни дуже високі. `{Existing=>Current:::Fluency} prices are very high.`

Table 5: Examples of annotation in each error category

Error type	Description
Grammar-related errors	
G/Case	incorrect usage of case of any notional part of speech
G/Gender	incorrect usage of gender of any notional part of speech
G/Number	incorrect usage of number of any notional part of speech
G/Aspect	incorrect usage of verb aspect
G/Tense	incorrect usage of verb tense
G/VerbVoice	incorrect usage of verb voice
G/PartVoice	incorrect usage of participle voice
G/VerbAForm	incorrect usage of an analytical verb form
G/Prep	incorrect preposition usage
G/Participle	incorrect usage of participles
G/UngrammaticalStructure	digression from syntactic norms
G/Comparison	incorrect formation of comparison degrees of adj. and adverbs
G/Conjunction	incorrect usage of conjunctions
G/Other	other grammatical errors
Fluency-related errors	
F/Style	style errors
F/Calque	word-for-word translation from other languages
F/Collocation	unnatural collocations
F/PoorFlow	unnatural sentence flow
F/Repetition	repetition of words
F/Other	other fluency errors

Table 6: Description of Grammar and Fluency fine-grained categories

calques, words inappropriate from a style perspective, rewriting syntactic structures that contain dysfluencies (repetitions, redundancies, etc.) or simply sound awkward to a native speaker.

`Fluency` accounts for 23.6% of all errors. This may be attributed to the fact that around 30% of respondents were not native Ukrainian speakers and therefore used a lot of calques, both lexical and structural, from other languages. Another reason is style correction: annotators corrected non-standard language into standard one to make the text sound more fluent and natural.

3.3 Inter-annotator agreement

Pass 1	Pass 2	Error rate	Unchanged
Ann. A	Ann. B	2.9%	64%
Ann. B	Ann. A	1.2%	75%

Table 8: Inter-annotator agreement based on the second-pass proofreading. *Error rate* is the density of annotations made on the already corrected text. *Unchanged* is the percentage of sentences that have not been changed on the second pass.

We follow the Rozovskaya and Roth (2010) setup for computing the inter-annotator agreement. A

Error type	Total	%	Per 1000 tokens
Grammar (all)	6,682	14.4	11.9
Fluency (all)	10,924	23.6	19.4
Spelling	8,771	19.0	15.6
Punctuation	19,871	43.0	35.3
F/Calque	2,397	5.2	4.3
F/Collocation	459	1.0	0.8
F/Other	245	0.5	0.4
F/PoorFlow	3,477	7.5	6.2
F/Repetition	621	1.3	1.1
F/Style	3,725	8.1	6.6
G/Aspect	92	0.2	0.2
G/Case	2,536	5.5	4.5
G/Comparison	135	0.3	0.2
G/Conjunction	417	0.9	0.7
G/Gender	539	1.2	1.0
G/Number	409	0.9	0.7
G/Other	236	0.5	0.4
G/PartVoice	99	0.2	0.2
G/Participle	2	0.0	0.0
G/Particle	60	0.1	0.1
G/Prep	542	1.2	1.0
G/Tense	223	0.5	0.4
G/Ungrammatical Structure	1,046	2.3	1.9
G/VerbAForm	52	0.1	0.1
G/VerbVoice	294	0.6	0.5
TOTAL	46,248	100.0	82.1

Table 7: Error distribution by category

text that was corrected by one annotator is passed to the other annotator. *Agreement* then is the percentage of sentences that did not require any changes during the second pass. This metric is important, given that our goal is to make a sentence well-formed, no matter whether the annotators propose the same changes (Rozovskaya and Roth, 2019). We run this evaluation on a set of 200 sentences. Table 8 shows that 64% of sentences corrected by Annotator A remained unchanged after the Annotator B's pass. The error rate has dropped from 7.1% to 2.9% errors. Similarly, Annotator A that proofreads after Annotator B leaves 75% of sentences unchanged.

This inter-annotator agreement (64%/75% of unchanged sentences) is in line with other GEC corpora: for English the reported numbers are 37%/59%, for Russian they are 69%/91% (Rozovskaya and Roth, 2010, 2019).

3.4 Comparison to other GEC datasets

Table 9 lists statistics of our corpus in relation to some similar GEC corpora in other languages.

Language	Corpus	Sent.	Er.
English	Lang-8	1,147,451	14.1
	NUCLE	57,151	6.6
	FCE	33,236	11.5
	W&I+L	43,169	11.8
	JFLEG	1,511	
	CWEB	13,574	1.74
Czech	AKCES-GEC	47,371	21.4
German	Falko-MERLIN	24,077	16.8
Romanian	RONACC	10,119	
Russian	RULEC-GEC	12,480	6.4
Spanish	COWS-L2H [3]	12,336	
Ukrainian	**UA-GEC**	**33,735**	**8.2**

Table 9: Statistics of related GEC corpora. *Er.* is the error rate, in percent. This work is highlighted in bold.

4 Model

To prove the utility of our dataset, we trained a simple baseline model. We fine-tuned mBART-50-large (Tang et al., 2021) on the UA-GEC train data without any preprocessing or data augmentation, similarly to (Katsumata and Komachi, 2020).

The model was fine-tuned for 3 epochs using Adam optimizer with a learning rate of 5e-5 and batch size of 8. We used greedy decoding. The full training cycle takes around 3 hours on a single Nvidia P100 GPU.

4.1 Results

Table 10 shows the results of our baseline model on the test set.

Task	Precision	Recall	$F_{0.5}$
GEC only	0.7706	0.5004	0.6955
GEC+Fluency	0.6996	0.4159	0.6156

Table 10: Results of the baseline model on the test set.

5 Conclusion

We release the first professionally annotated corpus. We hope it will facilitate further development of grammatical error correction in the Ukrainian language. The corpus is made publicly available at `https://github.com/grammarly/ua-gec` under the CC-BY 4.0 license.

[3]COWS-L2H statistics is for March 2021

Limitations

UA-GEC has some limitations that must be taken into account.

First, the dataset has been annotated with only two annotators, so their linguistic biases and preferences may affect the annotation of the dataset.

Second, despite our best efforts, it is not guaranteed that the accuracy of the corrected text will be perfect. It is possible that some errors may be overlooked by the annotators or that unnecessary corrections may be made.

Finally, a part of the dataset consists of translations from other languages. This could induce specific types of errors which are not generalizable across different types of text.

Acknowledgments

This work is supported by Grammarly. We thank Ira Kotkalova, Anna Vesnii, Halyna Kolodkevych, and everyone else who participated in the corpus creation.

References

Wasi Ahmad, Zhisong Zhang, Xuezhe Ma, Eduard Hovy, Kai-Wei Chang, and Nanyun Peng. 2019. On difficulties of cross-lingual transfer with order differences: A case study on dependency parsing. In *Proceedings of the 2019 Conference of the North American Chapter of the Association for Computational Linguistics: Human Language Technologies, Volume 1 (Long and Short Papers)*, pages 2440–2452, Minneapolis, Minnesota. Association for Computational Linguistics.

Adriane Boyd. 2018. Using Wikipedia edits in low resource grammatical error correction. In *Proceedings of the 2018 EMNLP Workshop W-NUT: The 4th Workshop on Noisy User-generated Text*, pages 79–84, Brussels, Belgium. Association for Computational Linguistics.

Christopher Bryant, Mariano Felice, Øistein E. Andersen, and Ted Briscoe. 2019. The BEA-2019 shared task on grammatical error correction. In *Proceedings of the Fourteenth Workshop on Innovative Use of NLP for Building Educational Applications*, pages 52–75, Florence, Italy. Association for Computational Linguistics.

Christopher Bryant and Hwee Tou Ng. 2015. How far are we from fully automatic high quality grammatical error correction? In *Proceedings of the 53rd Annual Meeting of the Association for Computational Linguistics and the 7th International Joint Conference on Natural Language Processing (Volume 1: Long Papers)*, pages 697–707, Beijing, China. Association for Computational Linguistics.

Sam Davidson, Qiusi Sun, and Magdalena Wojcieszak. 2020. Developing a new classifier for automated identification of incivility in social media. In *Proceedings of the Fourth Workshop on Online Abuse and Harms*, pages 95–101, Online. Association for Computational Linguistics.

Junjie Hu, Sebastian Ruder, Aditya Siddhant, Graham Neubig, Orhan Firat, and Melvin Johnson. 2020. Xtreme: A massively multilingual multi-task benchmark for evaluating cross-lingual generalization.

Satoru Katsumata and Mamoru Komachi. 2020. Stronger baselines for grammatical error correction using a pretrained encoder-decoder model. In *Proceedings of the 1st Conference of the Asia-Pacific Chapter of the Association for Computational Linguistics and the 10th International Joint Conference on Natural Language Processing*, pages 827–832, Suzhou, China. Association for Computational Linguistics.

Jakub Náplava and Milan Straka. 2019. Grammatical error correction in low-resource scenarios. In *Proceedings of the 5th Workshop on Noisy User-generated Text (W-NUT 2019)*, pages 346–356, Hong Kong, China. Association for Computational Linguistics.

Hwee Tou Ng, Siew Mei Wu, Ted Briscoe, Christian Hadiwinoto, Raymond Hendy Susanto, and Christopher Bryant. 2014. The CoNLL-2014 shared task on grammatical error correction. In *Proceedings of the Eighteenth Conference on Computational Natural Language Learning: Shared Task*, pages 1–14, Baltimore, Maryland. Association for Computational Linguistics.

Shauli Ravfogel, Yoav Goldberg, and Francis Tyers. 2018. Can LSTM learn to capture agreement? the case of Basque. In *Proceedings of the 2018 EMNLP Workshop BlackboxNLP: Analyzing and Interpreting Neural Networks for NLP*, pages 98–107, Brussels, Belgium. Association for Computational Linguistics.

Sascha Rothe, Jonathan Mallinson, Eric Malmi, Sebastian Krause, and Aliaksei Severyn. 2021. A simple recipe for multilingual grammatical error correction. In *Proceedings of the 59th Annual Meeting of the Association for Computational Linguistics and the 11th International Joint Conference on Natural Language Processing (Volume 2: Short Papers)*, pages 702–707, Online. Association for Computational Linguistics.

Alla Rozovskaya and Dan Roth. 2010. Annotating ESL errors: Challenges and rewards. In *Proceedings of the NAACL HLT 2010 Fifth Workshop on Innovative Use of NLP for Building Educational Applications*, pages 28–36, Los Angeles, California. Association for Computational Linguistics.

Alla Rozovskaya and Dan Roth. 2019. Grammar error correction in morphologically rich languages: The case of Russian. *Transactions of the Association for Computational Linguistics*, 7:1–17.

Sebastian Ruder. 2020. Why You Should Do NLP Beyond English. http://ruder.io/nlp-beyond-english.

Keisuke Sakaguchi, Courtney Napoles, Matt Post, and Joel Tetreault. 2016. Reassessing the goals of grammatical error correction: Fluency instead of grammaticality. *Transactions of the Association for Computational Linguistics*, 4:169–182.

Yuqing Tang, Chau Tran, Xian Li, Peng-Jen Chen, Naman Goyal, Vishrav Chaudhary, Jiatao Gu, and Angela Fan. 2021. Multilingual translation from denoising pre-training. In *Findings of the Association for Computational Linguistics: ACL-IJCNLP 2021*, pages 3450–3466, Online. Association for Computational Linguistics.

Reut Tsarfaty, Dan Bareket, Stav Klein, and Amit Seker. 2020. From SPMRL to NMRL: What did we learn (and unlearn) in a decade of parsing morphologically-rich languages (MRLs)? In *Proceedings of the 58th Annual Meeting of the Association for Computational Linguistics*, pages 7396–7408, Online. Association for Computational Linguistics.

Comparative Study of Models Trained on Synthetic Data for Ukrainian Grammatical Error Correction

Maksym Bondarenko
Columbia University
New York, USA
mb5018
@columbia.edu

Artem Yushko
Carleton College
Northfield, USA
yushkoa
@carleton.edu

Andrii Shportko
Northwestern University
Evanston, USA
andreshportko2026
@u.northwestern.edu

Andrii Fedorych
Taras Shevchenko
National University
Kyiv, Ukraine
andrii.t.fedorych
@gmail.com

Abstract

The task of Grammatical Error Correction (GEC) has been extensively studied for the English language. However, its application to low-resource languages, such as Ukrainian, remains an open challenge. In this paper, we develop sequence tagging and neural machine translation models for the Ukrainian language as well as a set of algorithmic correction rules to augment those systems. We also develop synthetic data generation techniques for the Ukrainian language to create high-quality human-like errors. Finally, we determine the best combination of synthetically generated data to augment the existing UA-GEC corpus and achieve the state-of-the-art results of 0.663 $F_{0.5}$ score on the newly established UA-GEC benchmark. The code and trained models will be made publicly available on GitHub and HuggingFace. [1] [2]

1 Introduction

Grammatical error correction (GEC) models have achieved significant results for English (Bryant et al., 2022). However, GEC for Ukrainian is an open challenge for multiple reasons. Even though Ukrainian is the official language of Ukraine with more than 40 million speakers worldwide[3], there are still few NLP corpora, studies, or tools available (Pogorilyy and Kramov, 2020). This lack of resources may be explained by the small pool of speakers (less than one percent of the world population), but also the many intrinsic difficulties of Ukrainian, including the historical suppression of the language by the USSR, the high prevalence of its mixture with Russian (surzhyk), and the formal context in which texts are commonly written (Buk and Rovenchak, 2003). The biggest difficulty is that Ukrainian is a low-resource language, and has only one annotated GEC dataset available (Syvokon and Nahorna, 2021) and few high-quality pre-trained transformer models compared to English[4]. Additionally, Ukrainian is a morphologically complex language, which makes its grammar correction more challenging with token-based models. The Ukrainian language also does not have rigid word order, which makes syntactic analysis more difficult. Finally, Ukrainian grammar contains lots of exceptions that are not widely known within the main body of native speakers, which makes GEC even more challenging (Syvokon and Nahorna, 2021).

In this paper, we outline the thought process behind and the development of seq2tag and NMT models for the Ukrainian language. Moreover, we outline the creation of algorithmic correction rules in addition to those architectures. We also assemble a clean corpus of 1mln sentences and develop generators of high-quality human-like errors for it. Finally, we compare our models and find the best combination of synthetically-made data with the existing UA-GEC corpus and achieve the best results on the newly established UA-GEC benchmark.

2 Related Work

2.1 Models for GEC

Two dominant state-of-the-art approaches for GEC in the English language are transformer-based neural machine translation (NMT) and sequence tagging (seq2tag) (Bryant et al., 2022). NMT approach treats GEC as a translation task, where the model must learn to translate from the errorful language to grammatically sound sentences (Sennrich et al., 2016). Recent advances in machine translation mean that many effective architectures and pre-trained models for translation exist, and applying them to GEC requires simple fine-tuning on GEC corpora. Sequence tagging as described in PIE (Awasthi et al., 2019) leverages the fact that

[1] https://github.com/pravopysnyk-ai/unlp
[2] https://huggingface.co/Pravopysnyk
[3] https://photius.com/rankings/languages2.html
[4] https://huggingface.co/models?pipeline_tag=fill-mask&language=uk&sort=downloads

Proceedings of the Second Ukrainian Natural Language Processing Workshop (UNLP), pages 103–113
May 5, 2023 ©2023 Association for Computational Linguistics

most tokens in the sentence do not need to be corrected and treats GEC as a token classification task, where each token is assigned a label to either keep it as it is, delete it, or replace it. In the GECToR paper (Omelianchuk et al., 2020), they build on this idea by introducing a number of G-transforms that decrease the number of required labels without sacrificing error coverage to achieve better data efficiency. Both approaches have their strengths and weaknesses in application to the Ukrainian GEC. As the recent research (Flachs et al., 2021) showed, NMT models for non-English languages require less pre-training since translation models for them already exist. On the other hand, they have longer inference times than sequence tagging due to the need to generate the entire sequence and lower interpretability and customization due to the black-box nature of the models. Sequence tagging approach as described in GECToR (Omelianchuk et al., 2020) requires the development of many complex g-transforms, which must be even more numerous for Ukrainian due to its morphological complexity. Additionally, seq2tag requires more pretraining because there are no existing models for Ukrainian.

2.2 Data Generation

A common technique used in English for training neural GEC models is synthetic data generation (Flachs et al., 2021). Synthetic data generation is even more crucial for Ukrainian since no large natural corpora exist. Most commonly used in English techniques include rule-based generation, back-translation, and round-trip translation, as well as leveraging public editing data through datasets such as Lang8 and Wiki Edits (Stahlberg and Kumar, 2021). The advantage of rule-based generation is that it leverages fundamental asymmetry that generating errors is much simpler than correcting them and therefore is possible to do programmatically (Awasthi et al., 2019). Back translation is a reverse task that uses deep learning (DL) models to recreate error patterns in existing human-annotated datasets (Sennrich et al., 2016). Round-trip-translation is based on the assumption that many translation models are still imperfect and that flow and style mistakes will be produced through the chain of translation (Lichtarge et al., 2019). Finally, the Wiki Edits and Lang8 datasets are available for any language (Faruqui et al., 2018).

3 Models

3.1 NMT

Most GEC systems that perform best on GEC benchmarks are based on the NMT architecture[5]. To extend those results to the Ukrainian language, we take the publicly available pre-trained mBART-50 model[6] and fine-tune it on UA-GEC augmented with our synthetically generated data. We choose to focus on mBART as it has previously shown the most promising results in the MT setting among comparable models (Tang et al., 2020). We train models with weight decay rate of 0.01 and the well-established and reliable native tokenizer and optimizer publicly available at HuggingFace[7]. All NMT models for 5 epochs with batch size of 32 and learning rate of 2e-5 on a single A100 Tensor Core GPU available at Google Colab. Average training time is 15 minutes.

3.2 SEQ2TAG

Despite showing the best results on GEC benchmarks (Bryant et al., 2017), NMT-based GEC systems suffer from multiple issues which make them far less convenient for deployment in the real world:

- Slow inference speed.
- Low interpretability and explainability; they require additional functionality to explain corrections, e.g., grammatical error type classification (Bryant et al., 2019)

To develop an alternative model of sequence tagging, we adopted GECToR's approach (Omelianchuk et al., 2020). Our GEC sequence tagging model is an encoder made of pre-trained Ukrainian-specific XLM-ROBERTa transformer [8] stacked with two linear layers and with softmax layers on the top.

We create a system of hand-made token-level transformations T(x_i) to match the target text by applying them to the corresponding source tokens ($x_1 ... x_N$). According to previous research, transformations increase the coverage of grammatical

[5] http://nlpprogress.com/english/grammatical_error_correction.html

[6] https://huggingface.co/facebook/mbart-large-50

[7] https://huggingface.co/docs/transformers/preprocessing

[8] https://huggingface.co/ukr-models/xlm-roberta-base-uk

error corrections for limited output vocabulary size for the most common grammatical errors, such as Spelling, Noun Number, Subject-Verb Agreement, and Verb Form (Yuan, 2017). Since no research has been conducted on native/non-native mistakes in the Ukrainian language, we adopt the classification used in the English language and applied by the GECToR team (Omelianchuk et al., 2020).

On the basic level, we use four types of token-level transformations, adopted from (Omelianchuk et al., 2020):

1. $KEEP – keeps the current token unchanged
2. $DELETE – deletes the current token
3. $APPEND – adds a new token to the current one, followed by a space
4. $REPLACE – replaces the current token with a different one.

Then, we add them to our custom-made G-Transformations, outlined in the Synthetic Data Generation section.

To correct the text, for each input sentence token x_i, $1 \leq i \leq N$ from the source sequence $(x_1 ... x_N)$, the model predicts the tag-encoded token-level transformation $T(x_i)$. These predicted tag-encoded transformations are then applied to the sentence, resulting in a modified sentence.

We train models of this type with variable training parameters for each run. We provide detailed overview of those for each model in the source code. On average, seq2tag models train for 8 hours on Google Colab GPUs.

3.3 Rule-Based Correction

The final approach that we try to apply to the Ukrainian language is rule-based correction. All existing services for Ukrainian GEC are rule-based[9], so we developed a few rule-based corrections to augment our models as well. However, we found that this approach requires additional research, which falls outside the scope of this paper.

4 Synthetic Data Generation

To train and test our models, we rely on the generation of synthetic data. In the following subchapters, we explain what techniques we use to imitate natural errors for the large corpus of correct sentences.

Many of our modules include detailed controls that allow us to modify data to suit our needs. This means we can provide high-quality data, with error patterns representative of those available in human-annotated corpora.

4.1 Clean data

Generating errors in existing sentences (errorification) necessitates the existence of a large, error-free corpus to errorify. To address this, we turn to web scrapping, since multiple authors have already addressed its usefulness for low-resource languages (Ghani et al., 2001). One commonly used technique is to send requests composed of mid-frequency n-grams to a search engine to gather bootstrap URLs, which use a breadth-first strategy to crawl the web page in search of meaningful information, such as documents or words (Sharoff, 2006). This is the technique that we apply to different news websites. The raw HTML content is fetched and converted to UTF-8 using a mixture of requests and BeautifulSoup. Then, we fix the remaining encoding artifacts with ftfy (Speer, 2019) and remove unicode emojis. Another crucial step is to normalize the Unicode points used for dashes, spaces, quotes etc., and strip any invisible characters. Furthermore, to simplify the process of tokenization, we enforce a single convention for all spaces around quotes and colons, e.g. no space inside quotes colons after the closing quote. Finally, to split text into sentences, we implement pymorphy in Python and apply it in three main ways: existing newlines are preserved, colons and semi-colons are considered segmentation hints, and sentences are required to start with an uppercase.

As a result, we compose a corpus of 1,030,582 high-quality error-free sentences from 62K URLs across 3,472 domains.

4.2 Punctuation

The first kind of error we use is punctuation errors. As they attribute the most errors in the UA-GEC dataset (Syvokon and Nahorna, 2021) and most English-language datasets (Bryant et al., 2019), we infer that this is the most common kind of mistake. To synthetically generate punctuation errors, we create the error probability matrix that replaces each mark (space between words was also counted as a mark) with any other one according to the randomly generated probability. Then, this matrix is applied to each sentence from our dataset. The resulting matrix looks like this:

[9] https://languagetool.org/

index		","	;	:	—	-	.	?	!	…
	0.95	0.05	0.00	0.00	0.00	0.00	0.00	0.00	0.00	0.00
","	0.41	0.59	0.00	0.00	0.00	0.00	0.00	0.00	0.00	0.00
;	0.80	0.09	0.11	0.00	0.00	0.00	0.00	0.00	0.00	0.00
:	0.86	0.05	0.00	0.05	0.04	0.00	0.00	0.00	0.00	0.00
—	0.87	0.05	0.00	0.00	0.08	0.00	0.00	0.00	0.00	0.00
-	0.80	0.00	0.00	0.00	0.03	0.17	0.00	0.00	0.00	0.00
.	0.16	0.00	0.00	0.00	0.00	0.00	0.84	0.00	0.00	0.00
?	0.80	0.00	0.00	0.00	0.00	0.00	0.04	0.12	0.04	0.00
!	0.80	0.00	0.00	0.00	0.00	0.00	0.10	0.10	0.00	0.00
…	0.80	0.00	0.00	0.00	0.00	0.00	0.00	0.00	0.00	0.20

Where row is the original mark, column is the new mark, number is the transformation probability.

English	Of course, the past cannot be changed, one can only observe and gently shrug.
corr	Звісно, минуле не можна змінити, тільки спостерігати і немічно розводити руками.
incorr	Звісно минуле не можна змінити тільки спостерігати і немічно розводити руками.

Table 1: Punctuation marks highlighted in red skipped in the incorr sentence

4.3 Grammar

To agree the gender of an adjective, verb, or pronoun with a corresponding head of the phrase, we develop an algorithm based on (Moskalevskyi) morphosyntactic parsing. For each correct sentence, the following conditions must be met:

$$\forall w, (w \in sent \land Ps(w)$$
$$\in \{PRON, NOUN, PROPN, ABBR\} \land w \in \Upsilon$$
$$\land (\exists a (a \in \mathbf{N}) : HL(w) = a) : \forall w_2 (w_2 \neq w$$
$$\land w_2 \in \{ADJ, VERB, PRON\}$$
$$\land HL(w_2) = HL(w)$$
$$\land R(w_2) = R(w)$$
$$\land N(w_2) = N(w) \land V(w_2) = V(w)))$$

Where:

- $\forall w$ means "for all w"
- $w \in sent$ means word "w is in a sentence"
- $Ps(w)$ is the part of speech of w
- Υ is a set of possible heads for the sentence
- $HL(w)$ is a function that determines the level relative to the head of the sentence (determined according to the rules of the Mova Institute: predicate > subj > nsubj > obj > iobj > obl > advmod > csubj > xcomp > ccomp > advcl)
- $R(w)$ is the gender of w, $N(w)$ is the number of w and $V(w)$ is the case of w

In simpler terms, this means that for a sentence to be grammatically correct in Ukrainian, all words in the sentence that are adjectives, verbs, or pronouns must agree in gender, number, and case with the noun, abbreviation, or pronoun that is the head of the phrase.

English	Bright curtain hung on the ledge.
corr	Яскравий тюль висів на карнизі.
incorr	Яскрава тюль висіла на карнизі.

Table 2: Words highlighted in red were modified to not agree in gender with the head of the phrase

4.4 Lexics

Russism is a word that has never existed in Ukrainian and was transliterated. For treating that object, we (0) check if the word doesn't exist in Ukrainian vocabulary Υ (I) observe letter patterns in transliterating russisms into Russian, (II) generate each possible way of transliterating a russism in Russian, (III) filter generated combinations through a Russian vocabulary Ω. (IV) Translate back.
More formally, let the Russian-Ukrainian dictionary be a Map $\mathcal{D}(w) = u$. Let $\mathcal{T}(r)$ be all possible Russian transliterations of the russism word r.
Therefore, a Ukrainian correspondence u of russism r may be:

$$\forall r \notin \Upsilon \exists u \in \{\mathcal{D}(i) : i \in \Omega \cap \mathcal{T}(r)\}$$

$\mathcal{T}(r)$ is a closed-form algorithm. We identify the most common russification patterns of the most commonly used words that suffer from the substitution of russisms in Ukrainian. Based on dictionary (Tyhyj, 2009), we generate a set of rules that allow for a double conversion between the russism and the correct word.

To generate datasets, we use a set of correct Ukrainian sentences, which are then translated into Russian with a certain probability. After the translation, we replace the Ukrainian word with the most commonly used Russian loanwords.

By using a probabilistic approach to the translation and substitution with a russism, we are able to generate datasets that accurately reflect the current state of Ukrainian language usage. This approach can be extended to other languages and can be used to develop strategies for improving language usage and reducing reliance on loanwords.

English	The owner of the house where storks nested, always was considered a respected man.
corr	Власник будинку, де гніздилися лелеки, завжди вважався шанованим чоловіком.
incorr	Владелец будинку, де гніздилися аїсти, всегда вважався шановним чоловіком.

Table 3: Words highlighted in red have been russified

4.5 Fluency

We developed 2 modules to generate errors in style and flow. In developing our errors, we relied on analyzing human-annotated data and rules of good writing for Ukrainian language. One module takes in a sentence, and identifies numbers written in words, after which it lemmatizes them and uses a custom dictionary to convert them to symbolic numbers. This error was based on occurence of similar errors in UA-GEC.

corr	I saw two of my friends today at the meeting.
incorr	I saw 2 of my friends today at the meeting.

Table 4: Words highlighted in red is number error

Another module performs word inversions at random. The two words must be at most two words apart. While Ukrainian does not have rigid word order, sentences written outside of dominant word order can seem odd to the reader and are annotated by the creators of UA-GEC corpora as stylistic error. As such, we created an error to generate word inversion to address that.

corr	I saw two of my friends today at the meeting.
incorr	I saw two of friends my today at the meeting.

Table 5: Words highlighted in red have been rearranged

4.6 Round Translation

The final technique that we investigated was round translation, which is known to be effective for low-resource monolingual datasets (Ahmadnia and Dorr, 2019). We would start by tokenizing and translating a sentence from Ukrainian to Russian through the Marian UK-RU (Tiedemann) encoder and transformer. Then, the sentence would be translated back, but using the UK-RU (instead of RU-UK) tokenizer and the correct transformer. In such a way, errorful sentences would be obtained through the usage of an incorrect tokenizer, yielding sentences resembling a mix of Russian and Ukrainian, also known as surzhyk.

English	In the document, Britain confirms Ukraine's right to reach its own security agreements, including with future NATO membership.
corr	Крім того, у документі Британія підтверджує право України досягати власних домовленостей щодо безпеки, включо з майбутнім членством в НАТО.
incorr	Кроме того, у документі британии підтвердять право України доносити свої суворі угоди про безпеності. в тому числі і будучому членство НАТО.

Table 6: Words highlighted in red have been modified with translation

5 Results

We train and evaluate more than 80 models to compare how well different model types, in conjunction with different synthetically generated data, perform for Ukrainian grammar correction. A full list of all models can be found in the appendix. We will provide the most important findings in this section. All models are trained using Google Colab GPUs.

We evaluate all our models on the UA-GEC development set (Syvokon and Nahorna, 2021) set using the M_2 scorer provided by the UNLP shared task.

5.1 Model comparison

In Table 7 we compare the performance of select models that we train. We train 10 different sequence tagging models on different combination of synthetic data and UA-GEC. We observe that models of this type do not benefit from synthetic data, and the baseline model trained on UA-GEC is the best model of this type by $F_{0.5}$ score. For comparison we also provide the seq2tag model trained on most data, which achieves highest recall of all seq2tag models.

The rule based models which we expected to augment neural-based models achieve very high rate of false positives and therefore are not appropriate to be used as additional layer of correction. In addition to that, we find that the true positives of rule-based models occur in the areas in which neural models already perform well (spelling and punctuation).

The NMT-based models performed better than both the rule-based models and seq2tag models on the evaluation test. The precision of those models especially is noticeable higher than the seq2tag models we train. We also find that models that use

Type	TP	FP	FN	Total P	Total R	Total F0.5
NMT (baseline)	685	302	1068	0.694	0.391	0.601
NMT (best)	691	241	1047	0.741	0.398	0.632
seq2tag (baseline)	399	753	953	0.346	0.295	0.335
seq2tag (most data)	461	1324	901	0.258	0.339	0.271
rule-based	104	1064	1194	0.089	0.080	0.087

Table 7: Comparison of precision, recall, and $F_{0.5}$ score between different models. The baseline is the UA-GEC dataset; $best$ is the best dataset we used.

a lot of synthetic data or do not use the core UA-GEC train corpus perform significantly worse than the baseline trained on UA-GEC only. This lead us to experiment with adding small amount (under 20k) of synthetically generated sentences to the core UA-GEC dataset to augment our model. Our best model is trained on such an augmented UA-GEC dataset. We discuss the impact of including different synthetic data in the next secion,.

5.2 Synthetic data comparison

To evaluate the impact of our synthetically generated data on model performance, we evaluate the results of the models trained with the UA-GEC train dataset and with several thousands of synthetically generated sentences of each error type mixed in. This allows us to determine if our synthetic data helped augment the performance in select target areas. The results for each category are presented below in Tables 8-12.

Model	Category TP	Precision	Recall	F0.5
ua-gec (baseline)	435	0.694	0.391	0.601
punct-assist (best)	488	0.742	0.375	0.620
ua-gec (baseline)	39	0.694	0.391	0.601
grammar-assist (best)	44	0.703	0.399	0.610
ua-gec (baseline)	153	0.694	0.391	0.601
spelling-assist (best)	83	0.738	0.317	0.583
ua-gec (baseline)	57	0.694	0.391	0.601
lexics-assist (best)	47	0.719	0.383	0.612
ua-gec (baseline)	57	0.694	0.391	0.601
fluency-assist (best)	41	0.712	0.365	0.599
ua-gec (baseline)	685	0.694	0.391	0.601
translation (best)	697	0.703	0.399	0.610

Table 8: Punct-assisted model is the model that was trained on synthetically generated punctuation errors. It achieves a higher target TP rate and overall $F_{0.5}$ score.

Model	Grammar TP	Precision	Recall	F0.5
ua-gec (baseline)	39	0.694	0.391	0.601
grammar-assist (best)	44	0.703	0.399	0.610

Table 9: Grammar-assisted model is the model that was trained on synthetically generated grammar errors. It achieves a higher target TP rate and overall $F_{0.5}$ score.

Model	Spelling TP	Precision	Recall	F0.5
ua-gec (baseline)	153	0.694	0.391	0.601
spelling-assist (best)	83	0.738	0.317	0.583

Table 10: Spelling-assisted model is the model that was trained on synthetically generated spelling errors. It achieves a lower TP rate and overall $F_{0.5}$ score.

Model	Lexics TP	Precision	Recall	F0.5
ua-gec (baseline)	57	0.694	0.391	0.601
lexics-assist (best)	47	0.719	0.383	0.612

Table 11: Lexics-assisted model is the model that was trained on synthetically generated lexical errors. It achieves a lower TP rate and overall $F_{0.5}$ score.

Model	Fluency TP	Precision	Recall	F0.5
ua-gec (baseline)	57	0.694	0.391	0.601
fluency-assist (best)	41	0.712	0.365	0.599

Table 12: Fluency-assisted model is the model that was trained on synthetically generated fluency errors (numerals-to-words, word order). It achieves a lower TP rate and overall $F_{0.5}$ score.

Model	Total TP	Precision	Recall	F0.5
ua-gec (baseline)	685	0.694	0.391	0.601
translation (best)	697	0.703	0.399	0.610

Table 13: Translation best model is the model that was trained on a synthetically generated back-translation (Ukrainian-Russian-Ukrainian). It achieves a higher TP rate and overall $F_{0.5}$ score.

We have determined that punctuation, grammar, and round-translation successfully augment the target category, and all but spelling and fluency successfully improve overall $F_{0.5}$ score. We believe that lexics and fluency errors did not improve the performance of the model due to intrinsic complexities of correction for those categories. The reason adding spelling failed to improve performance is a direction for future research.

5.3 The best model

When evaluating models augmented with synthetic data we noticed that the resulting F_{05} score some-

Model	TP	FP	FN	P	R	F0.5
ua-gec	685	302	1068	0.694	0.391	0.601
Dilute 20k	639	248	1074	0.720	0.373	0.607
Dilute 100k	544	184	1144	0.747	0.322	0.591

Table 14: Comparison of diluted model. Diluting increases precision at the cost of recall. Without extra data, the cost to recall is too high to justify

times went up compared to the baseline when the true positive rate for the target category actually went down. This increase in $F_0.5$ score can be accounted for by the increase in accuracy: adding that extra data did not make the model better at new type of errors, but made model already better at making fewer false positives.

Based on our previous research, it is found that the conventional approach of increasing the dataset size does not necessarily improve the model performance. Consequently, a decision was made to selectively generate mixed data to create a more diverse and representative dataset that could improve the performance of the model on a wider range of inputs.

For this study, the initial dataset UA-GEC (25k sentences) was selected, which contained a wide variety of errors. The objective was to achieve maximum accuracy in a specific category by artificially adding 10k sentences with only punctuation errors. As a result, the true positive (TP) rate increased by 53 points. Further tests were conducted by adding other inclusions, which resulted in an oversaturation of the model with only erroneous sentences. Therefore, around 5k absolutely correct sentences were added, resulting in a rapid decrease in the false negative (FN) rate.

The same process was repeated for other possible categories, but not as significant progress was made as before. This led to the conclusion that the type of error generation used in this study may be specific or simply not comparable to the test dataset.

It is important to note that mixing data in NLP can introduce new challenges, such as domain adaptation or language transfer issues. Therefore, it is essential to carefully evaluate the model's performance on a separate validation set to ensure that the mixing of data does not negatively impact its generalization ability.

6 Conclusions

We have investigated most of the state-of-the-art GEC approaches in the English language and tried to appropriate them for the Ukrainian language. We found that the most efficient GEC system can be developed using the NMT approach, however, seq2tag has a lot of room for research. Our best model gets the 0.632 $F_{0.5}$ score on the UA-GEC dataset, establishing the state-of-the-art benchmark.

Moreover, the results suggest that adding a mix of punctuation errors, russism errors, and clean data to the UA-GEC training data achieves the best results. Overall, we found that data quality is much more important than the amount of raw data. Therefore, we suggest that human-annotated GEC data is the most promising direction for future research.

Limitations

To the best of our knowledge, our paper is the first one outlining the application of the modern GEC techniques to the Ukrainian language, so it is bound by a lot of limitations.

1. We did not use neither Wiki Edits nor Lang8 datasets. Our initial overview observed that both of them included a lot of artifacts and grammatical mistakes in the "correct" options, so we concluded that cleaning up those datasets would take a lot of time and resources. Hence, both of them lay outside the scope of this paper.

2. Due to technical limitations of the resources we had, we did not have an option to test all available multi-language transformers. We know for a fact that there are multiple transformers, such as T5 and ELECTRA that can be adapted for both NMT and seq2tag architectures for the Ukrainian language. However, testing all of them was not technically feasible, therefore, this paper does not include that.

Model	TP	FP	FN	Precision	Recall	F0.5
ua-gec	685	302	1068	0.694	0.391	0.601
ua-gec + punct10k + dilute5k	644	221	1069	0.745	0.376	0.623
ua-gec + punct10k + dilule3.5k + lexics5k	691	241	1047	0.741	0.398	0.632

Table 15: Comparison of best NMT model data combinations

3. We found that the amount of data indeed scales well for the seq2tag architecture, however, the amount of truly error-free "clean" sentences was capped at 1 million. At the same time, most research for the English language used much more data, such as 9 million for GECToR, or even more for the mBART training. Therefore, the question of comparing seq2tag and NMT in the context of the Ukrainian language remains open.

4. For seq2tag, we realize that the total number of possible G-transformations is much higher than we have used, and that, despite covering most of the grammatical and punctuation errors, we did not cover everything. Therefore, there is still ample room for research of G-transformations.

5. Finally, this paper did not study back-translation models. All the ones that were used in the English language were trained on vast amounts of human-annotated data, while we have only UA-GEC. However, the usefulness of these models might be shown by future studies.

Acknowledgements

This work enjoyed selfless support from Anastasiia Teriokhina, Artur Zhdan, Maksym Matviievsky, Mykhailo Trushch, Nikita Masych, Tanya Melnyk, Taras Yaitskyi, and Vladyslav Verteletskyi. Thank you Veronika Kitsul for editing.

References

Benyamin Ahmadnia and Bonnie J. Dorr. 2019. Bilingual low-resource neural machine translation with round-tripping: The case of persian-spanish. In *Proceedings of the International Conference on Recent Advances in Natural Language Processing, RANLP 2019, Varna, Bulgaria, September 2-4, 2019*, pages 18–24. INCOMA Ltd.

Abhijeet Awasthi, Sunita Sarawagi, Rasna Goyal, Sabyasachi Ghosh, and Vihari Piratla. 2019. Parallel iterative edit models for local sequence transduction. *Proceedings of the 2019 Conference on Empirical Methods in Natural Language Processing and the 9th International Joint Conference on Natural Language Processing (EMNLP-IJCNLP)*.

Christopher Bryant, Mariano Felice, Øistein E. Andersen, and Ted Briscoe. 2019. The BEA-2019 shared task on grammatical error correction. In *Proceedings of the Fourteenth Workshop on Innovative Use of NLP for Building Educational Applications, BEA@ACL 2019, Florence, Italy, August 2, 2019*, pages 52–75. Association for Computational Linguistics.

Christopher Bryant, Mariano Felice, and Ted Briscoe. 2017. Automatic annotation and evaluation of error types for grammatical error correction. In *Proceedings of the 55th Annual Meeting of the Association for Computational Linguistics, ACL 2017, Vancouver, Canada, July 30 - August 4, Volume 1: Long Papers*, pages 793–805. Association for Computational Linguistics.

Christopher Bryant, Zheng Yuan, Muhammad Reza Qorib, Hannan Cao, Hwee Tou Ng, and Ted Briscoe. 2022. Grammatical error correction: A survey of the state of the art. *CoRR*, abs/2211.05166.

Solomija N. Buk and Andrij A. Rovenchak. 2003. The rank-frequency analysis for the functional style corpora in the ukrainian language. *CoRR*, cs.CL/0311033.

Manaal Faruqui, Ellie Pavlick, Ian Tenney, and Dipanjan Das. 2018. Wikiatomicedits: A multilingual corpus of wikipedia edits for modeling language and discourse.

Simon Flachs, Felix Stahlberg, and Shankar Kumar. 2021. Data strategies for low-resource grammatical error correction. In *Proceedings of the 16th Workshop on Innovative Use of NLP for Building Educational Applications*, pages 117–122, Online. Association for Computational Linguistics.

Rayid Ghani, Rosie Jones, and Dunja Mladenić. 2001. Mining the web to create minority language corpora. In *Proceedings of the Tenth International Conference on Information and Knowledge Management*, CIKM '01, page 279–286, New York, NY, USA. Association for Computing Machinery.

Jared Lichtarge, Christopher Alberti, Shankar Kumar, Noam Shazeer, Niki Parmar, and Simon Tong. 2019. Corpora generation for grammatical error correction. *CoRR*, abs/1904.05780.

Bohdan Moskalevskyi. Mova institute.

Kostiantyn Omelianchuk, Vitaliy Atrasevych, Artem N. Chernodub, and Oleksandr Skurzhanskyi. 2020. Gector - grammatical error correction: Tag, not rewrite. In *Proceedings of the Fifteenth Workshop on Innovative Use of NLP for Building Educational Applications, BEA@ACL 2020, Online, July 10, 2020*, pages 163–170. Association for Computational Linguistics.

S. D. Pogorilyy and A. A. Kramov. 2020. Method of noun phrase detection in ukrainian texts. *CoRR*, abs/2010.11548.

Rico Sennrich, Barry Haddow, and Alexandra Birch. 2016. Neural machine translation of rare words with subword units. *In Proceedings of the 54th Annual Meeting of the Association for Computational Linguistics (Volume 1: Long Papers)*, page 1715–1725.

Serge Sharoff. 2006. Creating general-purpose corpora using automated search engine queries. *WaCky*.

Robyn Speer. 2019. ftfy.

Felix Stahlberg and Shankar Kumar. 2021. Synthetic data generation for grammatical error correction with tagged corruption models.

Oleksiy Syvokon and Olena Nahorna. 2021. UA-GEC: grammatical error correction and fluency corpus for the ukrainian language. *CoRR*, abs/2103.16997.

Yuqing Tang, Chau Tran, Xian Li, Peng-Jen Chen, Naman Goyal, Vishrav Chaudhary, Jiatao Gu, and Angela Fan. 2020. Multilingual translation with extensible multilingual pretraining and finetuning. *CoRR*, abs/2008.00401.

Jörg Tiedemann. Marianmt.

Oleksa Tyhyj. 2009. *Slovnyk movnyh pokruchiv*.

Zheng Yuan. 2017. Grammatical error correction in non-native English. Technical Report UCAM-CL-TR-904, University of Cambridge, Computer Laboratory.

A Appendix

Category	TP	FP	FN	P	R	F0.5
Total	691	241	1047	0.741	0.398	0.632
F/Calque	5	0	72	1.000	0.065	0.258
F/Collocation	4	0	20	1.000	0.167	0.500
F/PoorFlow	10	0	129	1.000	0.072	0.279
F/Repetition	3	0	31	1.000	0.088	0.326
F/Style	18	0	125	1.000	0.126	0.419
G/Aspect	0	0	2	1.000	0.000	0.000
G/Case	13	0	73	1.000	0.151	0.471
G/Comparison	0	0	3	1.000	0.000	0.000
G/Conjunction	4	0	11	1.000	0.267	0.645
G/Gender	3	0	13	1.000	0.188	0.536
G/Number	2	0	17	1.000	0.105	0.370
G/Other	2	0	3	1.000	0.400	0.769
G/PartVoice	0	0	4	1.000	0.000	0.000
G/Participle	0	0	1	1.000	0.000	0.000
G/Particle	1	0	2	1.000	0.333	0.714
G/Prep	3	0	21	1.000	0.125	0.417
G/Tense	0	0	12	1.000	0.000	0.000
G/UngrammaticalStructure	2	0	42	1.000	0.046	0.192
G/VerbAForm	7	0	4	1.000	0.636	0.897
G/VerbVoice	0	0	9	1.000	0.000	0.000
M:NOUN	0	1	0	0.000	1.000	0.000
M:OTHER	0	2	0	0.000	1.000	0.000
M:PUNCT	0	46	0	0.000	1.000	0.000
Other	3	0	8	1.000	0.273	0.652
Punctuation	488	0	172	1.000	0.739	0.934
R:DET	0	1	0	0.000	1.000	0.000
R:NOUN	0	43	0	0.000	1.000	0.000
R:ORTH	0	8	0	0.000	1.000	0.000
R:OTHER	0	14	0	0.000	1.000	0.000
R:PUNCT	0	39	0	0.000	1.000	0.000
R:SPELL	0	46	0	0.000	1.000	0.000
R:VERB	0	1	0	0.000	1.000	0.000
R:WO	0	1	0	0.000	1.000	0.000
Spelling	123	0	273	1.000	0.311	0.693
U:NOUN	0	19	0	0.000	1.000	0.000
U:OTHER	0	1	0	0.000	1.000	0.000
U:PUNCT	0	19	0	0.000	1.000	0.000

Table 16: Full breakdown of the $F_{0.5}$ score of our best model

Model	ua gec	grammar	punct	spelling	lecxics	rus	dilute	backtranslation	RT	data	F0.5
5k punct + 10k ua_gec	10k		5k							5k punct + 10k ua_gec	0.5061
5k-rt-punct	full		5k						5k	UA-GEC + rt5k + punct5k	0.6101
5k-rt-punct-3e	full		5k						5k	UA-GEC + 5k backtranslated + 5k punct	0.6117
5k-rt-punct-diluted10k	full		5k				10k		5k	UA-GEC + 5k backtranslated + 5k punct + 10k clean	0.6111
press_f_gram_dilute	full	5k					5k			"ua-gec, 5k gram, 5k dilute"	0.6128
press_f_gram_typos_punct_dilute	full	5k		5k			5k			"ua-gec, 5k gram, 5k dilute, 5k punct"	0.6128
borshch_25_future_8	full					10k				russified_borshch_0.25er_10k	0.6118
borshch_40_future_7	full					10k				russified_borshch_0.4er_10k + gec	0.5793
combined-assist	full	2.5k	2.5k							ua-gec + 5k combined errorifer data from borsch-combined	0.5782
dilute-100k	full						100k			UA-GEC + 100k pure	0.5913
dilute-20k	full						20k			ua-gec + 20k pure	0.6073
future_10_punct5k_rus5k	10k		5k			5k				punct5k + russified_gec 5k + ua_gec10k	0.5828
future_10_punct5k_rus5k	full		5k			5k				gec_punct5k_rus5k	0.5828
future_12_punct5k_gec10k_punct5k_gec	full		10k							punct5k(low er) + gec10k + punct5k(er) + gec	0.6128
future_13_2ep	full		10k				5k			Punct10k + ua_gec + 5k dilute	0.6225
future_15_3ep	full		5k				3k			Punct5k + ua_gec + 3k dilute (shuffle)	0.6192
future_16_3ep	full		10k		5k	5k	5k				0.6299
future_17_3ep	full		10k		5k		3.7k				0.6321
future_9_punct5k_rus10k			5k		10k					punct5k + russified_gec10k	0.5795
future3					10k	10k				surzh10k(from 450kdataset)+ rusified_gec10k	0.3669
maksym-unlp-1	full									ua-gec	0.6107
maksym-unlp-2	full									ua-gec	0.6110
maksym-unlp-3	full									ua-gec	0.6107
maksym-unlp-5	full									ua-gec	0.6008
maksym-unlp-6	full									ua-gec	0.6125
press_f	12k	5k	5k			5k	5k			"12k UA-GEC, 5k inflection-preposition-gender, 5k rus, 5k dilute, 5k punct"	0.5914
press_f_typos	12k			5k			13k			"12k ua -gec, 13k ua-gec correct, 5k typos"	0.5832
punct-assist-1	fukk		5k							ua-gec + 5k punct errorifier with eror_prob=0.01	0.6172
punct-assist-2	full		10k							ua-gec + 10k punct errorifier with eror_prob=0.01	0.6152
punct-assist-3	full		20k							ua-gec + 20k punct errorifier with eror_prob=0.01	0.6204
rus 5k + punct_5k + ua_gec	full		5k			5k				rus 5k + punct_5k + ua_gec	0.5828
rus_45_future5	-				20k					russified_gec20k(medium_error)	0.5854
rus_60_future6	-				20k					russified_gec20k(0.6_error)	0.5767
rus_future4	-				20k					rusified_gec20k	0.5669
uagec-5k-rt	full							5k		UA-GEC + punct10k + dil4k + rus5k + rt5k mixed	0.6087
uagec-rt5k-punct10k-dilute4k-rus10k-mixed	full		10k			5k	4k		5k		0.6165
uagec-rt5k-punct10k-diluted1k-rus5k-mixed	full		10k				1k		5k	UA-GEC + punct10k + dil1k + rt5k + rus5k mixed	0.6065
uagec-rt5k-punct10k-diluted2k-rus10k-mixed	full		10k			5k	2k		5k	UA-GEC + punct10k + dil2k + rt5k + rus5k mixed	0.6187
uagec-rt5k-punct10k-rus10k-diluted1k-mixed	5k									5k	0.6226
uagec-rt5k-punct10k-rus10k-mixed	full		10k						5k	UA-GEC + punct10k + rt5k mixed	0.6097

Table 17: All models we have trained with their respective data and $F_{0.5}$ scores.

A Low-Resource Approach to the Grammatical Error Correction of Ukrainian

Frank Palma Gomez
Queens College, CUNY
frankpalma12@gmail.com

Alla Rozovskaya
Queens College, CUNY
arozovskaya@qc.cuny.edu

Dan Roth
University of Pennsylvania
danroth@seas.upenn.edu

Abstract

We present our system that participated in the shared task on the grammatical error correction of Ukrainian. We have implemented two approaches that make use of large pre-trained language models and synthetic data, that have been used for error correction of English as well as low-resource languages. The first approach is based on finetuning a large multilingual language model (mT5) in two stages: first, on synthetic data, and then on gold data. The second approach trains a (smaller) seq2seq Transformer model pre-trained on synthetic data and finetuned on gold data. Our mT5-based model scored first in "GEC only" track, and a very close second in the "GEC+Fluency" track. Our two key innovations are (1) finetuning in stages, first on synthetic, and then on gold data; and (2) a high-quality corruption method based on round-trip machine translation to complement existing noisification approaches.[1]

1 Introduction

This paper describes our submission in the shared task on the Grammatical Error Correction (GEC) of Ukrainian (Syvokon and Romanyshyn, 2023) that was organized as part of the Workshop on Ukrainian Natural Language Processing (UNLP 2023), in conjunction with EACL 2023.

Ukrainian is an Indo-European language from the East-Slavic language family, and is most closely related to Russian and Belarusian. In the context of GEC, Ukrainian is a low-resource language and is under-explored. A dataset of Ukrainian native and non-native texts annotated for errors was recently released (Syvokon and Nahorna, 2021), however, to the best of our knowledge, no systems have been benchmarked on this dataset.

We have developed two approaches. The first approach is based on the method proposed in earlier work (Rothe et al., 2021) that finetunes a multilingual mT5 model on gold GEC data.[2] Because mT5 is pre-trained with an objective that is not appropriate for GEC, we propose a 2-stage finetuning strategy, where we finetune first on native data with synthetic noise, and then further finetune on the gold GEC data. We show that this two-stage approach is beneficial and provides a large boost compared to an mtT5 model finetuned on gold data only. Our model scored first in the "GEC only" track and a very close second in the "GEC+Fluency" track (0.08 point difference from the top submission).

Our second system is a smaller seq2seq Transformer model pre-trained on synthetic data and finetuned on gold data. We propose a novel method of generating synthetic errors using back-translation. Unlike previous approaches, we do not use full-sentence translations but only extract back-translation pairs that are then used for introducing errors in native data.

We present related work on GEC in Section 2. Section 3 describes our approach. Section 4 briefly describes the Ukrainian GEC dataset. Section 5 presents our experimental results on the validation and test data, as well as additional evaluation by error type. Section 6 concludes.

2 Background

Most effort in GEC research concentrated on correcting errors made by English as second language writers. More recently, there has been interest in developing approaches and resources in GEC for other languages, including Arabic (Mohit et al., 2014), German (Naplava and Straka, 2019), Russian (Rozovskaya and Roth, 2014), Chinese, and Spanish (Rothe et al., 2021). Earlier approaches to GEC include rule-based methods and machine learning classifiers for correcting a specific type of mistake (e.g. article or preposition) (Tetreault

[1] Code is available at https://github.com/knarfamlap/low-resource-gec-uk

[2] We used the smaller (base and large) models only in our experiments, due to the sizes of mT5 models.

Proceedings of the Second Ukrainian Natural Language Processing Workshop (UNLP), pages 114–120
May 5, 2023 ©2023 Association for Computational Linguistics

et al., 2010; Foster, 2010; Rozovskaya and Roth, 2013; Dahlmeier and Ng, 2012). For an overview of approaches and methods in GEC, we refer the reader to Bryant et al. (2022).

Current approaches to GEC can be broken down into two categories: sequence-to-sequence (seq2seq) generation (Jianshu et al., 2017; Chollampatt and Ng, 2018; Grundkiewicz and Junczys-Dowmunt, 2019), and sequence-to-editing (seq2edits) (Omelianchuk et al., 2020; Awasthi et al., 2019; Li and Shi, 2021). Both approaches achieve state-of-the-art performance on English GEC. In the seq2edits framework, the task is viewed as a sequence labeling problem (Omelianchuk et al., 2020) that tags text spans with appropriate error tags, leaving the rest of the text unchanged.

Because the seq2edits approach requires human input, as it depends on constructing language-specific edit operations, we adopt the seq2seq framework. Seq2seq approaches have demonstrated strong empirical results in GEC (Chollampatt and Ng, 2018; Yuan and Briscoe, 2016; Grundkiewicz et al., 2019; Grundkiewicz and Junczys-Dowmunt, 2019; and R. Grundkiewicz and S. Guha and K. Heafield, 2018; Kiyono et al., 2019a; Zhao et al., 2019; Jianshu et al., 2017; Yuan and Briscoe, 2016; Katsumata and Komachi, 2019; Xie et al., 2018). Due to lack of gold training data, it is common to first *pre-train* a model on native data where the source side has been corrupted with artificial noise. The pre-trained model is typically further finetuned on the available gold data.

Pre-trained language models (PLMs) Recently, finetuning PLMs has become a standard paradigm for many NLP tasks. In GEC, PLMs have been mainly used in English where models have been finetuned on large amounts of hand-labeled data (Kaneko et al., 2020; Malmi et al., 2019; Omelianchuk et al., 2020). Katsumata and Komachi (2020) apply PLMs in a multilingual setting, by finetuning BART (Lewis et al., 2020). However, even when using a large number of hand-labeled examples, they achieve results that are way below state-of-the-art.

In this work we adopt the approach of Rothe et al. (2021) and make use of mT5 (Xue et al., 2021), a multilingual variant of T5 (Raffel et al., 2020), a pre-trained text-to-text Transformer. mT5 has been pre-trained on mC4 corpus, a subset of Common Crawl, covering 101 languages and composed of about 50 billion documents (Xue et al., 2021).

Rothe et al. (2021) finetune mT5 on GEC gold data for Russian, German, and Czech languages, although SOTA results are only achieved, when they re-train mT5 with a different objective and use an extremely large model xxl with 13B parameters. We use the original mT5 models of smaller sizes and show that it is possible to achieve competitive results by pre-training first on synthetic data.

3 The Models

We have implemented two approaches that draw on methods that showed competitive performance in multilingual low-resource settings. Our first (larger) model makes use of mT5 but is finetuned in two stages – on synthetic data (we refer to this stage as pre-training on synthetic data), and then finetuning on gold data. Our second (smaller) model is a seq2seq Transformer model pre-trained on synthetic data (from scratch) and finetuned on gold data. As our baseline for the second model, we use a model pre-trained on synthetic data generated using standard spell-based transformations. We show that adding synthetic noise from back-translations results in a 3-point improvement over the baseline. Because both approaches make use of synthetic data, we describe the data generation methods below.

Generating synthetic data Standard *data corruption methods* typically use a variety of heuristics: random character and token transformations (Schmaltz et al., 2016; Lichtarge et al., 2019a), confusion sets generated from a spellchecker (Grundkiewicz and Junczys-Dowmunt, 2019; Naplava and Straka, 2019), or a morphological analyzer (Choe et al., 2019), or round-trip translation (Lichtarge et al., 2019a).

We have experimented with two baseline data generation techniques for low-resource settings: (1) spell-based transformations and (2) part-of-speech (POS)-based transformations. Both of the methods rely on the idea of using *confusion sets* that specify for each target word occurring in a native corpus a list of highly confusable words. These lists are used to generate synthetic errors.

Spell-based transformations This approach showed state-of-the-art performance in English (Bryant et al., 2019; Grundkiewicz and Junczys-Dowmunt, 2019; Grundkiewicz et al., 2019), and other languages (Naplava and Straka, 2019; Flachs et al., 2021). Spell-based confusions include highly confusable words based on edit distance obtained from a dictionary available in a spellchecker. Because Aspell is an open-source spellchecker, it is common to use Aspell to generate spell-based confusion sets. We use Aspell with the Ukrainian dictionary in this work to create spell-based confusions. More detail about the method can be found in Naplava and Straka (2019). We follow Naplava and Straka (2019) for the parameter values for token replacement, deletions, and insertions.

POS-based transformations Confusion sets in this method are generated based on part-of-speech (POS) tag of the target word to be replaced: given a word and its POS tag (Choe et al., 2019), the target word is replaced with its inflectional variant that corresponds to the same base form (e.g. "walks" would be replaced with "walking", "walked" or "walk"). Flachs et al. (2021) use Unimorph morphological analyzer and tagger (McCarthy et al., 2020). Although POS-based transformations showed promising results for Russian, our initial experiments using pymorphy (Korobov, 2015) did not yield competitive results, and we do not report these experiments.

Back-translation (BT) The motivation for using BT is to generate more diverse errors that cannot be generated using the baseline spell-based transformations. We hypothesize that many fluency errors, such as choosing an incorrect word, will manifest themselves in the machine translation output as back-translated words that are semantically close to the target. The input to BT are sentences from a native Ukrainian corpus. The sentences are translated into another language (pivot), and then back into *Ukrainian*. We use English as the pivot: A sentence is translated into English, where top n translation hypotheses are generated. For each hypothesis, top m back-translations into *Ukrainian* are generated. For each unique word in *Ukrainian*, the back-translated words that are aligned to it are treated as potential synthetic errors.

Crucially, in contrast to other approaches that employ back-translation (Lichtarge et al., 2019b), we do not make use of the entire resulting back-translated sentences, but only generate targeted confusion sets of relevant errors that are used to corrupt the data. Further, we generate multiple hypotheses in each direction. We use the BT approach in conjunction with the spell-based transformations (see Section 5). We use the neural machine translation systems of Tiedemann and Thottingal (2020) to translation from Ukrainian into English and back.

	Percentage (%)		
Error	**Train**	**Valid (R_1)**	**Valid (R_2)**
Punctuation	36.9	32.8	29.8
Spelling	19.5	21.8	17.8
F/PoorFlow	8.9	12.1	16.0
F/Style	8.5	8.7	9.1
G/Case	6.2	6.5	3.7
F/Calque	6.4	4.1	4.9
G/Structure	2.3	2.2	3.8
F/Repetition	1.2	2.2	1.9
F/Collocation	1.2	1.6	1.2
F/Other	0.7	-	0.3
G/Prep	1.3	1.5	2.5
G/Number	0.9	1.0	1.3
G/Conjunction	1.1	1.0	0.7
G/Gender	1.3	0.9	0.7
G/VerbVoice	0.7	0.7	1.0
G/VerbAForm	0.2	0.7	0.1
G/Tense	0.4	0.6	1.4
Other	1.0	0.4	3.3
G/Other	0.6	0.4	-
G/PartVoice	0.3	0.3	0.1
G/Particle	0.2	0.2	0.2
G/Comparison	0.4	0.2	0.1
G/Participle	-	0.1	0.1
G/Aspect	0.2	0.1	0.3
Total	35,431	1,922	2,731

Table 1: Learner error distributions by category (on the training and validation data). *G* stands for grammar, and *F* stands for fluency. The validation data has two references per sentence (R_1 and R_2).

4 The Ukrainian GEC Data

The data used in the shared task comes from UA-GEC, a corpus of social media texts written by native speakers and learners of Ukranian (Syvokon and Nahorna, 2021). The shared task organizers have provided training and validation data. The training data is annotated with 1 reference, and the validation set is annotated with 2 references for each sentence. The gold corrections are provided in the standard M2 format (Ng et al., 2014), and the edits are labeled with the corresponding error tags. There are 24 error categories, broadly classified with a prefix into Grammar (G) and Fluency (F) corrections (with the exception of spelling and punctuation errors that do not have a prefix). The shared task includes 2 tracks: "GEC+Fluency", where the systems are evaluated with respect to all errors, and the "GEC only" track where the fluency edits are removed. Table 1 shows the distribution of errors in the training and validation data. As can be observed, punctuation and spelling errors constitute the majority of edits (over 50%), and grammar errors are less frequent. This may be because the Ukrainian corpus contains a lot of data from native speakers, as opposed to language learners (Syvokon and Nahorna, 2021).

5 Experiments and Results

Below, we present experimental results for the two models that we implemented. Our submissions for both tracks are the same, except that the models are finetuned on the gold data for each respective track. We first present a set of experiments on the data in the "GEC+fluency" track. We report results of the submitted systems for both tracks in Section 5.3.

Corrupting monolingual Ukrainian data Both models use synthetic data. We corrupt sentences from the Ukrainian partition of CC-100 (Wenzek et al., 2020), which contains high-quality data from Common Crawl. We tokenize the data using Stanza (Qi et al., 2020), the same tokenizer that is used to tokenize the gold data. We use spell-based transformations (see Section 3) to corrupt the monolingual data (but see also 5.2).

Evaluation We report the scores measured by ERRANT scorer (Felice and Briscoe, 2015), and report performance on correction.

5.1 mT5-Based Models

First, we evaluate mT5-based models. We have experimented with 2 models: base and large. Although xl and xxl models showed much stronger performance (Rothe et al., 2021), these models were too large (3.7B and 13B parameters, respectively). mT5 base and mT5 large have 580M and 1.3B parameters, respectively. We first finetune both models on the gold training data and evaluate on the validation set (see Table 2).

Pre-training on synthetic data Because mT5 has been pre-trained with span-prediction objective that is not optimal for GEC, Rothe et al. (2021) re-train the model, by splitting the paragraphs into individual sentences and corrupting the sentences with a set of operations that drop, insert, or swap tokens and characters. Their resulting gT5 model significantly outperforms the finetuned mT5 models. Since gT5 is not publicly available, we make use of the mT5 models, however, to account for the fact that mT5 may not be optimal for GEC, we introduce an additional pre-training step and pre-train mT5 on synthetic data with spell-based corruptions (see Section 3). We finetune mT5, using the original hyper-parameters in Xue et al. (2021). When finetuning, we utilize a max context length of 128 tokens, a batch size of 32, and a global seed of 42 for all experiments related to mT5.

	P	R	$F_{0.5}$
mT5 base	63.64	33.29	53.83
mT5 large	65.26	39.74	**57.83**

Table 2: mT5 models finetuned on gold training data. Results on **valid** ("GEC+Fluency"). Best result is in bold.

Model	P	R	$F_{0.5}$
mT5 base	63.64	33.29	53.83
mT5 large	65.26	39.74	57.83
mT5 base + 2M synth.	72.05	39.69	61.94
mT5 large + 2M synth.	73.95	41.84	64.11
mT5 large + 10M synth.	72.08	47.87	**65.45**

Table 3: mT5 pre-trained on synthetic data, and finetuned on gold training data. Results on **valid** ("GEC+Fluency"). Best result is in bold.

Results are shown in Table 3. Pre-training on synthetic data boosts the performance significantly, but almost 7 points. Increasing the size of the synthetic data used for pre-training further boosts the performance by 1 F-score point.

5.2 Transformer seq2seq Models Trained on Synthetic Data

The model We use the Transformer sequence-to-sequence model (Vaswani et al., 2017) implemented in the Fairseq toolkit (Ott et al., 2019). We use the "Transformer (big)" settings and the parameters specified in (Kiyono et al., 2019b) for `Pretrain` setting. The models are pre-trained on synthetic data until convergence using 3 seeds (1,2, and 3) and then further finetuned on gold training data. The gold training data is also used as the validation set. We ensemble the best checkpoints from each run during inference.

Pre-training with spell-based synthetic errors Table 5 shows experimental results on the validation set. The top two rows show models pre-trained on 15M synthetic sentences (single model results and an ensemble of 3 best checkpoints).

Back-translation based errors Our next experiment evaluates the contribution of back-translation based errors. The errors are introduced on top of

		GEC+Fluency			GEC only		
Model	**Number of params.**	**P**	**R**	**$F_{0.5}$**	**P**	**R**	**$F_{0.5}$**
mT5 large	1.3B	73.21	53.22	68.09	76.81	61.39	73.14
seq2seq	275M	69.91	53.78	65.96	72.32	63.13	70.27

Table 4: Results on the test data of the submitted systems for both tracks.

Model	**P**	**R**	**$F_{0.5}$**
Spell (15M, single)	62.0	46.8	58.2
Spell (15M, ens.)	65.6	47.4	60.9
Spell+BT (15M, single)	65.1	48.5	60.9
Spell+BT (15M, ens.)	68.3	49.0	63.3
Spell+BT (35M, single)	63.8	50.0	60.4
Spell+BT (35M, ens.)	67.8	50.5	**63.4**

Table 5: Seq2seq models pre-trained on synthetic data and finetuned on the gold training data. Results on the "GEC+Fluency" validation set (average over 3 random seeds for single models). *BT* stands for back-translation. Best result is in bold.

	Recall	
Error	**mT5 large**	**Seq2seq**
Calque	23.1	22.5
Case	23.3	15.0
Flow	8.0	10.6
Punc.	65.4	67.5
Spelling	48.6	51.2
Structure	13.5	11.7
Style	10.6	13.4

Table 6: Recall performance per error type for the most frequent error types on the validation set for the two submitted systems.

the spell-based confusions, with an error rate of 10%. We note that because these errors do not target every word, on average 5% of additional words are being corrupted in this stage. The second segment of Table 5 illustrates that adding back-translation errors improves the results by 3 points.

Effect of the synthetic data size Finally, we train models on more synthetic data (35M examples). We do not observe an improvement compared to using 15M examples (bottom segment of Table 5).

5.3 Submitted Systems

For the mT5-based model, we submitted an mT5 large pre-trained on 10M synthetic examples, and further finetuned on the gold data. The seq2seq model is pre-trained on 35M synthetic examples (Spell+BT) and finetuned on gold training data. We use 3 random seeds and the inference is an ensemble over the best checkpoints for the 3 runs. For each track, we finetune on the gold data for the corresponding track. Results are shown in Table 4. Note that the mT5 model is finetuned on the gold training and validation data in the "GEC+Fluency" track, and is finetuned on the gold training data in the "GEC only" track. Seq2seq models are finetuned on the gold training data for both tracks.

5.4 Evaluation by Error Type

Evaluating performance by individual error type is extremely useful, as it allows us to understand what type of mistakes each model is good at correcting, and which errors are more difficult. However, evaluating by error type requires classifying the edits made by the automated systems. In other languages, automatic tools for classifying edits have been built (Bryant et al., 2017; Belkebir and Habash, 2021; Rozovskaya, 2022). However, we can compute the recall of each model, by using gold error tags available in the M2 files. We report recall for the submitted systems (on the validation data) for the most frequent error types. Results are shown in Table 6. Note that because we cannot evaluate the precision of correcting these error types, these results cannot be used to directly compare performance on different errors. Nevertheless, this evaluation suggests that currently both systems mainly correct punctuation and spelling errors, whereas fluency errors, such as flow, and style prove to be the most challenging.

6 Conclusion

We have presented our submission that participated in the shared task on the Grammatical Error Correction of Ukrainian. Our submission includes two systems. The first system pre-trains mT5 on synthetic data and finetunes on the gold GEC data. We have shown that introducing this two-stage approach is crucial to achieving strong results when using mT5. We have also proposed a novel synthetic data generation method that extracts confusion pairs from multiple back-translation hypotheses that are aligned with the original sentence.

Limitations

The results shown in this work may not necessarily reflect performance on other languages with similar amounts of resources or even Ukrainian language error correction performed on a different domain. The methods described in this work require use of GPU resources that may not be available to all researchers.

Acknowledgments

We thank the anonymous reviewers for their insightful comments.

References

M. Junczys-Dowmunt and R. Grundkiewicz and S. Guha and K. Heafield. 2018. Approaching Neural Grammatical Error Correction as a Low-Resource Machine Translation Task. In *NAACL*.

A. Awasthi, S. Sarawagi, R. Goyal, S. Ghosh, and V. Piratla. 2019. Parallel iterative edit models for local sequence transduction. In *EMNLP-IJCNLP*.

R. Belkebir and N. Habash. 2021. Automatic error type annotation for arabic. In *CoNLL*.

C. Bryant, M. Felice, Ø. Andersen, and T. Briscoe. 2019. The BEA-19 shared task on grammatical error correction. In *Proceedings of the ACL Workshop on Innovative Use of NLP for Building Educational Applications (BEA-19)*.

C. Bryant, M. Felice, and T. Briscoe. 2017. Automatic annotation and evaluation of error types for grammatical error correction. In *ACL*.

C. Bryant, Z. Yuan, M. R. Qorib, H. Cao, H. T. Ng, and T. Briscoe. 2022. Grammatical error correction: A survey of the state of the art. *Computational Linguistics*.

Y. J. Choe, J. Ham, K. Park, and Y. Yoon. 2019. A neural grammatical error correction system built on better pre-training and sequential transfer learning . In *BEA Workshop*.

S. Chollampatt and H.T. Ng. 2018. A Multilayer Convolutional Encoder-Decoder Neural Network for Grammatical Error Correction . In *Proceedings of the AAAI*. Association for the Advancement of Artificial Intelligence.

D. Dahlmeier and H. T. Ng. 2012. A beam-search decoder for grammatical error correction. In *Proceedings of EMNLP-CoNLL*.

M. Felice and T. Briscoe. 2015. Towards a standard evaluation method for grammatical error detection and correction. In *NAACL-HLT*.

S. Flachs, F. Stahlberg, and S. Kumar. 2021. Data strategies for low-resource grammatical error correction. In *BEA Workshop*.

J. Foster. 2010. "cba to check the spelling": Investigating parser performance on discussion forum posts. In *NAACL*.

R. Grundkiewicz and M. Junczys-Dowmunt. 2019. Minimally-augmented grammatical error correction. In *Proceedings of the 5th Workshop on Noisy User-generated Text (W-NUT*.

R. Grundkiewicz, M. Junczys-Dowmunt, and K. Heafield. 2019. Neural grammatical error correction systems with unsupervised pre-training on synthetic data. In *Proceedings of the ACL Workshop on Innovative Use of NLP for Building Educational Applications (BEA-19)*.

J. Jianshu, Q. Wang, K. Toutanova, Y. Gong, S. Truong, and Jianfeng J. Gao. 2017. A nested attention neural hybrid model for grammatical error correction. In *ACL*.

M. Kaneko, M. Mita, S. Kiyono, J. Suzuki, and K. Inui. 2020. Encoder-Decoder Models Can Benefit from Pre-trained Masked Language Models in Grammatical Error Correction. In *ACL*.

S. Katsumata and M. Komachi. 2019. (almost) unsupervised grammatical error correction using synthetic comparable corpus. In *Proceedings of the ACL Workshop on Innovative Use of NLP for Building Educational Applications (BEA-19)*.

S. Katsumata and M. Komachi. 2020. Stronger baselines for grammatical error correction using a pre-trained encoder-decoder model. In *Proceedings of the 1st Conference of the Asia-Pacific Chapter of the Association for Computational Linguistics and the 10th International Joint Conference on Natural Language Processing*.

S. Kiyono, J. Suzuki, M. Mita, T. Mizumoto, and K. Inui. 2019a. An empirical study of incorporating pseudo data into grammatical error correction. In *EMNLP-IJCNLP*.

S. Kiyono, J. Suzuki, M. Mita, T. Mizumoto, and K. Inui. 2019b. An empirical study of incorporating pseudo data into grammatical error correction. In *EMNLP*.

M. Korobov. 2015. Morphological analyzer and generator for russian and ukrainian languages. In *Analysis of Images, Social Networks and Texts*.

M. Lewis, Y. Liu, N. Goyal, M. Ghazvininejad, A. Mohamed, O. Levy, V. Stoyanov, and L. Zettlemoyer. 2020. BART: Denoising Sequence-to-Sequence Pre-training for Natural Language Generation, Translation, and Comprehension. In *ACL*.

P. Li and S. Shi. 2021. Tail-to-tail non-autoregressive sequence prediction for Chinese grammatical error correction. In *ACL*.

J. Lichtarge, C. Alberti, S. Kumar, N. Shazeer, N. Parmar, and S. Tong. 2019a. Corpora Generation for Grammatical Error Correction. In *NAACL.*

J. Lichtarge, C. Alberti, S. Kumar, N. Shazeer, N. Parmar, and S. Tong. 2019b. Corpora generation for grammatical error correction . In *NAACL.*

E. Malmi, S. Krause, S. Rothe, D. Mirylenka, and A. Severyn. 2019. Encode, tag, realize: High-precision text editing. In *EMNLP-IJCNLP.*

A. D. McCarthy, C. Kirov, M. Grella, A. Nidhi, P. Xia, K. Gorman, E. Vylomova, S. J. Mielke, G. Nicolai, M. Silfverberg, T. Arkhangelskiy, N. Krizhanovsky, A. Krizhanovsky, E. Klyachko, A. Sorokin, J. Mansfield, V. Ernštreits, Y. Pinter, C. L. Jacobs, R. Cotterell, M. Hulden, and D. Yarowsky. 2020. UniMorph 3.0: Universal Morphology . In *LREC.*

B. Mohit, A. Rozovskaya, N. Habash, W. Zaghouani, and O. Obeid. 2014. The first QALB shared task on automatic text correction for Arabic. In *ANLP Workshop.*

J. Naplava and M. Straka. 2019. Grammatical error correction in low-resource scenarios. In *W-NUT Workshop.*

H.T. Ng, S.M. Wu, T. Briscoe, C. Hadiwinoto, R. Susanto, and C. Bryant. 2014. The conll-2014 shared task on grammatical error correction. In *Proceedings of CoNLL: Shared Task.*

K. Omelianchuk, V. Atrasevych, A. Chernodub, and O. Skurzhanskyi. 2020. GECToR ? Grammatical Error Correction: Tag, Not Rewrite . In *Building Educational Applications Workshop (BEA).*

M. Ott, S. Edunov, A. Baevski, A. Fan, S. Gross, N. Ng, D. Grangier, and M. Auli. 2019. fairseq: A Fast, Extensible Toolkit for Sequence Modeling. In *NAACL.*

Peng Qi, Yuhao Zhang, Yuhui Zhang, Jason Bolton, and Christopher D. Manning. 2020. Stanza: A Python natural language processing toolkit for many human languages. In *Proceedings of the 58th Annual Meeting of the Association for Computational Linguistics: System Demonstrations.*

C. Raffel, N. Shazeer, A. Roberts, K. Lee, S. Narang, M. Matena, Y. Zhou, W. Li, and P. J. Liu. 2020. Exploring the limits of transfer learning with a unified text-to-text transformer. *Journal of Machine Learning Research*, 21(140):1–67.

S. Rothe, J. Mallinson, E. Malmi, S. Krause, and A. Severyn. 2021. A simple recipe for multilingual grammatical error correction. In *ACL.*

A. Rozovskaya. 2022. Automatic Classification of Russian Learner Errors. In *LREC.*

A. Rozovskaya and D. Roth. 2013. Joint learning and inference for grammatical error correction. In *Proceedings of EMNLP.*

A. Rozovskaya and D. Roth. 2014. Building a State-of-the-Art Grammatical Error Correction System. In *Transactions of ACL.*

A. Schmaltz, Y. Kim, A. M. Rush, and S. M. Shieber. 2016. Sentence-level grammatical error identification as sequence-to-sequence correction . In *Proceedings of the NAACL Workshop on Innovative Use of NLP for Building Educational Applications (BEA-16).*

O. Syvokon and O. Nahorna. 2021. UA-GEC: Grammatical Error Correction and Fluency Corpus for the Ukrainian Language.

O. Syvokon and M Romanyshyn. 2023. The UNLP 2023 shared task on grammatical error correction for Ukrainian. In *Proceedings of the Second Ukrainian Natural Language Processing Workshop.*

J. Tetreault, J. Foster, and M. Chodorow. 2010. Using parse features for preposition selection and error detection. In *Proceedings of ACL.*

J. Tiedemann and S. Thottingal. 2020. OPUS-MT ? Building open translation services for the World. In *Proceedings of the 22nd Annual Conferenec of the European Association for Machine Translation (EAMT).*

A. Vaswani, N. Shazeer, N. Parmar, J. Uszkoreit, L. Jones, A. N. Gomez, Ł. Kaiser, and I. Polosukhin. 2017. 2017. Attention is all you need. *In I. Guyon, U. V. Luxburg, S. Bengio, H. Wallach, R. Fergus, S. Vishwanathan, and R. Garnett, editors, Advances in Neural Information Processing Systems.*

Guillaume Wenzek, Marie-Anne Lachaux, Alexis Conneau, Vishrav Chaudhary, Francisco Guzmán, Armand Joulin, and Edouard Grave. 2020. CCNet: Extracting high quality monolingual datasets from web crawl data. In *Proceedings of the Twelfth Language Resources and Evaluation Conference.*

Z. Xie, G. Genthial, S. Xie, A. Y. Ng, and D. Jurafsky. 2018. Noising and Denoising Natural Language: Diverse Backtranslation for Grammar Correction. In *NAACL.*

L. Xue, N. Constant, A. Roberts, M. Kale, R. Al-Rfou, A. Siddhant, A. Barua, and C. Raffel. 2021. mt5: A massively multilingual pre-trained text-to-text transformer. . In *NAACL.*

Z. Yuan and T. Briscoe. 2016. Grammatical error correction using neural machine translation. In *NAACL.*

W. Zhao, L. Wang, K. Shen, R. Jia, and J. Liu. 2019. Improving grammatical error correction via pre-training a copy-augmented architecture with unlabeled data. In *NAACL.*

RedPenNet for Grammatical Error Correction: Outputs to Tokens, Attentions to Spans

Bohdan Didenko
WebSpellChecker LLC / Ukraine
bogdan@webspellchecker.net

Andrii Sameliuk
WebSpellChecker LLC / Ukraine
andrii.sameliuk@webspellchecker.net

Abstract

The text editing tasks, including sentence fusion, sentence splitting and rephrasing, text simplification, and Grammatical Error Correction (GEC), share a common trait of dealing with highly similar input and output sequences. This area of research lies at the intersection of two well-established fields: (i) fully autoregressive sequence-to-sequence approaches commonly used in tasks like Neural Machine Translation (NMT) and (ii) sequence tagging techniques commonly used to address tasks such as Part-of-speech tagging, Named-entity recognition (NER), and similar. In the pursuit of a balanced architecture, researchers have come up with numerous imaginative and unconventional solutions, which we're discussing in the Related Works 4 section. Our approach to addressing text editing tasks is called RedPenNet and is aimed at reducing architectural and parametric redundancies presented in specific Sequence-To-Edits models, preserving their semi-autoregressive advantages. Our models achieve $F_{0.5}$ scores of 77.60 on the BEA-2019 (test), which can be considered as state-of-the-art the only exception for system combination (Qorib et al., 2022) and 67.71 on the UAGEC+Fluency (test) benchmarks.

This research is being conducted in the context of the UNLP 2023 workshop, where it will be presented as a paper for the Shared Task in Grammatical Error Correction (GEC) for Ukrainian. This study aims to apply the RedPenNet approach to address the GEC problem in the Ukrainian language. Public data related to this article may appear over time in this GitHub repository [1].

1 Introduction

The GEC challenge has been tackled with various techniques, including the traditional Autoregressive (AR) Neural Machine Translation (NMT) using the transformer architecture (Vaswani et al., 2017), as well as additional methods that we refer to collectively as Inference Optimized (IO). The existing IO methods for GEC can be broadly categorized into two groups, as described further.

The first group is non-autoregressive Feed Forward (FF) approaches which involve a single forward pass — through the model and provides token-level edit operations, such as the approach proposed in (Awasthi et al., 2019), (Omelianchuk et al., 2020). The advantage of FF approaches is their fast inference speed. However, their limitations lie in how they maintain consistency between interrelated edits, which leads to the need for iterative sentence correction approaches. The iterative sentence correction process solves some issues with interrelated corrections. However, it introduces new challenges. The absence of information about the initial input state could potentially lead to substantial modifications of the text meaning and structure, including rewording, word rearrangement, and the addition or removal of sentence components.

The second category consists of Inference Optimized Autoregressive (IOAR) models, which can be further separated into two subcategories: (i) sequence-to-edits (SeqToEdits). This category encompasses works such as (Malmi et al., 2019), (Chen et al., 2020), (Stahlberg and Kumar, 2020), and the RedPenNet model examined in this paper; (ii) the recently proposed Input-guided Aggressive Decoding (IGAD) approach (Ge et al., 2022), which has been proven effective for GEC tasks, as demonstrated in the study (Sun et al., 2021). More information about these model categories can be found in the Related Work 4 section.

In our study, we propose RedPenNet, which is an IOAR model of the SeqToEdits subtype. RedPenNet utilizes a single shallow decoder (Kasai et al., 2020) for generating both replacement tokens and spans. During the generation of edit tokens, the encoder-decoder attention weights are used to determine the edit spans. For these attentions, pre-

[1] https://github.com/WebSpellChecker/unlp-2023-shared-task

Proceedings of the Second Ukrainian Natural Language Processing Workshop (UNLP), pages 121–131
May 5, 2023 ©2023 Association for Computational Linguistics

softmax logits are fed as inputs to a linear transformation which predicts the position of the edit in the source sentence. This approach is similar to the method described in Pointer Networks (Vinyals et al., 2015). Additionally, we train compact task-specific decoder BPE vocabularies to reduce the cost of the pre-softmax dot operation, making it more efficient for predicting replacement tokens. The RedPenNet model is also capable of tackling the challenge of Multilingual GEC (Rothe et al., 2021). To achieve this, specialized shallow decoders need to be trained for different languages. This gives the ability to use a single model with a multilingual pre-trained encoder and language-specific decoders.

Our proposed solution has a design that enables converting the input sequence into any output sequence, achieving competitive results in solving the GEC task.

2 RedPenNet

2.1 General

Instead of predicting the target sequence directly, the RedPenNet model generates a sequence of N 2-tuples $(t_n, s_n) \in V \times \mathbb{N}_0$ where t_n is a BPE token obtained from the pre-computed decoder vocabulary 3 and s_n denotes the span positions. In the RedPenNet approach, we define each of the J edit operations $\mathbf{e}$ as a sequence of C 2-tuples (t_c, s_c), where $2 \leq C \leq N$. The first token for each edit e_j is represented as $t_{c=0} = \texttt{SEP}$. As previously mentioned, in our approach, a single edit can consist of multiple tokens. However, to determine the span of a single edit, only two positions are required: s_{start} and s_{end}. To accomplish this, we impose the following constraints for each e_j: $s\_start = s_{c_0}$ and $s\_end = s_{c_1}$. The remaining s_c values for $c \in 2, ..., C$ are not considered. In RedPenNet, if a correction requires inserting text at a position n in the source sequence, it is expressed as $s_{start} = s_{end}$. To handle the deletion operation, a special token DEL $\in V$ is used, which is equivalent to replacing the span with an empty string. If the input text is error-free, RedPenNet generates an EOS token in the first AR step, thereby avoiding unnecessary calculations.

The iterative process of applying edits to the source sequence is illustrated in Algorithm 1. Also, the process of generating GEC edits using the RedPenNet architecture can be visualized with the help of the following illustration 1.

Algorithm 1 editsToCorrect()

$s\_start \leftarrow 0$
$s\_end \leftarrow 0$ { Initialize spans}
$\mathbf{y} \leftarrow \mathbf{x}$ {Initialize $\mathbf{y}$ as tokenized input}
$\mathbf{z} \leftarrow \epsilon$ {Initialize $\mathbf{z}$ edit seq with the empty string.}
for $n \leftarrow 1$ **to** N **do**
  if $t_n = \texttt{EOS}$ **then**
    return $\mathbf{y}$
  else if $t_n = \texttt{SEP}$ **then**
    $\mathbf{y}_{s\_start}^{s\_end} \leftarrow \mathbf{z}$
    $\mathbf{z} \leftarrow \epsilon$
    $s\_start \leftarrow s_n$
  else
    if $t_n \neq \texttt{DEL}$ **then**
      $\mathbf{z} \leftarrow \mathsf{concat}(\mathbf{z}, t_n)$
    end if
    if $t_{n-1} = \texttt{SEP}$ **then**
      $s\_end \leftarrow s_n$
    end if
  end if
end for

In the case of RedPenNet, similar to the Seq2Edits approach (Stahlberg and Kumar, 2020), it is important to maintain a monotonic, left-to-right order of spans and ensure that SEP tokens are never adjacent to each other and the final edit token is always EOS. None of our models generated invalid sequences during inference without any constraints, as it is also the case with Seq2Edits.

2.2 Encoder

The utilization of pre-trained language models has been consistently shown to improve performance on a range of NLP downstream tasks, including GEC, as observed in numerous studies. To train RedPenNet, we deployed pre-trained models from the HuggingFace transformers library[2]. We have observed that models trained on Masked Language Modeling (MLM) tasks perform the best as encoders for the RedPenNet architecture. Therefore, in this work, we focus solely on this family of models. The availability of a range of models within the HuggingFace library offers the flexibility to choose a pre-trained model based on the required size, language, or a multilingual group. This opens up the potential for RedPenNet to (i) create multilingual GEC solutions using language-specific

[2]https://huggingface.co/models

Positions	1	2	3	4	5	5	6	7	8	9	10	11	12	13	14	15	16	17
Input Sentence	~~In~~	~~a~~	other	hand	∅	many	~~of~~	stars	sold	their	privacy	to	earn	more	and	more	money	.

Table 1: Visual representation of the tokenized encoder input sequence that includes visual markings, intended to improve the clarity of the editing process.

Autoregressive Steps	1	2	3	4	5	6	7	8
Input Tokens	SOS	SEP	On	the	SEP	,	SEP	DEL
Input Spans	0	1	3	∅	5	5	6	7
Output Tokens	SEP	On	the	SEP	,	SEP	DEL	EOS
Output Spans	1	3	∅	5	5	6	7	∅

Table 2: This example depicts a step-by-step demonstration of a RedPenNet autoregressive inference that encompasses multi-token edits, insertions and deletions.

decoders with a single multilingual encoder, and (ii) construct RedPenNet model ensembles based on different pre-trained models with comparatively less efforts.

2.3 Decoder

A transformer decoder stack was used as for the decoder in the RedPenNet model. During the training phase, the model learned an autoregressive scoring function $P(\mathbf{t}, \mathbf{s}|\mathbf{x}; \mathbf{\Phi})$, which is implemented as follows:

$$\mathbf{\Phi}* = \arg\max_{\mathbf{\Phi}*} \log P(\mathbf{t}, \mathbf{s}|\mathbf{x}; \mathbf{\Phi})$$
$$= \arg\max_{\mathbf{\Phi}*} \sum_{n=1}^{N} \log P(t_n, s_n | t_1^{n-1}, s_1^{n-1}, \mathbf{x}; \mathbf{\Phi})$$

where $\mathbf{t} = (t_1, ..., t_n)$ represents the sequence of ground-truth edit tokens with SEP tokens that are used to mark the start of each edit. Additionally, $\mathbf{s} = (s_1, ..., s_n)$ indicates the sequence of ground-truth span positions, which denote specific ranges in the input sequence $\mathbf{x}$.

In line with the standard Transformer architecture, the previous time step predictions are fed back into the Transformer decoder. At each step n, the feedback loop consists of the BPE token embedding of t_{n-1}, which is combined with a decoder-specific trainable positional encoding embedding p_{n-1}. The resulting sum is then concatenated with the span embedding of s_{n-1}.

The span embedding on step n can be defined as:

$$\mathbf{s\_emb}_n = s\_mask_n \cdot \mathbf{x\_emb}_{s_{n-1}}$$

$$s\_mask_n = \begin{cases} 0, & \text{if } n = 0 \\ 1, & \text{if } 0 < n \leq 2 \\ 0^{|tid_{n-1} - b|} & \\ +0^{|tid_{n-2} - b|}, & \text{otherwise} \end{cases}$$

where tid_n is an index of token t_n in decoder vocabulary V and is denoted as $\mathbf{tid} = \text{index}(\mathbf{t}, V)$, b is an index of SEP token in V and $\mathbf{x\_emb}_{s_{n-1}}$ is a vector embedding corresponding to $x_{s_{n-1}}$ token. In other words, there are two cases in how span embedding takes values depending on the preceding token sequence: (i) by using the embedding of the token $x_{s_{n-1}}$ from the encoder input sequence when $t_{n-2} = SEP \lor t_{n-1} = SEP$ or (ii) by using a zero-filled embedding ϵ with the same dimensions D as x_n. During training, similar to the MLM task, a binary spans target mask for spans sequences are used to regulate the given logic.

As a result, the inputs of the decoder at step $n-1$ can be expressed as follows:

$$\text{Concat}(\mathbf{t\_emb}_{n-1} + \mathbf{p}_{n-1}, \mathbf{s\_emb}_{n-1})$$
$$= [t\_emb_{n-1,1} + p_{n-1,1}, ..., t\_emb_{n-1,D} + p_{n-1,D},$$
$$s\_emb_{n-1,1}, ..., s\_emb_{n-1,D}] \in \mathbb{R}^{2D}$$

The technique of utilizing the pre-softmax attention weights from an encoder-decoder attention layer to represent the probabilities of positions in the input sequence was introduced in Pointer Networks (Vinyals et al., 2015) and later applied to the GEC task in the Seq2Edits approach (Stahlberg and Kumar, 2020). Additionally, to increase the number of trainable parameters at this stage, a dense layer has been added to the bottom of the spans output linear transform.

3 Training Decoder BPE Vocabularies

In the traditional implementation of the Transformer model, a shared source-target vocabulary is utilized for both the decoder and the encoder, as described in (Vaswani et al., 2017). It is evident that the pre-softmax linear transformation required to transform the decoder output into predicted next-token probabilities is computationally expensive.

Its computational complexity can be expressed as $O(d \cdot v)$, where d is the output dimension of the model and v is the decoder vocabulary size.

If the GEC task is approached by generating correction strings for the edits and using autoregressive decoding for this purpose, we tend to think that the information entropy of the generated sequences will be significantly lower compared to that of the input sequences. Our belief is based on the following two assumptions:

1. People tend to make mistakes in similar phrases and words.

2. Corrected versions of spelling words are statistically more frequent and can be represented by fewer BPE tokens.

Therefore, a smaller BPE vocabulary will be sufficient to create efficient representations of sequences of corrections. In section 5.1.2, we test this hypothesis on one of the languages, as the example shows.

4 Related Work

In the context of the GEC task, the closest family of approaches to RedPenNet is the Autoregressive approaches, specifically the SeqToEdits subtype. They include models such as Lasertagger, Erroneous Span Detection and Correction (ESD&ESC), and Seq2Edits comparison with which is important for understanding the impact of our work. These models share the advantage that the number of autoregressive steps are based on the number of necessary edits to the original text, rather than the length of the input text. We will evaluate each of these approaches to the GEC problem in this section. In this section, we will also discuss the Aggressive Decoding approach, which has evolved from the traditional sequence-to-sequence approach.

The Seq2Edits (Stahlberg and Kumar, 2020) approach predicts a sequence of N edit operations autoregressively from left to the right. Each edit operation is represented as a 3-tuple (tag, span, token) that specifies the action of replacing. The approach allows constructing an edit sequence for any pair (x, y). Tag prediction also improves explainability in the GEC task. For 3-tuple generation, a divided transformer decoder is used, and the tag and span predictions are located between its parts. Seq2Edits approach is similar to RedPenNet in the following (i) generation of spans and replacement tokens within the same autoregressive step, (ii) using Pointer Networks to predict spans. The difference between compared approaches is: 1. RedPenNet uses a single decoder stack to generate tokens and spans. 2. The Seq2Edits approach is different in terms of generating multi-token edits. According to (Bryant et al., 2017), an edit that has at least two tokens (multi-token edit) represents 10% of all edits from the CoNLL-2014 test set. As mentioned before, in the Seq2Edits approach, each step of the autoregressive process predicts an edit which consists of a 3-tuple (tag, end span, replacement token), where the replacement token is a sub--word. According to the cited articles (Stahlberg and Kumar, 2020), the Seq2Edits approach has the capability of representing multi-token edits as a list of single-token edits, where the tag and span remain unchanged, with only the replacement token being changed. In terms of the RedPenNet approach, a single edit can be represented by multiple autoregressive steps, allowing a more natural generation of multi-token edits. 3. In the RedPenNet approach, decoder-specific positional encodings are added to the decoder inputs at the bottom of the decoder stack. This allows the model to effectively utilize the order of multi-token edits. The approach presented in Seq2Edits does not clearly state the location in the divided Transformer decoder, where positional encodings can be utilized. The absence of such encodings can result in difficulty for the model in comprehending the order of the replacement tokens being inserted within the same span positions. 4. RedPenNet uses a pre-calculated, task-specific version of the BPE decoder vocabulary to generate edit tokens, thus reducing the cost of the pre-softmax linear transformation.

The Lasertagger (Malmi et al., 2019) approach deploys an autoregressive Transformer decoder to annotate the input sequence with tags from precalculated output vocabulary. With the limited size of the tags, vocabulary minimizes the cost of the pre-softmax linear transformation, making Lasertagger the fastest approach among the IOAR SeqToEdits architectures. However, the RedPenNet model presents several key differences: (i) it uses a BPE vocabulary instead of a tag vocabulary, (ii) it generates edits rather than tagging the input sequence, and (iii) it can produce a sequence of tokens for each edit.

In the ESD&ESC (Chen et al., 2020) approach, the task of solving the GEC editing problem is divided into two subtasks: Erroneous Span Detection (ESD), where incorrect spans are identified through binary sequence tagging, and Erroneous Span Correction (ESC), where the correction of these spans is performed using a classic autoregressive approach that implies generation of edits for tokens surrounded by annotated span tokens. RedPenNet shares some similarities with this architecture, as it also utilizes autoregressive generation of a sequence of edit tokens, separated by control tokens that are part of the decoder vocabulary. The ESD&ESC approach differs from RedPenNet in several key aspects. 1. Firstly, RedPenNet predicts the span positions in a one-by-one manner at the decoder level, while the ESD&ESC approach uses a separate encoder to generate spans. However, the ESD approach has the same limitations as the FF family, since the ESD tags may not always be consistent, leading to difficulties in maintaining consistency between interrelated edits. The ESC decoder during generation will not have the capability to fully rectify the situation, as it will be confined to the range of the annotated span tokens. 2. RedPenNet approach is capable of decomposing neighboring errors in the input text into multiple edit operations, if necessary. Conversely, the ESD approach merges nearby errors in a single span.

The Aggressive Decoding (Sun et al., 2021) method accelerates the AR calculations for the task by utilizing the input tokens as drafted decoded tokens and autoregressively predicting only those portions that do not match. This leads to a significant improvement in inference speed. The disadvantage of the IGAD approach is that it requires the use of a shared vocabulary with the encoder during decoding. Therefore, even when the input and output sequences are the same, IGAD requires a significant number of floating point operations for the pre-softmax linear transformation in the decoder which is calculated using the formula: $O(v \cdot d \cdot l)$, where v is the vocabulary size, d is the model depth, and l is the input length. This problem becomes more obvious in the case of using pre-trained multi-language models, which traditionally have larger encoder vocabularies and corresponding matrix embeddings. The impact of decoder vocabulary is analyzed in section 3. Additionally, since the length of the output sequence in IGAD is directly tied to the length of the input sequence, the issue of quadratic complexity in attention mechanisms remains in the decoder. This can be a challenge when dealing with long sequences and requires the use of specialized transformer architectures in the decoder.

It is worth mentioning, that the Highlight and Decode Technique described in our previous study (Didenko and Shaptala, 2019). Similar to the Erroneous Span Detection (ESD) component in the ESD&ESC approach, a binary sequence tagging model was used to identify incorrect spans. Subsequently, a broadcast binary sequence mask was element-wise multiplied to a special "highlight" embedding. The result of this operation was added to the encoder output at the bottom of the decoder stack. This allowed the decoder to predict the replacement tokens only for the "highlighted" spans. However, as outlined in the mentioned article, this approach had a list of limitations.

5 Experiments

5.1 UNLP 2023 Shared Task

The UNLP-2023 conference hosted the first Shared Task (Syvokon and Romanyshyn, 2023) in GEC for Ukrainian. One of the primary difficulties in addressing the GEC problem for the Ukrainian language lies in the scarcity of high-quality annotated training examples — a common issue for Non-English GEC. The Ukrainian language also poses an additional challenge due to its rich morphological structure and fusional nature. (Syvokon and Nahorna, 2021). The foundation of this Shared Task was established by Grammarly's efforts to develop a corpus that has been professionally annotated for GEC and fluency edits in the Ukrainian language, referred to as the UA-GEC corpus. The Shared Task consists of two tracks: (i) GEC-only, which focuses on automatically identifying and correcting grammatical errors in written text, and (ii) GEC+Fluency, which encompasses corrections for grammar, spelling, punctuation, and fluency. Given that the RedPenNet architecture is capable of handling any type of editing, including rephrasing, reordering words, and sentence splitting, we decided to participate in the GEC+Fluency track.

GEC+Fluency Baseline: Furthermore, the organizers offered a baseline model [3] based on facebook/mbart-large-50. This model was trained for a NMT task with the objective of autoregressively generating correct text from erroneous input. The score of baseline can be found in table 3.

[3]https://huggingface.co/osyvokon/mbart50-large-ua-gec-baseline

5.1.1 Data

In the case of GEC tasks, data is typically stored in the m2 format (Dahlmeier and Ng, 2012), where each instance consists of a source text and a list of edits required to transform it into the target text. To adapt the m2 training examples for the RedPenNet architecture, we (i) deployed the pre-trained encoder tokenizer to tokenize the erroneous input text, (ii) used the decoder tokenizer 3 to tokenize the edits correction strings, and (iii) converted the span offsets from the word count separated by spaces to the corresponding BPE tokens (sub-words) offsets.

UA-GEC: In the GEC+Fluency track of the Shared Task, the participants were given access to the gec-fluency public dataset [4]. The training data comprises 32,734 examples, where 15,161 contain at least one annotated error edit, while 17,573 are error-free. The evaluation dataset consists of 1,506 dev set and 1,350 test set instances. In this Shared Task, two annotators annotated all examples from the development set of the dataset and some examples from the training set. They also annotated all examples from the evolution dev sets, as well as some examples from the training data. For the Shared Task, all the data was tokenized using the stanza library [5]. To categorize the dataset edits by error types, we utilized a set of 20 tags. They included 14 grammar types and 6 fluency types.

Synthetic Data: Much of the research on the GEC problem shows that the use of pre-generated synthetic data reduces model training time and also improves overall quality. For the UNLP 2023 Shared Task, we generated over $160K$ Ukrainian erroneous data sentences based on error-free texts taken from data corpora presented on lang.org.ua [6] website. For our error generation approach, we utilized mbart-large-50 as a pre-train model, which we trained using the back translation method (Xie et al., 2018) on the training data from the UA-GEC dataset. Our task was to transduce the error-free input text sequence into the erroneous one. The synthetic data generation model was trained on a Google Colab Premium GPU instance for 8 epochs with a batch size of 4, a learning rate of 1e-5, and a maximum input and output length of 128 tokens each. The performance of the RedPenNet architecture trained on this pre-training data is presented in Table 4.

[4]https://github.com/asivokon/unlp-2023-shared-task

[5]https://stanfordnlp.github.io/stanza/

[6]https://lang.org.ua/uk/corpora/

5.1.2 Decoder vocabulary for Ukrainian GEC

Multiple BPE decoder vocabularies were trained with varying sizes and evaluated based on the resulting output token count (refer to Figure 1). A training text file was created specifically for this purpose, consisting of correction strings extracted from the m2 edits. The (gec-fluency/train.m2) file from the UNLP-2023 Shared Task was used as the source. Also, we added additional 50,000 of the most frequent words from the Ukrainian Frequency dictionary of lexemes of artistic prose.[7] to the vocabularies training text file extracted from (gec-fluency/train.m2). The (gec-fluency/valid.m2) was utilized to evaluate and compare the different sizes of the decoder vocabularies.

The evaluation was performed by extracting and concatenating the correction strings from all edits for each annotated m2 sentence into a space-separated sequence. This sequence was then tokenized using different decoder vocabularies. Example: annotated m2 sentence:

```
S Нечіткі бенефітс співпраці ,
натомість вихначені зобовязання
A 5 6|||Spelling|||визначені|||...|||0
A 6 7|||Spelling|||зобов'язання|||...|||0
A 1 2|||Spelling|||бенефіціари|||...|||1
A 5 6|||Spelling|||визначені|||...|||1
A 6 7|||Spelling|||зобов'язання|||...|||1
A 7 7|||Punctuation|||.|||...|||1
```

concatenated edits corrections:

```
визначені зобов'язання бенефіціари
визначені зобов'язання .
```

To compare the advantages of using a shorter task-specific decoder vocabulary for the Ukrainian GEC task, we will use the mbart-large-50 baseline model 5.1 as a reference. For this model, the number of operations required for the pre-softmax linear transformation is $(1024 \cdot 250,054) =$ 256,055,296 floating-point operations. In contrast, our trained vocabulary with a size of 16,384 performs the same task using only $(1024 \cdot 16,384) =$ 16,777,216 operations while maintaining a smaller encoding length than the baseline.

5.1.3 Model Configuration

Encoders: For the encoder part of RedPenNet, we chose pre-trained models from those available

[7]http://ukrkniga.org.ua/ukr_rate/hproz_92k_lex_dict_orig.csv

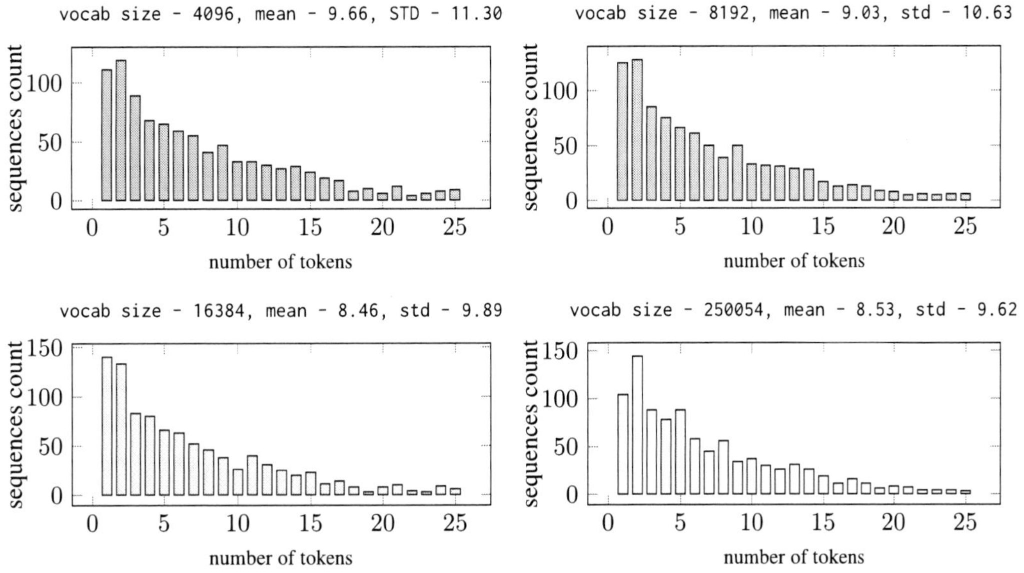

Figure 1: The x-axis depicts the number of tokens required to represent the concatenated correction of sequences for each m2 instance. The y-axis represents the total count of the concatenated corrections extracted from the (gec-fluency/valid.m2) that meet a specific number of tokens. The results show that as the vocabulary size increases, the mean number of tokens needed to encode one concatenated correction decreases. However, when the vocabulary reaches 16,384, a vocabulary trained on corrections and frequent words outperforms the native vocabulary of mbart-large-50 in terms of the mean parameter.

on the Hugging Face Hub [8]. Our main requirement during the selection process was that the models were trained on the Ukrainian language corpora. We built and compared a few models based on different encoders: **RPN(R_{LARGE})** – RoBERTa Large [9] transferred to Ukrainian using the method from the NAACL2022 paper (Minixhofer et al., 2022), **RPN(XLM_{BASE})** – a smaller version of the XLM-RoBERTa [10] model with only Ukrainian and some English embeddings left. Comparative results for these models can be seen in the table 3

Decoder: We utilized a shallow RedPenNet Decoder stack 2.3 for the decoder part of our architecture. It consists of two layers, and we kept the model depth and dropout parameters the same as the encoders. We utilized a previously computed decoder vocabulary (refer to Section 5.1.2) which was set to a size of $16,384$.

Setup: Tensorflow 2 on a Google Colab TPU instance was used for training and evaluation. In most of the combinations, we conducted pre-training on synthetic data for 20 epochs, followed by training on UA-GEC erroneous data for 30 epochs using a batch size of 32 and a learning rate of 2e$-$5. Afterward, we fine-tuned the model on UA-GEC (erroneous + error-free) data for 5 epochs, with a batch size of 16 and a learning rate of 5e$-$6. In the Results section 5.1.5, we present the results of the approaches that showed the best performance.

5.1.4 Evaluation

For the evaluation, the organizers of the Shared Task provided the script based on Errant [11]. Although Errant isn't able to handle specific error types in Ukrainian, it is common practice to use this library for other non-English languages, such as Spanish (Davidson et al., 2020). We have also evaluated scores on the free version of LanguageTool and Hunspell for comparison 3.

In RedPenNet, we implemented a *minimum edit probability* parameter to filter out low-probability edits and to improve precision at the cost of recall. To achieve this, we averaged the probabilities of all predicted edit tokens, as well as the predicted start span and end span for each edit. We assessed the probability of all edits in the model output and discarded those that have probabilities below the *min-*

[8] https://huggingface.co/models

[9] https://huggingface.co/benjamin/roberta-large-wechsel-ukrainian

[10] https://huggingface.co/ukr-models/xlm-roberta-base-uk

[11] https://github.com/chrisjbryant/errant

Approach	min edit prob	dev P	dev R	dev $F_{0.5}$	test P	test R	test $F_{0.5}$
Hunspell	-	12.9	04.0	08.9	-	-	-
Langtool(free)	-	21.8	05.9	14.2	-	-	-
Langtool(free)+Hunspell	-	19.1	09.0	15.6	-	-	-
MBart-50$_{\text{LARGE}}$		67.51	39.48	59.11	73.06	44.36	64.69
RPN(XLM$_{\text{BASE}}$)	0.94	74.9	31.2	58.51	-	-	-
RPN(R$_{\text{LARGE}}$)	0.95	75.31	35.11	**61.28**	76.54	41.93	**65.69**
1×RPN(XLM$_{\text{BASE}}$) + 2×RPN(R$_{\text{LARGE}}$)*	58.5/59	80.28	36.58	**64.80**	80.86	41.03	**67.71**

Table 3: displays the performance comparison between RedPenNet (RPN) and other existing public methods on the UA-GEC+Fluency dataset. The *min edit prob* column shows the edit probability threshold required for accepting an edit.

Approach	UA-GEC+Fluency (dev) P	R	$F_{0.5}$
Synt. pre-train & freeze encoder	08.0	08.9	08.2
Synt. pre-train	07.18	**17,27**	08.13

Table 4: Performance of RPN(R$_{\text{LARGE}}$) after pre-training on synthetic data.

imum edit probability. All edits with probabilities surpassing the threshold were applied. A similar prediction filtering method for GEC was proposed in the GECToR paper and was called "Inference tweaking". And in both cases, the method proved to be effective in improving precision. We also experimented with an iterative correction process, where the output of a previous correction round is used as input for the next one.

Ensembles To create an ensemble of the RedPenNet models, we calculated the average edit probabilities and applied an algorithm that follows the subsequent scenario: 1. For matched edits, we summed their probabilities. 2. For intersecting edits, we choose the more probable one. 3. We kept all remaining non-intersecting edits in the result. Then we tuned the *minimum edit probability* parameter to maximize the F0.5 score on the UA-GEC+Fluency dev set.

5.1.5 Results

We began by pre-training models solely on erroneous data, as proposed in the GECToR research. During this stage, we froze encoders and used synthetic data for pre-training. In the next stage, we unfroze the encoders and trained the models on UA-GEC erroneous data. Our experiments indicate that a low learning rate of $\pm$5e$-$6, a small batch size, a few training steps (less than epoch), and an increase in dropouts to ± 0.2 are useful during the initial stages of fine-tuning on a combination of (erroneous + error-free) data. This approach enables us to capture a good checkpoint when the model shifts from recall to precision.

To implement ensembles, we trained two RPN(R$_{\text{LARGE}}$) models and one RPN(XLM$_{\text{BASE}}$) model. The only difference between the two RPN(R$_{\text{LARGE}}$) models is that one of them was trained on erroneous data before being trained on (error-free + erroneous data). The model that was trained only on (error-free + erroneous data) has higher recall.

To enhance the quality of the results, we performed two rounds of iterative correction and applied the ensemble technique to the output of each round. During the first iteration, we set the *minimum edit probability* to 0.585, and for the second iteration, it was set to 0.59. During iterative correction, we selected the value of the *minimum edit probability* parameter that maximizes the precision score.

During the experiment, we demonstrated that our custom architecture, RedPenNet can be applied to the GEC task, with performance that competes with large Seq2Seq models like mbart-large-50 and significantly outperforms classical algorithmic approaches.

5.2 BEA 2019 Shared Task

To further demonstrate the capabilities of the RedPenNet architecture, we applied it to the BEA-2019 Shared Task on English GEC.

Data: The combination of erroneous data obtained from several sources was used for pre-training. We used 20 million samples from the synthetic *tagged corruption* dataset (Stahlberg and Kumar, 2021)[12], approximately 500K English samples from the (Rahman, 2022) study, and around 500K English samples from the *lang-8* dataset. The

[12] https://huggingface.co/datasets/liweili/c4_200m

data was sampled in the following proportions: 50% of *tagged corruption*, 25% of *lang-8*, and 25% of samples from the (Rahman, 2022) study. Only data samples that had at least one error were selected. After pre-training, we used the combination of *W&I+LOCNESS* train set with 13,574 sentences from CWEB(G+S) evaluation dataset (Flachs et al., 2020) [13] that are used as training data for fine-tuning.

Model Configuration: We trained several different-sized RedPenNet models: two based on XLNet [14] pre-trains - RPN(XLNBASE) and RPN(XLNLARGE), and two models based on Muppet Roberta [15]: RPN(MPRBASE) and RPN(MPRLARGE).

The decoder stack consists of two layers, and we utilized a pre-computed decoder vocabulary trained on text corrections extracted from `ABC.train.gold.bea19.m2`. The chosen vocabulary size is 8192.

For pre-training, we conducted 500K steps with a batch size of 128 for BASE models and 64 for LARGE, setting the learning rate to 3e−5. For fine-tuning, we performed 4-6 epochs (depending on the model) to obtain the maximum $F_{0.5}$ score on the *W&I+LOCNESS* dev set. During fine-tuning, we used a batch size of 32 and a learning rate of 5e−6 for all models.

Table 5: BEA-2019 (Test)

Model	P	R	$F_{0.5}$
(Qorib et al., 2022)∗	86.6	60.9	79.9
(Lichtarge et al., 2020)	75.4	64.7	73.0
(Omelianchuk et al., 2020)	79.4	57.2	73.7
(Stahlberg and Kumar, 2021)	77.7	65.4	74.9
(Rothe et al., 2021)	-	-	75.9
RPN(MPR$_{BASE}$)	80,80	56,71	74,47
4×RPN ensemble	**86.62**	54.80	**77.60**

Table 6: A comparison of the performance of various modern GEC approaches, including RedPenNet on the BEA-2019 test set. (Qorib et al., 2022)∗ provides results of combination several systems outputs.

Evaluation and Results: We evaluated RedPenNet models on *W&I+LOCNESS* test set. For our best result, we used an ensemble of RPN(XLNBASE), RPN(XLNLARGE), RPN(MPRBASE) and RPN(MPRLARGE) models. We merged the output using the same scenario as for the UNLP 2023 Shared Task 5.1.4 and determined the best *minimum edit probability* to be 0.68. Interestingly, the second round of processing, in which the outputs from the previous round served as model inputs, did not lead to an improvement in the $F_{0.5}$ score. As it is shown in Table 6, our approach yields state-of-the-art results on BEA-2019 (Test) benchmark, surpassed only by the System Combination result by (Qorib et al., 2022). Furthermore, it is worth mentioning that the RedPenNet ensemble consisting of four BASE/LARGE models outperforms the BEA-2019 (Test) $F_{0.5}$ score of the T5-XXL 11B model from (Rothe et al., 2021) study.

[13] `https://github.com/SimonHFL/CWEB`

[14] `https://huggingface.co/xlnet-large-cased`

[15] `https://huggingface.co/facebook/muppet-roberta-large`

6 Conclusion

While there has been a significant amount of research in the field and many tailored architectures have been proposed, a universally accepted neural architecture for text editing tasks that involves highly similar input and output sequences has yet to be established. This has prevented the creation of an industry standard that can be included in default toolkits for popular machine learning libraries and MLOps tools. Our proposed RedPenNet is an attempt to create a universal neural architecture that is not overloaded with design nuances and is capable of implementing any source-to-target transformation using a minimal number of autoregressive steps. The RedPenNet architecture is a classic transformer, and the only differences lie in how we form decoder input embeddings and interpret outputs and attention scores.

Limitations

While the RedPenNet approach has demonstrated several strengths, such as superior inference capabilities for seq2seq tasks with highly similar inputs and outputs, and some advantages over other SeqToEdits approaches highlighted in the Related Works 4 section, it is not without its limitations:

Due to the tailored architecture of RedPenNet, there are no off-the-shelf solutions for data preprocessing, training, and fine-tuning, as is the case of tasks such as common classification or sequence-to-sequence. Consequently, it is not possible to use convenient tools like the HuggingFace Estimator or cloud platforms for rapid model fine-tuning and deployment.

Additionally, the implementation of a non-greedy beam search approach is complicated by the presence of multiple sequence outputs.

One more fundamental limitation is that for each edit, the model needs to generate at least two tokens (SEP, token). This does not provide an advantage in reducing the number of autoregressive steps, particularly for short and error-crowded sentences.

Additionally, while RedPenNet has the ability to express any type of input sequence transformation through a number of editing operations, it may not be able to express a single "conceptual" edit, such as transferring a word within a sentence, using a single edit operation. In such cases, two edits — deletion and insertion — may be required to accomplish the desired transformation.

Ethics Statement

Our study focuses on the development of a neural architecture for text editing tasks. The research was conducted in accordance with ethical principles, and no sensitive or personal data was used or collected during the study. The UA-GEC dataset and corpora presented on lang.org.ua used in the study have been obtained from public sources, and their authors assure the privacy and confidentiality of the original texts. The results of the study are intended to improve the efficiency and accuracy of text writing and may be useful for other NLP tasks. We ensure that the study does not raise any ethical concerns or has no negative impact on individuals or groups.

Acknowledgments

We would like to acknowledge and give our thanks to WebSpellChecker LLC for the support and resources allocated to this project. We are also grateful to the WebSpellChecker team, especially Julia Shaptala and Viktoriia Biliaieva, for their assistance and advice during the competition. We are expressing our gratitude to the Program Committee reviewers for organizing the first Shared Task in Grammatical Error Correction (GEC) for Ukrainian, their guidance and insightful recommendations. Also, we would like to mention that the competition took place and this paper was written in Ukraine during wartime. We extend our sincere thanks to all Ukrainian defenders and all supporters of our country and people during these tough times. We also wish to acknowledge our friends who are defending the country with arms — Andrey Boychuk and Georgiy Bondarenko. We would like to honor the memory of Andrey Avilov who died during the liberation of Balakliya.

References

Abhijeet Awasthi, Sunita Sarawagi, Rasna Goyal, Sabyasachi Ghosh, and Vihari Piratla. 2019. Parallel iterative edit models for local sequence transduction. *CoRR*, abs/1910.02893.

Christopher Bryant, Mariano Felice, and Ted Briscoe. 2017. Automatic annotation and evaluation of error types for grammatical error correction. In *Proceedings of the 55th Annual Meeting of the Association for Computational Linguistics (Volume 1: Long Papers)*, pages 793–805, Vancouver, Canada. Association for Computational Linguistics.

Mengyun Chen, Tao Ge, Xingxing Zhang, Furu Wei, and Ming Zhou. 2020. Improving the efficiency of grammatical error correction with erroneous span detection and correction. In *Proceedings of the 2020 Conference on Empirical Methods in Natural Language Processing (EMNLP)*, pages 7162–7169, Online. Association for Computational Linguistics.

Daniel Dahlmeier and Hwee Tou Ng. 2012. Better evaluation for grammatical error correction. In *Proceedings of the 2012 Conference of the North American Chapter of the Association for Computational Linguistics: Human Language Technologies*, pages 568–572, Montréal, Canada. Association for Computational Linguistics.

Sam Davidson, Aaron Yamada, Paloma Fernandez Mira, Agustina Carando, Claudia H. Sanchez Gutierrez, and Kenji Sagae. 2020. Developing NLP tools with a new corpus of learner Spanish. In *Proceedings of the 12th Language Resources and Evaluation Conference*, pages 7238–7243, Marseille, France. European Language Resources Association.

Bohdan Didenko and Julia Shaptala. 2019. Multi-headed architecture based on BERT for grammatical errors correction. In *Proceedings of the Fourteenth Workshop on Innovative Use of NLP for Building Educational Applications*, pages 246–251, Florence, Italy. Association for Computational Linguistics.

Simon Flachs, Ophélie Lacroix, Helen Yannakoudakis, Marek Rei, and Anders Søgaard. 2020. Grammatical error correction in low error density domains: A new benchmark and analyses.

Tao Ge, Heming Xia, Xin Sun, Si-Qing Chen, and Furu Wei. 2022. Lossless acceleration for seq2seq generation with aggressive decoding.

Jungo Kasai, Nikolaos Pappas, Hao Peng, James Cross, and Noah A. Smith. 2020. Deep encoder, shallow decoder: Reevaluating non-autoregressive machine translation.

Jared Lichtarge, Chris Alberti, and Shankar Kumar. 2020. Data weighted training strategies for grammatical error correction. *Transactions of the Association for Computational Linguistics*, 8:634–646.

Eric Malmi, Sebastian Krause, Sascha Rothe, Daniil Mirylenka, and Aliaksei Severyn. 2019. Encode, tag, realize: High-precision text editing.

Benjamin Minixhofer, Fabian Paischer, and Navid Rekabsaz. 2022. WECHSEL: Effective initialization of subword embeddings for cross-lingual transfer of monolingual language models. In *Proceedings of the 2022 Conference of the North American Chapter of the Association for Computational Linguistics: Human Language Technologies*, pages 3992–4006, Seattle, United States. Association for Computational Linguistics.

Kostiantyn Omelianchuk, Vitaliy Atrasevych, Artem Chernodub, and Oleksandr Skurzhanskyi. 2020. Gector – grammatical error correction: Tag, not rewrite.

Muhammad Qorib, Seung-Hoon Na, and Hwee Tou Ng. 2022. Frustratingly easy system combination for grammatical error correction. In *Proceedings of the 2022 Conference of the North American Chapter of the Association for Computational Linguistics: Human Language Technologies*, pages 1964–1974, Seattle, United States. Association for Computational Linguistics.

Chowdhury Rafeed Rahman. 2022. Judge a sentence by its content to generate grammatical errors.

Sascha Rothe, Jonathan Mallinson, Eric Malmi, Sebastian Krause, and Aliaksei Severyn. 2021. A simple recipe for multilingual grammatical error correction. In *Proceedings of the 59th Annual Meeting of the Association for Computational Linguistics and the 11th International Joint Conference on Natural Language Processing (Volume 2: Short Papers)*, pages 702–707, Online. Association for Computational Linguistics.

Felix Stahlberg and Shankar Kumar. 2020. Seq2Edits: Sequence transduction using span-level edit operations. In *Proceedings of the 2020 Conference on Empirical Methods in Natural Language Processing (EMNLP)*, pages 5147–5159, Online. Association for Computational Linguistics.

Felix Stahlberg and Shankar Kumar. 2021. Synthetic data generation for grammatical error correction with tagged corruption models. In *Proceedings of the 16th Workshop on Innovative Use of NLP for Building Educational Applications*, pages 37–47, Online. Association for Computational Linguistics.

Xin Sun, Tao Ge, Furu Wei, and Houfeng Wang. 2021. Instantaneous grammatical error correction with shallow aggressive decoding.

Oleksiy Syvokon and Olena Nahorna. 2021. UA-GEC: grammatical error correction and fluency corpus for the ukrainian language. *CoRR*, abs/2103.16997.

Oleksiy Syvokon and Mariana Romanyshyn. 2023. The UNLP 2023 shared task on grammatical error correction for Ukrainian. In *Proceedings of the Second Ukrainian Natural Language Processing Workshop*, Dubrovnik, Croatia. Association for Computational Linguistics.

Ashish Vaswani, Noam Shazeer, Niki Parmar, Jakob Uszkoreit, Llion Jones, Aidan N. Gomez, Lukasz Kaiser, and Illia Polosukhin. 2017. Attention is all you need.

Oriol Vinyals, Meire Fortunato, and Navdeep Jaitly. 2015. Pointer networks.

Ziang Xie, Guillaume Genthial, Stanley Xie, Andrew Ng, and Dan Jurafsky. 2018. Noising and denoising natural language: Diverse backtranslation for grammar correction. In *Proceedings of the 2018 Conference of the North American Chapter of the Association for Computational Linguistics: Human Language Technologies, Volume 1 (Long Papers)*, pages 619–628, New Orleans, Louisiana. Association for Computational Linguistics.

The UNLP 2023 Shared Task on Grammatical Error Correction for Ukrainian

Oleksiy Syvokon
Microsoft
osyvokon@microsoft.com

Mariana Romanyshyn
Grammarly
mariana.romanyshyn@grammarly.com

Abstract

This paper presents the results of the UNLP 2023 shared task, the first Shared Task on Grammatical Error Correction for the Ukrainian language. The task included two tracks: GEC-only and GEC+Fluency. The dataset and evaluation scripts were provided to the participants, and the final results were evaluated on a hidden test set. Six teams submitted their solutions before the deadline, and four teams submitted papers that were accepted to appear in the UNLP workshop proceedings and are referred to in this report. The CodaLab leaderboard is left open for further submissions.

1 Introduction

Grammatical Error Correction (GEC) is an important task in natural language processing (NLP) that aims to automatically detect and correct grammatical errors in a given text. With the rapid growth of digital communication, GEC has become increasingly important in improving the quality of written communication. However, GEC is a complex task, especially for languages with complex grammar rules and rich morphology such as Ukrainian. Lack of large annotated and unlabeled datasets poses another challenge.

Shared tasks were a major contributing factor to the GEC progress in other languages: HOO-2011, HOO-2012, CoNLL-2013, CoNLL-2014, BEA-2019 (Dale and Kilgarriff, 2011; Dale et al., 2012; Ng et al., 2013, 2014; Mizumoto et al., 2012; Napoles et al., 2017; Bryant et al., 2019). Following that trend and to promote the development of GEC systems for Ukrainian, we organized the UNLP 2023 Shared Task on Grammatical Error Correction for Ukrainian. The shared task was organized as part of the Second Ukrainian NLP Workshop (UNLP 2023) colocated with EACL'2023.

The remainder of the paper is organized as follows. Section 2 describes the task. Section 3 describes the dataset. Section 4 explains how the submissions were evaluated. Finally, Section 5 presents the results of the participating teams.

2 Task description

The UNLP 2023 shared task required the participating systems to correct a text in the Ukrainian language to make it grammatical or both grammatical and fluent. Consequently, two tracks were suggested: GEC-only and GEC+Fluency. We made this distinction because fluency errors are more subjective and thus harder to correct.

In the GEC-only track, the participating systems were expected to correct grammar, spelling, and punctuation errors in the test set. The GEC+Fluency track added fluency errors to that list. Fluency errors include word calques, stylistically inappropriate words, repetitions, or any other constructions that sound unnatural to a native speaker. It was not mandatory to participate in both tracks, i.e., participating in either GEC-only or GEC+Fluency was acceptable.

Error classification was out of the scope of the shared task.

We provided the participants with a preprocessed version of the UA-GEC corpus (Syvokon et al., 2023) for training and validation (see Section 3 for details) but also encouraged them to use any external data of their choice. Evaluation scripts were provided together with the data.

We set up a CodaLab environment[1] to manage system submissions and the leaderboard. The participants submitted their system results to CodaLab, which automatically evaluated their results on a hidden test set and returned the scores. We used $F_{0.5}$ computed by Errant (Felice and Briscoe, 2015) as the primary metric. The leaderboard is still open for further submissions.

Proceedings of the Second Ukrainian Natural Language Processing Workshop (UNLP), pages 132–137
May 5, 2023 ©2023 Association for Computational Linguistics

Split	Documents	Sentences	Tokens	Annotations
Train	1,706	31,038	457,017	26,123
Valid	87	1,422	23,692	1,393
Test	79	1,274	19,911	1,081

Table 1: The GEC-only data statistics. Validation and test sets were independently annotated by two annotators.

Split	Documents	Sentences	Tokens	Annotations
Train	1,706	31,038	457,017	35,460
Valid	87	1,419	23,692	1,923
Test	79	1,271	19,911	1,423

Table 2: The GEC+Fluency data statistics. Validation and test sets were independently annotated by two annotators.

3 Data

The UNLP 2023 shared task for grammatical error correction utilizes the UA-GEC dataset (Syvokon et al., 2023) as the primary source for training, evaluation, and test data. We chose this dataset due to its relevance to the task at hand. Table 1 and Table 2 provide statistics of data used in GEC-only and GEC+Fluency tracks, respectively. The minor difference in the number of sentences is an artifact of source and target sentence alignment.

The training set comprises 1,706 documents, which amount to a total of 31,028 sentences.

For hyperparameter tuning and evaluation during development, we created a separate validation set by extracting 87 documents (1,419 sentences) from the UA-GEC test set.

In order to assess the final performance of the participating models, we formed a test set containing another 79 documents (1,271 sentences) from the remaining samples in the UA-GEC test set. Each sentence in both test set and validation set was annotated by two independent annotators. This dual annotation approach ensures a more accurate evaluation of model performance, taking into account the discrepancies and variations between human annotators.

We provide training and validation data in three formats:

- unprocessed parallel text;
- tokenized parallel text;
- .m2 files (Ng et al., 2014).

Test data is provided only as tokenized and non-tokenized source text files.

[1]https://codalab.lisn.upsaclay.fr/competitions/10740

The participants had the freedom to choose which version of the data to utilize for training their models. We employed the Stanza tokenization tool (Qi et al., 2020) to tokenize the data and prepared a tokenization script for the participants.

Preserving the document structure allowed the participants to make use of document-level context in their models. To achieve this, sentences were kept in the order in which they appeared within their respective documents. Document headers were appended before a sequence of a document's sentences to retain this structure. These headers followed a specific format: "# [0-9]{4}", where an example would be "# 1234". This approach facilitated the incorporation of document-level context while maintaining consistency across the datasets.

4 Evaluation

The primary evaluation metric used for the shared task is the $F_{0.5}$ score, which combines the precision and recall metrics while weighing precision more than recall. This metric was computed using the Errant tool (Bryant et al., 2017), a widely-accepted tool for evaluating grammatical error correction.

In addition to reporting the $F_{0.5}$ scores, the evaluation script also reports other metrics: precision, recall, true positives (TP), false positives (FP), and false negatives (FN).

Furthermore, the evaluation script reports error detection metrics. However, these are provided merely for reference and are not considered while comparing the participating models. Detection metrics can be insightful in understanding how well a system identifies errors in the text, without necessarily focusing on the correction.

All evaluation is done on tokenized data. If the participants choose to train a model that produces

Rank	Participant	TP	FP	FN	Prec	Rec	$F_{0.5}$
1	QC-NLP (fpg)	636	192	400	76.81	61.39	**73.14**
2	UA-GEC	508	**139**	496	**78.52**	50.60	70.71
3	QC-NLP (rozovska)	**661**	253	**386**	72.32	**63.13**	70.27
4	WebSpellChecker	458	170	502	72.93	47.71	65.96

Table 3: Official shared task results for all teams in Track 1. GEC-only. The best values are shown in bold.

Rank	Participant	TP	FP	FN	Prec	Rec	$F_{0.5}$
1	Pravopysnyk	580	153	742	79.13	43.87	**68.17**
2	QC-NLP (fpg)	735	269	646	73.21	53.22	68.09
3	WebSpellChecker	528	**125**	759	**80.86**	41.03	67.71
4	GrammarUA	526	138	776	79.22	40.40	66.45
5	QC-NLP (rozovska)	**739**	318	**635**	69.91	**53.78**	65.96
6	UA-GEC	594	219	745	73.06	44.36	64.69
7	Final Submission	483	212	796	69.50	37.76	59.50

Table 4: Official shared task results for all teams in Track 2. GEC+Fluency. The best values are shown in bold.

non-tokenized outputs, it must be tokenized first. We provide a tokenization script to ensure there's no mismatch in preprocessing between submission and golden data.

The train and validation sets, as well as tokenization and evaluation scripts, are published on GitHub[2].

5 Participating Systems

A total of fifteen teams registered for the UNLP 2023 shared task, but only six teams submitted their solutions before the deadline. Four teams submitted papers that were accepted to appear in the UNLP workshop proceedings and are referred to in this report. Two more teams provided their system descriptions by email.

Three teams submitted their results for both GEC-only and GEC+Fluency tracks, and three more teams submitted their results only for GEC+Fluency. We briefly review the systems here; for complete descriptions, please see the corresponding papers. Table 3 and Table 4 present the leaderboards for the two tracks.

Pravopysnyk (Bondarenko et al., 2023), the winners of the GEC+Fluency track, combined a transformer-based model with a rule-based spelling correction system. For the transformer-based model, they fine-tuned MBart (Tang et al., 2021) on UA-GEC augmented by synthetically generated errors. To generate more data, the team used round-trip translation, a custom punctuation error generation script, and replacing Ukrainian words with their Russified versions. For spelling correction, the team applied the SymSpell algorithm (Garbe, 2012) to the Ukrainian language. This algorithm uses a word frequency dictionary and a bigram frequency dictionary based on the dataset of 500k sentences collected from Ukrainian books. The most frequent word that passes the spelling criteria is then selected. The transformer-based model was responsible for most corrections. The advantages of the system include high performance, low training cost (training takes 10 minutes on Google Colab A100 GPU), and its end-to-end training setup, which allows combining different sources of synthetic data. However, the system is slower when compared to sequence tagging models.

The authors published the system on the Huggingface platform: `https://huggingface.co/Pravopysnyk/best-unlp`.

QC-NLP (Gomez et al., 2023), the winners of the GEC-only track and second place holders of the GEC+Fluency track, submitted 2 systems: (1) fpg and (2) rozovska. Both systems participated in the two tracks of the shared task. System (1) achieved stronger performance in both tracks than system (2), but system (1) requires more computational resources.

In system (1), the authors fine-tuned a pre-trained mT5-large (Rothe et al., 2021; Xue et al., 2021) to correct ungrammatical sentences to their grammatical counterparts. They first fine-tuned the model with 10M synthetically generated grammati-

[2]`https://github.com/asivokon/unlp-2023-shared-task`

cal error correction examples for three epochs and then with the shared task dataset for 10 additional epochs. The synthetic examples were generated using the approach based on the Aspell confusion sets proposed in Náplava and Straka (2019). The method was applied to the native Ukrainian data from the WNT News Crawl corpus. Fine-tuning on synthetic and learner data was done with 8 Nvidia 80GB GPUs taking approximately 16 hours to train in total.

System (2) is a transformer model proposed in Náplava and Straka (2019) pre-trained on 35M synthetic examples that use Aspell confusions and additional noise from round-trip translation and fine-tuned on the gold learner training data. Three models were trained with three different seeds, and the final model is an ensemble of the three best checkpoints. Pre-training on 1 Nvidia 32GB GPU took 7 hours per epoch for about 10 epochs until convergence. Fine-tuning took about an hour until convergence.

The authors published the systems on GitHub: `https://github.com/knarfamlap/low-resource-gec-uk`.

WebSpellChecker (Didenko and Sameliuk, 2023) used a custom transformer-like architecture called RedPenNet. The architecture leverages a pre-trained MLM encoder along with a shallow decoder to generate both replacement tokens and spans for editing GEC cases. During the generation of edit tokens, the encoder-decoder attention weights determine the edit spans (start and end) that point at the position of the edit in the source sentence. Edit tokens are predicted in the autoregressive way. SEP tokens separate edits in the output sequence. At each step of the feedback loop, the edit BPE token embedding is combined with a decoder-specific trainable positional encoding embedding. The resulting sum is then concatenated with the span embedding. Additionally, compact GEC task-specific decoder BPE vocabularies are trained to lower the cost of the pre-softmax dot operation, thus improving the efficiency of predicting replacement tokens.

The main advantage of RedPenNet is the ability to implement any source-to-target transformation using a minimal number of autoregressive steps, which makes it possible to effectively solve the GEC cases, including interrelated and multi-token edits. However, due to the tailored architecture of RedPenNet, there are no out-of-the-box solutions available for data preprocessing, training, or fine-tuning. Thus, convenient tools like the HuggingFace infrastructure cannot be used for rapid model fine-tuning and deployment.

The system repository: `https://github.com/WebSpellChecker/unlp-2023-shared-task`.

Final Submission by Maksym Tarnavskyi uses a sequence tagging GECToR model (Omelianchuk et al., 2021) that contains a transformer-based encoder stacked with two output linear layers that are responsible for error detection and error correction. The author trained the model only on UA-GEC data without any synthetic data pre-training or hyperparameter optimization. An ukr-roberta-base[3] model is used to initialize the encoder.

The system repository: `https://github.com/MaksTarnavskyi/gector-large`.

Model checkpoints: `https://drive.google.com/drive/folders/1ZWjJwZrTQAcs48Z_h4T1Mivzf5nU3h_0`.

GrammarUA by Anastasiia Hudyma uses mBART50 (Tang et al., 2020), a sequence-to-sequence model that was fine-tuned on the shared task training and validation data. This model was chosen because of good results for low-resource languages.

The author published the system on the Huggingface platform: `https://huggingface.co/smartik/mbart-large-50-finetuned-gec`

UA-GEC system is the baseline for Ukrainian GEC presented in Syvokon et al. (2023). The team used mBART50-large (Katsumata and Komachi, 2020; Tang et al., 2020) fine-tuned on the unprocessed training data. Training takes around 3 hours on a single Nvidia P100 GPU.

6 Conclusion

We believe that the UNLP 2023 shared task was instrumental in facilitating research on grammatical error correction for the Ukrainian language, and we hope the insights from the teams' research will be useful to the NLP community. All the data and evaluation scripts used in the shared task are available on GitHub, and the competing systems were openly published, which contributes to the reproducibility of the shared task results. The CodaLab environment remains open for further submissions, although any such submissions will be considered outside of the UNLP 2023 competition.

[3] `https://huggingface.co/youscan/ukr-roberta-base`

The most successful systems were submitted by Pravopysnyk (Bondarenko et al., 2023) and QC-NLP (Gomez et al., 2023), scoring 68.17% and 68.09% $F_{0.5}$ respectively on GEC+Fluency. The teams set the first state of the art results for the task of Ukrainian GEC. Notably, the common themes among the best-performing systems are fine-tuning of large pre-trained transformer-based models and synthetic data.

In the next iterations of this shared task, we plan to increase the hidden test set, include error classification, and present restricted and unrestricted tracks.

Limitations

Due to limited resources, the test set of the shared task is relatively small. More labelled data would provide for more representative results.

The $F_{0.5}$ scores in our shared task are higher when compared to similar shared tasks in other languages (Bryant et al., 2019). We attribute this to the fact that 43% of errors in the data are punctuation errors, which are easier to correct (Syvokon et al., 2023).

Breaking down system outputs by error categories would help in analyzing model performance.

Ethics Statement

Upon entering the competition, all participants of the shared task accepted the following terms and conditions of the competition:

- All participants agree to compete in a fair and honest manner in the shared task and not use any illegal, malicious, or otherwise unethical methods to gain an advantage in the shared task.
- All participants agree to not distribute or share the test data obtained during the shared task with any third parties.
- All participants agree to make their solutions publicly available upon the completion of the shared task in order to facilitate knowledge sharing and developments of the Ukrainian language.

To the best of our knowledge, the shared task participants followed these terms and conditions.

Acknowledgements

We are extremely grateful to the creators of the UA-GEC corpus who made this shared task possible. Thank you, Nastasiia Osidach, Olena Nahorna, and Pavlo Kuchmiichuk! We thank Danylo Mysak for numerous fixes and improvements of the corpus.

References

Maksym Bondarenko, Artem Yushko, Andrii Shportko, and Andrii Fedorych. 2023. Comparative study of models trained on synthetic data for Ukrainian grammatical error correction. In *Proceedings of the Second Ukrainian Natural Language Processing Workshop*, Dubrovnik, Croatia. Association for Computational Linguistics.

Christopher Bryant, Mariano Felice, Øistein E. Andersen, and Ted Briscoe. 2019. The BEA-2019 shared task on grammatical error correction. In *Proceedings of the Fourteenth Workshop on Innovative Use of NLP for Building Educational Applications*, pages 52–75, Florence, Italy. Association for Computational Linguistics.

Christopher Bryant, Mariano Felice, and Ted Briscoe. 2017. Automatic annotation and evaluation of error types for grammatical error correction. In *Proceedings of the 55th Annual Meeting of the Association for Computational Linguistics (Volume 1: Long Papers)*, pages 793–805, Vancouver, Canada. Association for Computational Linguistics.

Robert Dale, Ilya Anisimoff, and George Narroway. 2012. HOO 2012: A report on the preposition and determiner error correction shared task. In *Proceedings of the Seventh Workshop on Building Educational Applications Using NLP*, pages 54–62, Montréal, Canada. Association for Computational Linguistics.

Robert Dale and Adam Kilgarriff. 2011. Helping our own: The HOO 2011 pilot shared task. In *Proceedings of the 13th European Workshop on Natural Language Generation*, pages 242–249, Nancy, France. Association for Computational Linguistics.

Bohdan Didenko and Andrii Sameliuk. 2023. RedPenNet for grammatical error correction: Outputs to tokens, attentions to spans. In *Proceedings of the Second Ukrainian Natural Language Processing Workshop*, Dubrovnik, Croatia. Association for Computational Linguistics.

Mariano Felice and Ted Briscoe. 2015. Towards a standard evaluation method for grammatical error detection and correction. In *Proceedings of the 2015 Conference of the North American Chapter of the Association for Computational Linguistics: Human Language Technologies*, pages 578–587, Denver, Colorado. Association for Computational Linguistics.

Wolf Garbe. 2012. SymSpell.

Frank Palma Gomez, Alla Rozovskaya, and Dan Roth. 2023. A low-resource approach to the grammatical error correction of Ukrainian. In *Proceedings of the Second Ukrainian Natural Language Processing Workshop*, Dubrovnik, Croatia. Association for Computational Linguistics.

Satoru Katsumata and Mamoru Komachi. 2020. Stronger baselines for grammatical error correction using a pretrained encoder-decoder model. In *Proceedings of the 1st Conference of the Asia-Pacific Chapter of the Association for Computational Linguistics and the 10th International Joint Conference on Natural Language Processing*, pages 827–832, Suzhou, China. Association for Computational Linguistics.

Tomoya Mizumoto, Yuta Hayashibe, Mamoru Komachi, Masaaki Nagata, and Yuji Matsumoto. 2012. The effect of learner corpus size in grammatical error correction of ESL writings. In *Proceedings of COLING 2012: Posters*, pages 863–872, Mumbai, India. The COLING 2012 Organizing Committee.

Jakub Náplava and Milan Straka. 2019. Grammatical error correction in low-resource scenarios. In *Proceedings of the 5th Workshop on Noisy User-generated Text (W-NUT 2019)*, pages 346–356, Hong Kong, China. Association for Computational Linguistics.

Courtney Napoles, Keisuke Sakaguchi, and Joel Tetreault. 2017. JFLEG: A fluency corpus and benchmark for grammatical error correction. In *Proceedings of the 15th Conference of the European Chapter of the Association for Computational Linguistics: Volume 2, Short Papers*, pages 229–234, Valencia, Spain. Association for Computational Linguistics.

Hwee Tou Ng, Siew Mei Wu, Ted Briscoe, Christian Hadiwinoto, Raymond Hendy Susanto, and Christopher Bryant. 2014. The CoNLL-2014 shared task on grammatical error correction. In *Proceedings of the Eighteenth Conference on Computational Natural Language Learning: Shared Task*, pages 1–14, Baltimore, Maryland. Association for Computational Linguistics.

Hwee Tou Ng, Siew Mei Wu, Yuanbin Wu, Christian Hadiwinoto, and Joel Tetreault. 2013. The CoNLL-2013 shared task on grammatical error correction. In *Proceedings of the Seventeenth Conference on Computational Natural Language Learning: Shared Task*, pages 1–12, Sofia, Bulgaria. Association for Computational Linguistics.

Kostiantyn Omelianchuk, Vipul Raheja, and Oleksandr Skurzhanskyi. 2021. Text Simplification by Tagging. In *Proceedings of the 16th Workshop on Innovative Use of NLP for Building Educational Applications*, pages 11–25, Online. Association for Computational Linguistics.

Peng Qi, Yuhao Zhang, Yuhui Zhang, Jason Bolton, and Christopher D. Manning. 2020. Stanza: A Python natural language processing toolkit for many human languages. In *Proceedings of the 58th Annual Meeting of the Association for Computational Linguistics: System Demonstrations*.

Sascha Rothe, Jonathan Mallinson, Eric Malmi, Sebastian Krause, and Aliaksei Severyn. 2021. A simple recipe for multilingual grammatical error correction. In *Proceedings of the 59th Annual Meeting of the Association for Computational Linguistics and the 11th International Joint Conference on Natural Language Processing (Volume 2: Short Papers)*, pages 702–707, Online. Association for Computational Linguistics.

Oleksiy Syvokon, Olena Nahorna, Pavlo Kuchmiichuk, and Nastasiia Osidach. 2023. UA-GEC: Grammatical error correction and fluency corpus for the Ukrainian language. In *Proceedings of the Second Ukrainian Natural Language Processing Workshop*, Dubrovnik, Croatia. Association for Computational Linguistics.

Yuqing Tang, Chau Tran, Xian Li, Peng-Jen Chen, Naman Goyal, Vishrav Chaudhary, Jiatao Gu, and Angela Fan. 2020. Multilingual translation with extensible multilingual pretraining and finetuning.

Yuqing Tang, Chau Tran, Xian Li, Peng-Jen Chen, Naman Goyal, Vishrav Chaudhary, Jiatao Gu, and Angela Fan. 2021. Multilingual translation from denoising pre-training. In *Findings of the Association for Computational Linguistics: ACL-IJCNLP 2021*, pages 3450–3466, Online. Association for Computational Linguistics.

Linting Xue, Noah Constant, Adam Roberts, Mihir Kale, Rami Al-Rfou, Aditya Siddhant, Aditya Barua, and Colin Raffel. 2021. mT5: A massively multilingual pre-trained text-to-text transformer. In *Proceedings of the 2021 Conference of the North American Chapter of the Association for Computational Linguistics: Human Language Technologies*, pages 483–498, Online. Association for Computational Linguistics.

Author Index